SALVATION FROM DESPAIR

ARCHIVES INTERNATIONALES D'HISTOIRE DES IDEES

INTERNATIONAL ARCHIVES OF THE HISTORY OF IDEAS

59

ERROL E. HARRIS

SALVATION FROM DESPAIR

A REAPPRAISAL OF SPINOZA'S PHILOSOPHY

ERROL E. HARRIS

Professor of Philosophy in the Northwestern University

SALVATION FROM DESPAIR

A REAPPRAISAL OF SPINOZA'S PHILOSOPHY

MARTINUS NIJHOFF / THE HAGUE / 1973

ISBN 90 247 5158 6

PRINTED IN THE NETHERLANDS

TABLE OF CONTENTS

Preface   IX

Frontispiece   XI

PART I

INTRODUCTION

CHAPTER I. CONTEMPORARY DESPAIR AND ITS ANTIDOTE   3

    1. Forebodings   3
    2. Reactions against the Past   4
    3. Groundspring of Philosophy   8
    4. Spinoza's Scientific Attitude   11

CHAPTER II. GEOMETRICAL METHOD   15

    1. The Primacy of Knowledge   15
    2. Critics of Spinoza's Method   19
    3. Deduction   21
    4. Geometry and Metaphysics   28

PART II

GOD

CHAPTER III. THE ABSURDITY OF ATHEISM   33

    1. Is Spinoza an Atheist?   33
    2. The Conception of God   35
    3. The Existence of God   39
    4. Dismissal of the Indictment   46

CHAPTER IV. GOD'S CREATIVITY   48

    1. *Natura Naturans* and *Natura Naturata*   48
    2. Attributes and Modes   50
    3. Modes, Infinite and Finite   55
    4. The Causality of God   57

5. Interpretations, Comment and Criticism 58
6. Solution of the Problem 64
7. Residual Difficulties 69

PART III

MAN

CHAPTER V. BODY AND MIND 77

1. The Material World 77
2. Mind as Felt Body 80
3. Substantial Identity 82
4. Rejection of Parallelism 84
5. Alleged Ambiguity of 'Idea' 85
6. *Idea Ideae* 87
7. Passivity and Activity 89
8. *Imaginatio* 93
9. The Common Order of Nature – Time, Measure and Number 98
10. Adequate Knowledge 103

CHAPTER VI. PASSION AND ACTION 110

1. Affects 110
2. *Conatus* 110
3. Primary and Secondary Affects 113
4. Active Emotions 118
5. 'Human Nature' 119
6. Freedom 122
7. Teleology 126
8. The Will and Human Responsibility 132

PART IV

HUMAN WELFARE

CHAPTER VII. GOOD AND EVIL 141

1. Aids to the Imagination 141
2. True Good and Supreme Good 143
3. Perfection 144
4. One coherent Doctrine 145
5. Spinoza and Plato on the Good and the Expedient 147
6. Moral Weakness 149
7. The Reality of Evil 152

CHAPTER VIII. THE MASTERY OF FATE 160

1. Of Human Bondage 160
2. The Mastery over the Passions 166

3. The Dictates of Reason   172
4. Selfishness and Self-sacrifice   174
5. Vice and Virtue   176

CHAPTER IX. THE STATE AND POLITICS

1. Ethics, Politics and History   181
2. Philosophical Roots   182
3. Natural Law, Natural Rights and the State of Nature   183
4. Sovereignty and Law   188
5. The Rights and Powers of the Sovereign   191
6. Limitations on the Power and Action of the State   193
7. Political Freedom   196
8. Practical Considerations   197

CHAPTER X. RELIGION   201

1. Philosophy and Religion   201
2. The Intellectual Love of God   202
3. The *Tractatus Theologico-Politicus*   205
4. Revealed Religion and Superstition   207
5. Biblical Criticism   210
6. Prophecy   215
7. The Election of the Jews   219
8. Miracles   221
9. The True and Universal Religion   222
10. Spinoza's Attitude to Christianity   225

CHAPTER XI. HUMAN IMMORTALITY   227

1. The final Problem   227
2. Traditional Ideas of Immortality   228
3. A Common Interpretation of Spinoza   231
4. Difficulties and Criticisms   232
5. Idea as Transcendent   235
6. Time and Eternity   237
7. Mind as Idea of Body   239
8. Misinterpretations and Misconceptions   243
9. Blessedness   246

Epilogue   247

Chapter XII Spinoza in Retrospect   249

Bibliographical Appendix   259

Index   263

PREFACE

My purpose in this book is to re-interpret the philosophy of Spinoza to a new generation. I make no attempt to compete with the historical scholarship of A. H. Wolfson in tracing back Spinoza's ideas to his Ancient, Hebrew and Mediaeval forerunners, or the meticulous philosophical scrutiny of Harold Joachim, which I could wish to emulate but cannot hope to rival. I have simply relied upon the text of Spinoza's own writings in an effort to grasp and to make intelligible to others the precise meaning of his doctrine, and to decide whether, in spite of numerous apparent and serious internal conflicts, it can be understood as a consistent whole. In so doing I have found it necessary to correct what seem to me to be misconceptions frequently entertained by commentators. Whether or not I am right in my re-interpretation, it will, I hope, contribute something fresh, if not to the knowledge of Spinoza, at least to the discussion of what he really meant to say.

The limits within which I am constrained to write prevent me from drawing fully upon the great mass of scholarly writings on Spinoza, his life and times, his works and his philosophical ideas. I can only try to make amends for omissions by listing the most important works in the Spinoza bibliography, for reference by those who would seek to know more about his philosophy. This list I have added as an appendix. Here I shall, at the outset, mention only Spinoza's own philosophical writings and the abbreviations I have used in referring to them in footnotes:

K.V.   *Korte Verhandeling van God, de Mensch, en deszelfs Welstand* (Short Treatise on God, Man and Human Welfare).

P.P.C.   *Principia Philosophiae Cartesianae, More Geometrico Demonstratae* (Principles of Cartesian Philosophy, demonstrated geometrically).

Cog. Met.	*Cogitata Metaphysica* (Metaphysical Reflections).
TdIE.	*Tractatus de Intellectus Emendatione* (Treatise on the Improvement of the Intellect).
T.Th.P.	*Tractatus Theologico-Politicus* (Theologico-Political Treatise).
T.P.	*Tractatus Politicus* (Political Treatise).
Ethics	*Ethica, Ordine Grometrico Demonstrata* (Ethics, demonstrated in Geometrical Order).
Epp.	*Epistolae doctorum quorundum virorum ad B.d.S. et Auctoris Responsiones* (Letters of certain learned men to B.d.S. and the Author's answers).
V.V.L.	*Benedicti de Spinoza Opera Quotquot Reperta Sunt,* J. van Vloten and J. P. N. Land, The Hague, 1914.

My thanks are due to the American Philosophical Society for financial assistance, and acknowledgements to *The Monist, The Canadian Journal of Philosophy,* and *Idealistic Studies* for permission to reprint those portions of Chapters IV, VI and XI which have appeared as articles in those journals.

FRONTISPIECE

If Wolfson's conviction is correct, "that much of the criticism levelled at Spinoza is due to lack of knowledge regarding the personality and character of this rare man," [1] an account of his philosophy ought to be preceded by a character study and a history of his life and times. To be well done this would require the expertise of a qualified historian, and that I cannot claim. The best I can do is to select from the work of others more competent and refer the reader to sources (see Appendix) where, as he wishes, he can find more adequate and reliable information.

Truth to say, not very much is reliably known of Spinoza's life, possibly because he was very modest and retiring and sought neither fame nor notoriety, possibly because during his lifetime he was anathematized, his opinions were attacked as pernicious and heretical, and his person and doctrine vilified by his theological and philosophical opponents, so that in an age of intolerance those who knew and admired him feared to defend him, or to give any public account of his activities. After his death several, including Leibniz, who had benefited by studying his ideas, used them without acknowledgement, and he was remembered, if at all, only as the despised propagator of an abominable creed. Hume, in his *Treatise of Human Nature* describes Spinoza's doctrine as a "hideous hypothesis" for which he is "universally infamous" – a theory which is "the fundamental principle of atheism." [2]

It was not until approximately two centuries after his death that interest in his philosophy was revived and its merits were fully appreciated, and, by then, much of the historical documentation of his biography had disappeared. Consequently, obscurities persist as to certain periods and events in his life, and the earliest biographies are still among the best:

---

[1] A. Wolfson, *Spinoza, A Life of Reason* (New York, 1969), p. xiii.
[2] *Op. cit.*, I, iv, 5. Selby-Bigge Edn., (Oxford, 1888), pp. 240 ff.

those of J. M. Lucas, who knew him personally, and John Colerus, who
was Lutheran minister at the Hague not long after Spinoza died in the
house still to be seen in the Paviljoensgracht, and who numbered among
his parishioners one, van der Spijck, Spinoza's landlord.

The liberation of the Seven Provinces of the Netherlands from the
power of Spain, and of their protestant sects from Catholic persecution,
brought into being a regime in Holland that was both republican in
form and relatively tolerant (by contemporary standards) of divergent
religious persuasions. There, particularly in Amsterdam, Jews from Spain
and Portugal, who had suffered cruelly under the Inquisition, found
asylum and flourished unmolested. Among them were the forebears of
Baruch de Spinoza. He was the son of Michael de Spinoza by a second
marriage, but his mother, Hannah Deborah, died when he was a child
of only six.

His early brilliance excited the hopes of the rabbinate that he would
become a celebrity and a pillar of the Synagogue, for before he was twenty
he had mastered the Hebrew language, the literature of the Bible, the
Old Testament scholarship of the Talmud and the Mediaeval Jewish
philosophers such as Maimonides, Chasdai ben Crescas, Gersonides, Ibn
Ezra and Ibn Gabriol. It was not long, however, before the young Baruch
began to question the beliefs both of the orthodox and of the philosophers
and to thirst after wider knowledge to be found in the gentile world. His
questions confounded his teachers, Rabbi Manassah ben Israel and
Rabbi Saul Levi Mortiera, who could give him only unsatisfactory
answers; but for the time being his youth and modesty prompted him to
refrain from pressing awkward difficulties and pursuing embarrassing
inquiries.

However, at the age of about 18, he went further afield, and under
the instruction of a free thinking scholar who set up a private school in
Amsterdam, one Francis van den Enden, he studied Latin, the Cartesian
philosophy, mathematics and the science of the day. This interest in
secular and gentile learning dismayed the authorities of the Synagogue,
and when, after his father's death (whom he had not wished to grieve by
open rebellion), Spinoza began to neglect religious observances in which
he could no longer see any significance, the rabbis became alarmed and
angry. Spinoza's half-sister attempted to disinherit him of his patrimony
on the ground that he held heretical views; but he took the case to the
civil courts and won it, only to give up everything his sister had claimed,
except his mother's bedstead and a few trifles of purely sentimental value.

Lucas reports that two former school fellows, acting as *agents provo-*

cateurs, inveigled him into expressing views, disapproved by the rabbis, about God and Immortality, as well as disbelief in the election of the Israelites, and these they reported to the leaders of the Synagogue. Spinoza was summoned before them but refused to recant. Unwilling to acquire a reputation for harbouring atheists, they tried in every way to persuade him to conform, at least outwardly, to Jewish custom, even offering him a stipend of 1,000 florins for his silence on points of disagreement. But he was not to be bribed, and finally was excommunicated with awesome ritual and expelled from the Jewish community.

This took place in 1656, when he was 24 years old, and it freed him to pursue his own studies and ideas. He temporarily took up residence with the van den Enden family, where he assisted in the private academy as a tutor. One legend has it that he fell in love with Clara Marie, van den Enden's daughter, who was 10 years his junior. If so, his suit was unsuccessful, for she later married one of Spinoza's friends and admirers, Dr. Dirck Kerckrink. Now a group of students and intellectuals began to gather around Spinoza and to take interest in the ideas he was developing. Many of them were Collegiants, a sect similar to the Quakers, with whom he had much in common, but whose Society he never joined. Several of his fellow students and pupils formed a discussion group to study his philosophical position, and they continued to meet and to correspond with Spinoza, long after he was forced to leave Amsterdam.

The hostility of the Jewish authorities persisted and was increased by his continued unrepentant presence in the city. There is a story (also reported by Lucas) that an attempt was made on his life one night as he was leaving the theatre; but the would-be assassin's knife did no more damage than a rent in Spinoza's cloak. The rabbis then denounced him to the city government as one who taught doctrines subversive of religion and morality, and he was banished from Amsterdam for a period of some months.

He retired to the house of a Collegiant friend on the Ouwerkerk Road just outside the city, earning his living by the craft of lense-grinding, which he had learned earlier in accordance with the ancient Jewish requirement that every man acquire some manual skill. It is possible that at this time he wrote the *Short Treatise on God, Man and Human Welfare* for the benefit of his friends and disciples. It was written apparently for private circulation and the original Latin manuscript has been lost. Only late in the nineteenth century was a Dutch translation discovered, which is the version we now have.

In a not dissimilar way the *Principles of the Cartesian Philosophy, geometrically demonstrated,* came to be written. After a brief return to Amsterdam Spinoza withdrew once again into the country; this time to Rijnsburg near Leyden, where there was a Collegiant community. His purpose seems to have been to find seclusion and opportunity to write down the philosophical system developing in his mind. But he soon attracted visitors and pupils, not only from among the Collegiants, but also from the neighbouring University of Leyden, a great centre of Cartesian studies. In the eighth and ninth epistles, mention is made of a young man, Casearius, who was lodging with Spinoza and receiving instruction from him in the philosophy of Descartes. It was for his benefit that Spinoza reformulated Descartes's arguments, as he himself had suggested in his Reply to the Second set of Objections, in geometrical form.[3] The manuscript obviously was circulated also among the group in Amsterdam, and Spinoza was persuaded to allow his friends, Ludowijk Meyer, who wrote a preface to the work, and Jan Rieuwertz, to publish it in book form, with a long appendix, which Spinoza added under the title *Cogitata Metaphysica* (Metaphysical Reflections). In one of his letters to Henry Oldenburg, Spinoza says that he agreed to the publication in the hope of attracting the attention of certain influential people in Holland who might then approve the publication of more of his writings, expositions of his own philosophy on which he was then at work (Cf. *Ep.* XIII).

The *Treatise on the Improvement of the Intellect* may well have been what he had in mind, for in an earlier letter to Oldenburg he says that he has written a booklet "on the Improvement of the Understanding, in the rewriting and correction of which" he was then engaged (*Ep.* VI). But apparently the progress of the work was interrupted by the constant visits of friends and would-be students, for he later complains that he has scarcely been able to be his own master because of the friends who have visited him (*Ep.* XIII). And, indeed, after only a few years in Rijnsburg, he removed to Voorburg near the Hague, partly in search of undisturbed peace and partly, no doubt, to be nearer to those powerful and influential friends in the government whose literary patronage and protection he needed.

Among these the most notable was Johan de Witt, the Grand Pensionary of Holland, a liberal anti-clerical republican who was constantly and bitterly opposed by the reactionary and intolerant Calvinist faction. Spinoza, who became convinced that much social evil and civil unrest was traceable to religious and intellectual intolerance, was a friend and sup-

---

[3] Cf. Haldane and Ross, *The Philosophical Works of Descartes* (Cambridge University Press, 1934) II, p. 48 f.

porter of the Grand Pensionary, who so admired and valued the philosopher that he settled on him an annuity of 200 florins.

L. S. Feuer believes that Spinoza's reasons for moving nearer to the
Hague were more definitely political than those I have mentioned: that
he had grown impatient with the political withdrawal of his Collegiant
friends, and as an active political reformer, he went to the Hague (perhaps even on invitation) to become the official philosopher of the republican party of Johan de Witt in succession to Jean de la Court who
had recently died.[4] There may be some truth in this allegation but such
evidence as can be found in Spinoza's correspondence supports it only
slightly and is equally capable of being understood to mean that Spinoza
was simply seeking the means to pursue his continued quest for truth.
This, moreover, would be in keeping with his renunciation of public
honours, along with wealth and pleasure, in the *Treatise on the Improvement of the Understanding,* as well as with his habitual aversion to
publicity. Feuer's belief, however, is not incompatible with views Spinoza
expresses in the *Theologico-Political Treatise* and the *Ethics* about men's
duty to serve the community and to participate in the activities of society.
It is also the case that he wrote the *Theologico-Political Treatise* in large
measure to vindicate and support the policies of de Witt, as well as to
expound his own ideas on the authority of the Scriptures and the divine
election of the Jews. A statement which he had written earlier on these
topics in reply to the accusations for which he was expelled from the
Synagogue was the last straw which had moved the rabbis to take final
action. Of the original statement no trace has survived, but much of
it, if not all, may be repeated in the *Tractatus Theologico-Politicus.*

The book, though published anonymously, rapidly went through five
editions and had a wide impact. It excited bitter attacks from opponents,
both ecclesiastical and secular, and Spinoza's hopes, expressed in Epistle
XXX, were far from fulfilled that it would prove a defence against the
accusations of atheism which were being levelled against him, for it
seemed only to intensify them. At this time he had already completed a
large part of the *Ethics,* and, whether from political pressure by the de
Witt party, or concern about the accusations made against himself, he
had interrupted his work on the comprehensive exposition of his system
to write the *Theologico-Political Treatise.* By the time the *Ethics* was
completed the fortunes, both of de Witt and of Spinoza had so changed

---

[4] Cf. L. S. Feuer, *Spinoza and the Rise of Liberalism* (Beacon Press, Boston, 1964),
pp. 58-9.

for the worse, that the publication of his greatest work had to be delayed and it was not printed until after its author's death.

Meanwhile Spinoza, ailing in health, suffering from phthisis aggravated by his lense-grinding, and in straitened financial circumstances, moved to the Hague, taking up quarters first in the Stille Veerkade and shortly afterwards in the house of the painter, Hendrik van der Spijck, in the Paviljoensgracht, where he ended his days.

Poverty Spinoza bore with equanimity, living with extreme frugality to keep within his slender means. He was no ascetic but was entirely free of mercenary desires. There is evidence that before his expulsion from the Jewish Community in Amsterdam he had conducted a business in partnership with his brother Gabriel, but he seems never to have had much aptitude and certainly little taste for mercenary pursuits. After the ban, he had naturally to withdraw from the business. His brother sold it and emigrated to the West Indies. His great friend and fellow student Simon de Vries was a successful merchant, and, according to Colerus, he at one time offered Spinoza a gift of a thousand florins to enable him to live more comfortably, but Spinoza would not accept it. Then, as he was a bachelor, de Vries expressed the intention of making Spinoza his heir, but Spinoza dissuaded him, contending that de Vries' duty lay towards his brother, Isaac. This advice was followed but the will stipulated that Isaac de Vries should pay Spinoza an annual allowance of 500 florins. When eventually Isaac inherited the estate Spinoza accepted only 300 of the 500 florin allowance, saying that that was sufficient for his needs.

In 1673, Spinoza received an invitation from the Elector Palatine to become Professor of Philosophy at the University of Heidelberg. Had he accepted, he would finally have been relieved of financial stringency and his social status would have been greatly enhanced. But the letter, written by the Elector's Councillor, J. Ludovicus Frabitius, himself a Professor in the University, contained the proviso: "You will have the fullest freedom of philosophizing, which he [his Serene Highness the Prince] believes you will not misuse to disturb the publicly established religion." Despite the fact that the invitation probably resulted from the reputation of the *Theologico-Political Treatise,* Spinoza declined, replying:

"I do not know within what limits that freedom of philosophizing ought to be confined so that I may not seem to be disturbing the publicly established religion: since schisms arise, not so much from the ardent study of religion, as from the differing emotions of men or the zeal for dispute by which they are wont to pervert and condemn all things, even if rightly stated." (*Epp.* XLVII, XLVIII)

He was also averse to sacrificing the creative work that he was doing to the labour of instructing the young, for, he says, it was never his intention to teach publicly.

The victory of the Dutch admiral de Ruyter over the English fleet and the conclusion of a favourable peace with England in 1665 improved the fortunes of de Witt's administration, but not for very long. For Charles II went back on his treaty obligations and sided with Louis XIV in his claim to the Spanish Netherlands. In the ensuing war the Dutch initially fared badly and the royalist party blamed de Witt and demanded the elevation of the House of Orange to the Dutch monarchy. De Witt's brother, Cornelius, was arrested and thrown into prison for alleged high treason. The royalists stirred up the mob to riot. They broke into the prison when Johan was visiting his brother and brutally murdered them both.

Spinoza was deeply upset by this event. He broke down and wept at the news and had to be restrained forcibly from rushing to the scene of the murder to post a placard denouncing "the very lowest of all barbarians." De Witt's legatees tried to deprive him of his pension and his friends pressed him to contest the matter in the courts. But Spinoza deposited the document assigning him the annuity in the hands of his opponents, and acted so disinterestedly that they were shamed into continuing the payments.

William of Orange, who was later to become King of England as well, now took over the government of the Netherlands. He was by no means a despotic ruler and retained the services of many of the more liberal party not only to offset the bigotry of the Calvinist clerics but also to take advantage of the skill and experience of several of his erstwhile opponents.[5] Some of Spinoza's friends, notably Jan Hudde, Burgomaster of Amsterdam, continued in their offices. Nevertheless, after the removal of de Witt's protective presence Spinoza's enemies attacked him more freely and more viciously. The Cartesians joined forces with the theologians to denigrate his views and intrigued to have the projected edition of the *Ethics* banned on publication. Spinoza, in consequence delayed its printing and it never appeared during his lifetime.

Meanwhile, the gifted and enlightened Prince of Condé leading the French armies of invasion, having heard of the controversial author of

---

[5] Cf. Pieter Geyl, *History of the Low Countries* (London, 1964), p. 126: "He was sensible enough to make use of the services, and listen to the advice, of experienced regents like Van Beuningen and Van Beverningh, both experts in foreign policy . . ." Also P. J. Blok, *History of the People of the Netherlands* (New York and London, 1907), Part IV, p. 406.

the *Tractatus Theologico-Politicus,* invited him to Utrecht where he was
encamped. The fact that Spinoza undertook the journey, holding not
only a safe conduct from the French Army but also one from the Dutch
authorities, indicates that some of the notables at the Hague had entrusted
him with a diplomatic mission, possibly in the hope of securing favourable
conditions of peace. Prince Condé was called away from Utrecht before
the philosopher arrived leaving a message of regret and instructions that
Spinoza should be suitably entertained until his return. Lieutenant-
Colonel Jean Baptiste Stouppe, the Marshall's staff officer, himself something of a scholar and a former Lutheran minister, who was the person
first to draw the attention of the Prince to Spinoza, carried out the
instruction faithfully and enjoyed two weeks of learned discussion with
Spinoza. But the Prince did not return and no visible political result
accrued from the mission. Stouppe suggested to Spinoza that he dedicate
his next book to King Louis, who, if he did, would certainly provide him
with a pension. But Spinoza, a convinced democrat, was neither syco-
phant nor turncoat, nor was he moved by the prospect of financial gain,
and of all men he was the least covetous of easy notoriety. He ignored the
suggestion and went home to the Paviljoensgracht.

His return met with an unfriendly reception from the people of the
Hague. His visit to the camp of the enemy aroused the suspicion that he
was a spy, and people gathered round the house in a threatening crowd.
Spinoza, however, allayed the fears of his landlord by saying, as Colerus
reports:

"There are people enough, and even some of the most considerable persons
in the State, who know very well what put me upon that journey. But, however, as soon as the mob make the least noise at your door, I'll go and meet
'm, tho' they were to treat me as they treated good Messieurs de Witt. I am
a good republican, and I always aimed at the glory and welfare of the
State."

This was virtually the last remarkable event of his life. His illness had
advanced upon him and his physician Dr. Schuller wrote forebodingly
to Leibniz in February 1677 that he "greatly feared our good friend, M.
Benedict de Spinoza,[6] is not going to remain much longer among us . . ."

He had begun work on the *Tractatus Politicus* about which he wrote
to a friend, whose identity has not been discovered, that he had completed six chapters of the work setting out an introduction and dealing
with Natural Law, the right of the Sovereign power, political affairs

---

[6] Spinoza changed his name to Benedict, the latin version of the Hebrew Baruch,
after his expulsion from the Jewish Community.

within the jurisdiction of the supreme power, the ultimate end and the highest good of society, and the constitution of monarchical government so as to prevent tyranny. He projected further chapters on Aristocracy and Democracy, Law "and other special questions relating to politics." The treatise was never completed but breaks off in the eleventh chapter, just as the discussion of popular government is beginning.

On the 21st of February, in his 45th year, Spinoza died, Dr. Schuller being in attendance, but nobody else, for van der Spijck and his wife had gone to Church leaving him apparently in no great danger. He left few possessions, the sale of which produced barely enough to pay for his funeral. His manuscripts were carried off to Amsterdam by his faithful friends who promply prepared and published an edition of his works, first in Latin under the title of *Opera Posthuma,* and then in Dutch translation, the *Nagelaten Schriften.* Respecting the author's wishes and for fear of vicious persecution by opponents, Spinoza's name was not attached to them, except for the initials B.d.S., and it was not until 1802 that a complete edition of Spinoza's writings was published in Jena, under the editorship of Professor Paulus.

The eulogy with which Lucas ends his biography will make a fitting conclusion to this brief and sketchy frontispiece. He writes:

"He had a great, penetrating mind and a very complacent disposition. He had a wit so well seasoned that the most gentle and the most severe found very peculiar charms in it.

His days were few, but one may say nevertheless that he lived much, for he had acquired all that is truly good, namely virtue, and had nothing more to desire after the great reputation which he acquired through his profound knowledge. Sobriety, patience and veracity were but his lesser virtues; and he may be declared fortunate because he died at the summit of his glory, unstained by any blemish, and leaving to the world of sage scholars the regret of seeing themselves bereft of a luminary that was not less useful to them than the light of the sun."

PART I

INTRODUCTION

CHAPTER I

CONTEMPORARY DESPAIR AND ITS ANTIDOTE

1. Forebodings

The prevalent mood of contemporary mankind is one of despair, for never before have the prospects of civilization seemed gloomier or the situation of mankind more helpless. The extinction of the race within the foreseeable future seems threatened from every quarter, whether by the exhaustion of the resources of the earth, or by the pollution of the sea and its life-giving waters, or by the destruction of the ecological systems in which living species cooperate to maintain themselves and one another. All these deleterious processes seem to be happening at an accelerating pace without any deliberate action on the part of man and despite such feeble efforts as he has yet made or seems likely to make to stem the tide of deterioration.

Meanwhile, long cherished ideals of social justice and political emancipation seem today as far from realization as they ever were. The corruption of tried political methods has disillusioned the rising generation and positive aspirations have been reduced to purely destructive anarchism. Nor are we nearer to an equitable distribution of the world's goods among the peoples of the earth or to any international system that can guarantee peace among the nations. Even revolutionaries who look forward to a socialist millennium through the implementation of Marxist doctrine must recognize the precariousness of the future of any regime which must rely, as all do now, for its security on superiority in nuclear weaponry. Today the nations seek to protect their ways of life with military devices, which, if actually put to the use for which they are designed, would annihilate the human race and obliterate everything they were supposed to protect.

In the midst of these menaces the young see no gleam of hope. They seek desperately for some means of spiritual succour but find nothing in which to pin their faith. Traditional religions have lost their hold, as much as anything because in their long history they seem to have achieved such meagre practical consequences. As a result, any expedient is sought that will provide release from tension and anxiety, and resort is had to self-hallucination or the oblivion that narcotics can provide. Contemporary philosophy induces only further disillusionment with traditional ideals, or greater anarchy and capricious nihilism. The prevalent belief, if any does indeed prevail, is relativism, a subjectivism implying the abandonment of all objective standards either of conduct or of judgement.

In a cultural milieu of so confused and dismal a character, one casts about for some philosophical ground for hope and faith. It may seem a far cry to return to the philosophy of the seventeenth century, but this has already been done by both Husserl and Heidegger, not in order to find spiritual reassurance, but in the attempt to explain the contemporary predicament as a long-term consequence of critical intellectual attitudes adopted at that time.[1] Important and interesting as their contentions are, my purpose is not to discuss them, for in the philosophy of the same period there is to be found another, and in some subtle ways divergent, doctrine, which, I believe, does hold (at least in principle) the antidote to our contemporary despair. It is the doctrine expounded by Benedict de Spinoza.

Such a claim may well be met with some astonishment. What purpose, it may be asked, can be served by returning to the study of the thought of an excommunicated Jew of the seventeenth century? What relevance can that have to the anguish and bewilderment of our own times?

2. Reactions against the past

Many excellent books have been written and published about Spinoza, almost (in spite of a long period of neglect) since his death. In the comparatively recent past at least four series on great thinkers have included admirable volumes on Spinoza: John Caird's in 1910, Leon Roth's in 1929, Stuart Hampshire's in 1951, and H. G. Hubbeling's in 1966. Why now another? Must we always be harking back to the past? What can the 17th Century teach us that will be of any help in the 20th? Are not the abstruse language and involved arguments of Spinoza totally out of date, obsolete and even antiquarian? In any case, have not Wittgenstein and Carnap once and for all put an end to the belief that any sense or "wisdom" can be derived from such superannuated metaphysics? And if not they, then Heidegger and Sartre – metaphysicians of a sort though

---

[1] See below, p. 5 n. 3.

they are – have they not made all attempts, such as Spinoza's, seem futile? To construct a purely logical, "objective," system explaining the entire universe, they would contend, would be a misguided and unnecessary exercise. It could never satisfy our existential urge to be authentically ourselves, and can only falsify the reality that must be "lived" to be properly grasped and cannot simply be beheld.

The answer to the last two questions is, briefly, No. But before I say more about them let me consider those preceding. The past, especially the intellectual activity of its great men, is not dead and gone, it is that out of which the present is made, that from which the present has developed. If we are to understand our present situation, in any way adequately, so as to be able to cope with its problems, we must know its history. Collingwood has warned us that "a philosophy which ignores its own history is a philosophy which spends its labour only to rediscover errors long dead." [2] Today we cannot afford to lose time so ill spent. It is, therefore, far from a waste of labour to seek to know and understand the philosophy of the past, to "praise famous men and our fathers that begat us."

Our own era began with the Renaissance and Reformation along with the rise of modern science marked by the Copernican revolution. Contemporary philosophy and politics, as well as science, and many of the most urgent and perplexing problems of our cultural situation can be traced back to the intellectual ferment of the sixteenth and the seventeenth centuries, of which Spinoza's philosophy was a product. [3] The Copernican revolution especially brought with it a new conception of the world and of the nature of things which was to pose questions for philosophy and religion and set the seed of moral, social and political problems, which have persisted steadily and continuously unsolved, until today they threaten the very existence of our civilization. It is not with these matters that this book is to be directly concerned, but the thought of Spinoza is by no means irrelevant to them, as I hope will become apparent to the reader as he proceeds.

Spinoza's terminology as well as his method of exposition (at least in the *Ethics* and the *Principia Philosophiae Cartesianae*) often prove obstacles to the modern reader. But I hope to be able to show that neither

---

[2] *Essays in the Philosophy of History* (Ed. William Debbins, Texas University Press, Austin, 1965), p. 4.

[3] Cf. Edmund Husserl, *Die Krisis der Europäischen Wissenschaften*; Martin Heidegger, "The Foundation of the Modern World-Picture through Metaphysics," in *Holzwege*; Hans Jonas, *The Phenomenon of Life* (New York, 1966), esp. second Essay, App.; R. G. Collingwood, *The Idea of Nature* (Oxford, 1945), Part II, Ch. I.

was arbitrarily or capriciously adopted, that both have intelligible purpose, which, once it is appreciated, makes them comprehensible, and that
they are integral characteristics of Spinoza's thought.

As to Analytic philosophy and Existentialism, I shall not enter into
polemics (merited or otherwise), but shall content myself with these few
considerations.

A deep concern for the ultimate purpose of human life and the consequent search for the most satisfactory way of living, are the fundamental
springs of all genuine philosophy. But this has been denied by contemporary Analytic philosophers. To discover "the purpose of life," if any
meaning is conceded for the phrase, they no longer consider to be the
philosopher's business; and how life ought to be lived is not, on this view,
for the philosopher to dictate. They hold that the values by which we
direct our actions are, in the last resort, psychologically determined, and
that the philosopher can, at best, decide whether or not ways of speaking
about them are clear, whether our reasoning is valid about the facts that
must be taken into consideration when making decisions, and whether
our practical judgements are mutually consistent. Questions about the
validity of values themselves, if they are at all legitimate, are not within
his province and for him to prescribe which values ought to be adopted
would (it is held) be both presumptuous and useless.

It is not my purpose here to enter upon a critique of this conception
of philosophy. As a method of clarifying our language, it has been thought
by some to exercise a therapeutic effect upon those afflicted with an urge
to indulge in metaphysics, for it is supposed to reveal the linguistic con-
fusions which are the source of metaphysical puzzles. But the doctrine in
more recent times has fallen into disrepute and metaphysical investigation
has continued despite prophesies of its imminent demise. Analytic philosophy has also claimed to analyse the language of science so as to clarify
its concepts. But scientists, though they sometimes seek philosophical aid,
need no outsiders to teach them the meaning of their own terms, which
they themselves define precisely to serve the purposes of their science.
Nevertheless, it may be argued, even though Analytic philosophy may
have become a rather specialized expertise, acquired for no clearly as-
signable purpose, it is a fascinating intellectual exercise, the pleasure of
which is not to be denied to those who have a penchant for it. That may
well be the case, as can be said of many other pastimes, but if this were
all that could be said in its favour, it would have no bearing upon the
issue from which we began, and Analysts would have no legitimate right
to interdict philosophical reflection upon the fundamental questions

which are Spinoza's concern. The age-old questions, how men should direct their lives and towards what ultimate aims, remain insistent, and they have never been more urgent than they are at the present time.

On the wall of Spinoza's dwelling there appear to this day the lines:

> "Ach waren alle Menschen wijs
> En wilden daarbij wel!
> De Aard' waar haar een Paradijs
> Nu is ze meest een Hel" [4]

If they were appropriate in the 17th Century they are even more apt in the late 20th. Never was there more doubt or more confusion in men's minds, particularly those of the young, about the ultimate aims and purposes of life. Never was there more bewilderment or dissension over the most satisfactory way to live. We are faced by problems of the greatest magnitude affecting the entire population of the earth: the dangers of atomic warfare, the spread of environmental deterioration, the pressures of overpopulation; the contradictions and iniquities of economic practices and the inequalities of distribution; the conflict of social relations and the breakdown of communication between the old and the young. They are all inter-connected problems and their solutions all depend upon the answer we find to the fundamental question of ultimate human purposes.

The urgency and reality of the question has been well recognized by Existentialist thinkers, but they too tend to deny the right of the philosopher to pontificate, and they rightly insist that it is a question each individual must and can only decide for himself. They repudiate, therefore, any claim of reason to universal authority and reject as impossible any effort at deductive system-building claiming the assent of every sane mind. To live according to reason is but one (and not necessarily the best) among many possible alternative choices, which neither savant nor priest has any right to impose upon others. The only valid decision is what each person genuinely and authentically makes by his own free will, be it judged "rational" or otherwise, and by whatever extrinsic criterion. But Existentialists who hold this sort of view do not and cannot consistently adhere to it if they publish their philosophy and advocate its tenets to others. For, not only must they defend their position rationally if they are to be heeded, but also they must advocate it as objectively right if they are to be believed. Further, were each person to choose arbitrarily and

---

[4] "Oh, if but all men were wise and acted accordingly! Earth would then be Paradise. Now it is mostly Hell." A verse by Dirk R. Camphuyzen inscribed on the house at Rijnsburg in which Spinoza lived between 1660 and 1662.

according to inclination, nothing but confusion and conflict could result.[5] Some principle must guide our choice and it is this principle that we must seek to know. True it is that each must seek it for himself and no one can take it on trust from any other. Nevertheless, the search is by no means easy. It is not even easy to be clear for what precisely we are seeking. The guidance, therefore, of other men's thought and experience on these major questions is not to be scorned, and where better do we find this if not among the great philosophers of the past; especially as they, like Socrates, Plato and Spinoza, were themselves responding to the same existential urge to find ultimate satisfaction of spirit.

3. Groundspring of philosophy

One must go far to find any more authentic or convincing witness to the initial unease and the urge to find final satisfaction than Spinoza's. At the beginning of his unfinished *Treatise on the Improvement* [6] *of the Intellect* he states the reasons which led him to choose a life of contemplation, and he gives expression to what is the genuine motive for philosophizing. I can do no better than begin my account of Spinoza's philosophy by quoting his own words:

"After experience had taught me that everything which is usually met with in common life is vain and futile; when I saw that all things about which I was wont to be anxious held nothing in themselves of good or evil, except so far as the mind was moved by them; I decided at length to inquire whether there was anything which was a true good, capable of imparting itself, and by which alone, all else having been given up, the mind might be affected; in short, whether there was anything by the discovery and acquisition of which I might enjoy happiness continually and for all eternity . . .

"For things, which for the most part, offer themselves in life, and are held by men, as one may gather from their actions, to be the highest good, are reducible to these three: riches, honour and sensual pleasure. The mind is so distracted by these three that it can by no means think of any other good. For, with respect to sensual pleasure, the mind is so obsessed with it, as if absorbed in something good, that it is entirely prevented from thinking of anything else. But after the enjoyment of that kind of pleasure, the greatest depression follows, which, if it does not engross the mind altogether, yet confuses and dulls it. The pursuit of honours and wealth distracts the mind no less, especially when they are

---

[5] This, we shall see, was recognized by none more clearly than Spinoza.
[6] Perhaps better translated "Rectification."

sought exclusively for their own sake ... But if our hope is in any event frustrated, then the deepest dismay arises. Honour, moreover, is a great hindrance because, to attain it, one must direct one's life according to other men's views, avoiding what they commonly avoid and seeking what they commonly seek ...

"These evils, moreover, seemed to arise from this, that all happiness or unhappiness depends solely upon the quality of the object to which we attach ourselves by love. For on account of that which is not loved, no strife will arise, there will be no sorrow if it perishes, no envy should another possess it, no fear, no hatred, in a word, no agitation of the mind; all of which, however, occur for the love of those things that are perishable, like all those about which we have just been speaking. But love towards an eternal and infinite object feeds the mind with joy alone, from which all sorrow is excluded, and that is mightily to be desired and to be sought with all one's strength."

Because this is the genuine starting point of all philosophy and because it is still the crying need of our generation, the satisfaction of which is sought by all kinds of devious methods and in the most unlikely places, even in resort to drugs – because this is indeed so, Spinoza's philosophy remains relevant in our day; and if we trace the development and inter-connexion of his ideas, woven as they are into a system of the most elegant unity, we see just how relevant this starting point remains to the most mundane and practical problems of day to day life and politics.

"An eternal and infinite object," one may question, "what could be more remote from the demands and pressures of every-day life? – and does not Spinoza himself say that we must renounce all pursuit of pleasure, gain and social recognition, in the search. This is to become an academic recluse, as Spinoza himself was. If every man were to follow his example, the practical affairs of life would be utterly neglected and its whole social and political structure would collapse."

But if Spinoza speaks here for himself and not necessarily for others – certainly not for all – he was by no means averse to sharing his discovery with his fellow men and he believed (for reasons that will appear) that ultimate satisfaction, once found, neither could or should be enjoyed in isolation. Whoever achieves it must of necessity wish others to achieve it likewise. So, at the end of the *Short Treatise on God, Man and Human Welfare*, he appeals to the friends for whose benefit it was written: "Be-cause you are not unaware of the conditions of the age in which we live, I would urge you most strongly to be careful about imparting these matters to others. I shall not say that you should keep them solely to yourselves, but only that, if ever you proceed to impart them to anybody, you have no other aim or purpose than the welfare of your neighbour, as one on whom you are unmistakably assured that the reward of your labour will not be lost."

Although pursuit of pleasure, wealth and honour is renounced (not altogether, but only as ends in themselves),[7] Spinoza was no ascetic. He approved of moderate indulgence in worldly pleasures, so far as they are necessary for health and happiness. "Nothing," he says, "save stern and dismal superstition prohibits enjoyment. For why should it be more becoming to relieve hunger and thirst than to dispel melancholy? This is my principle and thus am I persuaded: No deity nor any except the envious takes pleasure in my weakness or discomfort, or ascribes to us as virtue tears, sobs, fear and other things of this sort, which are signs of weakness of spirit, but, on the contrary, the more we are moved to delight, the more perfect we become, that is, to that extent, we necessarily participate the more in the divine nature. Thus it is characteristic of the wise man to use things and to take pleasure in them as much as he can (not indeed *ad nauseam,* for that is not to take pleasure). It is, I say, the part of a wise man to nourish himself with congenial food and drink in moderation and to refresh himself with perfumes, the delight of growing plants, adornments, music, sport and theatre, and other recreations of this kind that anyone can enjoy without harm to others." (*Ethics,* IV, xlv, S.) [8]

Nor was Spinoza really a mere academic recluse, not only did he have pupils and correspondents and a circle of studious admirers,[9] but he also had friends among public men and politicians who (we have good reason to believe) consulted him on practical matters and at least once enlisted his services on a quasi-diplomatic mission. Further, he believed and taught that men should conscientiously perform their civic duties, writing in the *Theologico-Political Treatise*:

"It is certain that duty (*pietas*) to one's country is the highest that anyone can be responsible for; for if government is abolished, nothing good can be accomplished, but everything comes into dispute, and only hostility (*ira*) and disloyalty, but most of all fear, prevail." [10]

It takes all sorts to make a world, and many different interdependent

---

[7] Cf. *TdIE.,* II, 2.

[8] Cf. also, *TdIE.,* II, 14, and *Ep.* XXI: "I endeavour to pass my life not sorrowing and complaining, but in tranquility, joy and cheerfulness . . ."

[9] Eg. Simon de Vries and his brother, Peter Balling, Ludovicus Meyer, Jarig-Jelles, Johan Bouwmeester, Georg Schuller, etc.

[10] *T.Th.P.,* XIX.

functions to constitute a society, and Spinoza thought it neither advisable nor possible that everybody should follow the same course as he adopted for himself. But he did believe it was possible under certain conditions for everybody to enjoy satisfaction and peace of mind, what he called "salvation." Though it might not be possible for all to achieve this through philosophy, yet the majority could achieve it through good government and a purified form of religion, which he considered universal and independent of the various doctrinal and theological trappings attached to it by the different sects. His philosophy is a genuine search for this salvation, not by way of wishful thinking, but by the most rigorous and exact reasoning, rejecting anything, however otherwise attractive it may seem, if it is not consistent in itself and deducible from first principles that are wholly clear and distinct. Spinoza's desire above all is for truth, through which alone he believed salvation was to be found, and he would tolerate no method of discovery that was not rigorously scientific. So his first approach to his self-appointed task is to seek a method of purifying, or clarifying, the understanding, so that nothing doubtful, confused or ill-founded should be entertained. Only knowledge of the best and most adequate kind, he held, is efficacious for salvation.

4. Spinoza's Scientific Attitude

This is another important way in which Spinoza's thought is relevant to our modern situation. Today we turn to science for the solution of all our problems – not always wisely, but at least because we have come to believe, as we should, that nothing is reliable which has not been demonstrated and reasoned out on strict scientific principles. Religion today has lost its hold on many because it cannot, or does not, establish its doctrine scientifically and cannot, so they think, be made consistent with what science has established. This modern scientific attitude is precisely Spinoza's; but where he excels is in combining it completely with what can only rightly be called a religious outlook and in developing by strictly rational argument a religious conclusion. So he addresses himself to both of our most urgent and most significant modern needs. He provides an answer (and no trivial one) to our moral and religious perplexities, and he does so in a way which satisfies our demand for scientific precision and reliability.

This last point would very probably be repudiated by some contemporary thinkers. In the first place there are those who would deny that Spinoza's deductive method [11] is scientific in the proper sense of the word,

[11] See Ch. II below.

because it claims to deduce matters of fact *a priori* from premisses taken to be self-evident. We shall find, however, that this is not a correct description of Spinoza's proceeding and involves misunderstanding. Equally it is based on a misconception of sound scientific method and on philosophical preconceptions which are unwarranted (and which, incidentally, Spinoza rejected). The presumption behind this criticism of Spinoza's method is that science proceeds by observation of facts, knowledge of which can only be obtained in the first instance through sense-perception, and then constructs its theories by generalization from the primary observation, checking them finally by deducing consequences from them and submitting those to further observational test. This is a long-standing empirical view, but contemporary philosophy of science has demonstrated its error and its falsity to the actual practice of scientists,[12] and has made it clear that genuine science has more in common with Spinoza's reasoning than either Empiricists or idealistic commentators have been wont to allow.

In the second place, from a very different quarter, a reaction against the scientific attitude has recently set in, which sees in it the source of all our ills and problems. Heidegger [13] has argued that the scientific rationalism, adopted as the norm of Western thought at the Renaissance, has increasingly subjected our outlook and culture to the dominance of technique – organised, systematic, method. But technique is essentially and solely a means to the achievement of ends, which must be selected on other grounds, and which rational and scientific methods can never determine. But contemporary thinking is limited to rational standards and recognizes no other as capable of validating its findings. The consequence is increasing technical efficiency, which, while it seems to solve some problems, continually creates others more intractable, stimulating the invention of new and more complicated techniques in a vicious circle that tends towards no discoverable objective. Similarly Hans Jonas has shown with great lucidity how the scientific revolution of the seventeenth century, in the service of a strictly rational analysis, conceived the world as a lifeless machine.[14] Thus the phenomena of life and mind were either left outside of this mechanical universe, inexplicable by scientific methods, or else reduced to a material mechanism that belied their essential char-

---

[12] Cf. K. Popper, *The Logic of Scientific Discovery* (London, 1959; New York, 1961); N. R. Hanson, *Patterns of Discovery* (Cambridge, 1958); T. Kuhn, *The Structure of Scientific Revolutions* (Chicago, 1962); I. Lakatos and A. Musgrave, *Criticism and the Growth of Knowledge* (Cambridge, 1970); and my *Hypothesis and Perception* (London, 1970).

[13] Cf. *op. cit.*

[14] Cf. *op. cit.*, First Essay and Appendix to Second Essay.

acter and virtually eliminated them from the scientific scene. In such a world the human spirit feels abandoned. It is a dead purposeless universe into which man feels himself simply to have been "thrown." So far from "rational," it now appears totally absurd, and man, finding no response in it to his search for "meaning," no satisfaction of his urge and aspiration, no rest for his spirit, is relinquished to despair and ultimate frustration.

The root and origin of this debacle is identified as rationalism – the very rationalism of which Spinoza is an outstanding advocate and of which his philosophy is perhaps the most typical and complete example. How, then, can it offer any solace to our modern ills, or solution to our modern perplexities?

There are, however, at least two conceptions of reason of which only one is represented in the Heideggerian and existentialist critique. Reason may be viewed, used and treated merely as an analytic instrument – simply as a method of deducing conclusions from premises derived from experience – as it was by Hume when he declared that reason was "the slave of the passions." This is the characteristic empiricist view. When reason is conceived in this way all the consequences follow which the existentialist critique deplores. But reason, in a higher form is constructive and prescriptive, the source of order and systematic completeness which establishes the ultimate standards of truth and perfection.[15] This ambiguity of "reason" is recognized by many of the great philosophers, one among whom is Spinoza. It is reflected in Plato's distinction between διάνοια and ἐπιστήμη, in Hegel's contrast of *Verstand* with *Vernunft,* and in Spinoza it is seen in the advance from *ratio* to *scientia intuitiva*.[16] The problems, practical and theoretical, which prove insoluble for instrumental reason, may well be transformed and resolved by a more adequate and more truly philosophical approach.

If the use of reason generates problems, it can only be by the further exercise of the intellect that they can, if ever, be solved. The philosophers who condemn and castigate reason do not and cannot relinquish its use, and it is still by reasoning and arguments, which they present as having universal force, that they develop their own critique. To abandon reason is to abandon all comprehensible knowledge. Practical activity which is irrational can solve problems, if at all, only by accident, and is more liable to create confusion and chaos in which none of us should see salvation.

---

[15] Cf. H. Horkheimer's discussion in *The Eclipse of Reason* (O.U.P., 1947).

[16] These terms will be explained below (p. 105-109) they correspond generally to "understanding" and "speculative reason."

Our perplexities arise out of conflicts in our experience and practice, and our efforts at solution are the promptings of our rational propensities. Questions can be answered, therefore, only by taking thought; and answers, if they are to be found, can satisfy only if they are intellectually acceptable. Of this, Spinoza was fully aware and his philosophy is one of the most systematic and coherent presentations ever made of the human situation, the conflicts and failings of passionate human nature, and its ultimate source of satisfaction.

CHAPTER II

GEOMETRICAL METHOD

1. The primacy of knowledge

The ultimate concern of Spinoza's philosophy, as we have seen, is not simply a theoretical interest in ethics but a deep practical desire to discover the best way to live. Spinoza was no mere theorist; he put his philosophy into practice and lived the kind of life he found on theoretical grounds to be the most satisfactory. And he did so only when and because he was rationally convinced. Though experience taught him that the pursuit of mundane advantages was frustrating and unsatisfying, he was not content to accept experience as the final arbiter of the truth and to rest his convictions upon it. That experience was real and bitter. The Synagogue, in which his learning and great intellectual powers might have qualified him for distinction, rejected him with the most awesome curses and expelled him from the Jewish community. His own sister attempted to exclude him from his heritage, so that he had to resort to the law to establish his rights (which he then voluntarily relinquished). In trade he found men all too ready to swindle and defraud; and, if Lucas' report is to be trusted, an attempt was made upon his life for no stronger reason than that his opinions and neglect of religious observance displeased the Jewish authorities. With reason he was able to write that experience had taught him that all things usually encountered in common life were futile and vain.

Yet it was not to experience that Spinoza appealed to convince himself of the superiority of the contemplative life, but only to the unshakable demonstration of sound reasoning. The treatise, from which I have quoted above, while setting out the ultimate moral aim of his philosophy at the very beginning, proceeds at once to assert that the first and indispensable condition of success in the quest for moral satisfaction is the purification of the intellect, the discovery of the best and surest kind of knowledge,

and the best method of investigation. That, forthwith, is acknowledged
as the main subject matter of the *Tractatus*.[1]

The search for the right method and the best kind of knowledge, however, threatens *prima facie* to lead us into an infinite regress. Before we
know how to proceed to discover the right method, should we not seek
the right method of such proceeding? But that would imply a prior search
for a prior method, and so on *ad infinitum*.[2] But we are not really in any
such predicament, for methodology is a reflective study – a knowledge
about knowledge, an idea of an idea.[3] Before we can embark upon it,
therefore, all that is required is that we have some knowledge on which to
reflect, some idea the nature of which we may investigate. And unless
we do already have some such idea reflection cannot begin.

Now an idea, for Spinoza, is an act of knowing [4] and he uses the term
almost with verbal force, so that he calls its object *ideatum* (what is
"ideated"). The idea, he explains, is the "objective essence" of the
ideatum, while the actual existence of the *ideatum* is called its "formal
essence." [5] These two kinds of "essence," we shall see later, are in reality
the same. So Spinoza maintains that a true idea, one which exactly
corresponds to the actual (formal) essence of its *ideatum*, is nothing other
than the objective essence. Accordingly, we need no extrinsic mark by
which to recognize a true idea. To have one is *ipso facto* to know that it
is true. It is, so to speak, self-validating or self-guaranteeing. The truth,
he says, is like light, which reveals both itself and darkness. It is its own
criterion and also that of falsity.[6] In other words, we judge false ideas to

---

[1] *V.V.L.* I, p. 7. *TdIE.*, IV, 18.

[2] Cf. *Ibid.*, VI. 30 (*V.V.L.*, I, p. 10): "Now that we know what sort of knowledge
is necessary to us, the way and method must be set out by which we may know the
things which are knowable by this knowledge. In order that that should be done, it
comes to be considered first that this inquiry will not be one *in infinitum*; that is to
say, there is no need, in order to find the best method of investigating the truth, of
another method to investigate the method by which truth should be sought; and to
investigate the second method, there is no need of a third, and so *in infinitum*: for in
such a manner, knowledge of the truth, indeed knowledge of any kind, would never
be reached."

[3] The doctrine of *idea ideae* will occupy us at more length below, p. 87.

[4] Cf. *Ethics* II, Def. III: "By idea I understand a conception of the mind, which
the mind forms because it is a thinking thing.

Explanation: I say 'conception' rather than 'perception' because the word,
perception, seems to indicate that the mind is passive to the object; but conception
is seen to express action of the mind."

[5] Cf. *TdIE.*, VI, 33 (*V.V.L.* I. p. 11). *Essentia formalis* and *essentia objectivis* are
technical terms in the scholastic language of Spinoza's time. The term "objective" was
used in almost exactly the opposite sense to ours today. Objective was what was
represented in the idea (its ideal content), whereas the external existence of the
thing "ideated" was said to be its "formal" or "subjective" being.

[6] *Ethics*, II, xliii, S.

be such by comparison with true ones which rank as the standard for all knowledge. The intrinsic criterion by which a true idea reveals itself as true is a sort of internal coherence or "perfection," the nature of which we shall come to understand better at a later stage (when Spinoza's use of the words "perfection" and "reality" have been fully explained). An engineer examining a plan for a newly invented machine can tell from its internal organization and arrangement whether or not it will work. If it will it ranks as a "true" representation of the machine – its true idea – and there would be no need to compare it with an actually existing model to discover this. Likewise, a geometer examining the idea of a triangle and proving Euclid's theorems about it can tell that they are true from their internal coherence without examining (or measuring) actually existing triangular things. Accordingly, to have a true idea is to know it to be true, and we need no special method to discover the criterion of truth, but "the true method is the way in which truth itself, or the objective essences or ideas of things . . . must be sought in their proper order." [7]

To discover the right method, therefore, all we need is a true idea; for the method "is nothing other than reflexive knowledge, or idea of an idea; and because an idea of an idea is not given unless an idea is first given, so there would be no method unless there were first an idea." [8] Further, an idea (or "objective" essence) stands in relation to another idea as the formal essences of their *ideata* are related, so that reflection upon the idea of a perfect being will be more excellent than reflection upon that of some lesser object. It follows that the best method will be that derived from reflection upon the idea of the most perfect object – "that which shows, according to the standard of a given idea of the most perfect being, in what manner the mind should be directed." [9] In short, the right method must be derived from reflection upon the idea of God.

Spinoza's own reflection upon the nature of God led him, as we shall shortly see, to the conclusion that all things, and the knowledge of all things (all truths), follow from God's nature in a necessary and eternal order, as the properties of a triangle follow necessarily from its definition in geometry. It was, therefore, natural for him to conclude that once we had grasped the idea of God, everything else should be deducible from that idea in geometrical order. God, he found, was the immanent cause of all things. Nothing can either be or be conceived apart from God, and everything can and must be conceived only through God. It follows,

---

[7] *TdIE.*, VII, 36 (*V.V.L.* I, p. 12). This theory of truth will be further considered below (pp. 89-109).
[8] *Ibid.*, 38.
[9] *Ibid.*

clearly, that all adequate knowledge can be attained only if it is deduced
by consecutive steps from the nature of God. Spinoza, accordingly, proceeds forthwith to adopt this method and deduces the entire system of
his philosophy in geometrical order from the definition of God as an
absolutely infinite being.

I say that Spinoza proceeded forthwith to use the geometrical method.
He did so in the *Ethics,* but it does not, of course, immediately appear in
the unfinished *Tractatus de Intellectus Emendatione.* There he proceeds,
after some general defence of his argument against possible objections
from persistent sceptics, to explain the nature of fictions, false ideas, doubt
and forgetfulness, and then to lay down rules for definition. The *Treatise*
breaks off as he is proceeding to examine the properties of the intellect
in preparation for the formulation of an adequate definition of it. From
this, he says, when we have acquired it, we can deduce the way in which
the intellect can attain to the knowledge of eternal things. The *Treatise*
is an early work, and though there is evidence in his correspondence that
Spinoza always intended to complete it, there is some doubt whether he
would ever have continued it as it now is rather than have rewritten it
entirely. It seems not unlikely that he broke off when he did, realizing
that his opening argument really required him to define, not the intellect,
as a first step, but God or Substance, and then to proceed *geometrico
ordine* from that. And this he had already begun to do by 1663 in what
was probably the first draft of the *Ethics.*[10] Once he had developed his
entire system, as he did in that work, there was no call to return to an
introductory treatise, which (as internal and external evidence indicates)
was intended to lead up to the exposition of material, covering the same
ground as the *Ethics.* To this projected work Spinoza refers in footnotes
to the *Treatise* as "my philosophy." [11]

Although the geometrical method had already been suggested by
Descartes and Spinoza had, at an early date, developed that suggestion,
setting out Descartes's philosophy at length in geometrical order, his use
of it in the *Ethics* is just one of the many examples of Spinoza's relentless
consistency. He had decided, as a result of his own reflection upon the
nature of things, that everything flows of necessity from the infinite essence of God and that (as will appear later) the order and connexion of

---

[10] Cf. *Epp.* II, III (in which reference is made to geometric method and quotations
of axioms and propositions not identical with those which appear in the Appendix to
K.V.), and *Epp.* VIII, IX, X.
[11] Cf. *TdIE.*, VI, 31 nn 1 and 2; VII, 36 n, IX, 76, n 1. (*V.V.L.* I, pp. 10, 12
and 24).

ideas was the same as that of things.[12] All that was needed, then, was to purify the mind from confusion (the source of which we shall shortly see is sensuous imagination) in order to be able to develop in logical order the entire system of reality – not in detail, but according to its essential structural principles. That system, Spinoza held, was single and integral, with every distinguishable part dependent for its character and existence upon its systematic relationship to every other, and to their interconnexion in the whole. The whole was absolutely prior to the parts (terms not wholly appropriate to express the true relationship) and was the source both of the conception and of the occurrence in space and time, of finite entities.[13] If, therefore, things are to be known as they really are, and are to be properly understood, they must be seen in their actual relation within the entire system, and that, in the nature of the case, must be demonstrable by deduction from the essence of the ultimate being or totality – God – the fundamental ordering of the entire structure.

2. Critics of Spinoza's method

Spinoza's use of the geometrical method of exposition, apart from the difficulty it occasions for students approaching his philosophy for the first time, has been much criticized by commentators, and has been blamed for many of the difficulties and obscurities in his philosophy, even for what the critics view as philosophical errors. Hegelian commentators, like John Caird and Harold Joachim consider the use of the method a confusion of levels of knowledge which Spinoza himself had distinguished. The method of mathematics, they maintain, is appropriate to science and to subject matters which are quantitative and mechanistic in character, and it must be limited to them. Philosophy is concerned with mind and spirit which can neither be conceived nor treated under categories of quantity. To the distinction (to which reference has already been made above [14]) between *ratio* and *scientia intuitiva* (or Understanding and Reason), there corresponds a similar distinction of method between science and philosophy, and while Spinoza has recognized the first, he has failed to observe the second.

Caird points out that geometry (like all special sciences) is hypothetical in character. It is founded upon assumptions which philosophy cannot

---

[12] Cf. *Ethics II*, vii and H. H. Joachim, *Study of the Ethics of Spinoza* (Oxford, 1901, New York, 1964), Introduction. Hereafter abbreviated *Study*.

[13] The place of space, time and finite events in Spinoza's system is hedged about with difficulties, which are discussed below, pp. 98-103.

[14] P. 13.

leave unquestioned. It is abstract and achieves clarity by sacrificing concrete content, and simplicity by sacrificing depth. Its method is adapted to the treatment of quantity and extension, the essentially self-external, and is therefore unsuited to the study even of chemical and biological facts, let alone psychological and moral. Spinoza's use of the geometrical method, therefore, (so Caird argues) misleads him into confusing the infinite with the indefinitely extensive, and so causes him to define infinity as what excludes all negation. It leads him likewise to regard all natural events including human action and psychological experience as mechanically determined and so to deny teleology in nature and free will to man.[15]

Joachim clearly understands Spinoza's reasons for adopting the geometrical order of exposition and acknowledges that it never occurred to the author of the *Ethics* that he was distorting his subject matter by forcing it into an alien mould.[16] But Joachim certainly believed that the method had just such distorting effects and is largely responsible for many of the difficulties which he finds in Spinoza's doctrine.[17]

But such criticisms are surely misplaced. Whether or not Spinoza's philosophical opinions are sound, all those to which Caird raises objections appear in the *Short Treatise* where the geometrical method is not used. An experimental attempt is made in the Appendix at the end of that Treatise to cast the first principles of the system in geometrical form, but only after the doctrines have been set out and argued in straightforward prose. It cannot, therefore, be the method that generates the philosophical difficulties, so far as they exist. Similarly, Joachim finds much the same obscurities (along with some others) in the *Treatise on the Improvement of the Understanding*, which is not written in geometrical order.[18] Everything that Spinoza set out *geometrico ordine* could easily (much more easily) have been expounded in the more common form of philosophical argument, as Joachim's admirable and faithful paraphrases, throughout his commentary, bear witness. There can be little doubt that Spinoza adopted the method because it seemed to him to follow logically from his philosophical conception of the nature of things, and not the other way round. His philosophical views are not the consequences of his

---

[15] Cf. John Caird, *Spinoza* (London, 1910), Ch. VI. Also H. G. Hubbeling, *Spinoza's Methodology*, (Assen, 1967), p. 10 and passim.

[16] Cf. *Study*. Introd.

[17] Cf. *op. cit.*, Appendix to Book I, pp. 115-119, Book II, Ch. III, pp. 189-90, Appendix, pp. 230-232.

[18] Cf. Joachim, *Spinoza's Tractatus de Intellectus Emendatione* (Oxford, 1940), Ch. II, § 6, Ch. III, Excursus, Ch. IV, § 21 and passim. (Hereafter abbreviated as *Spinoza's Tractatus*).

method of presentation,[19] but the method is dictated by his metaphysics.

Indeed, Spinoza did not believe (whether rightly or wrongly) that the method was solely appropriate to the second kind of knowledge (*ratio*). It is undoubtedly the case that he considered his own philosophizing, especially in the *Ethics*, to be an example of *scientia intuitiva*. If then mathematics is held to be typical only of *ratio*, the method of the *Ethics*, must be regarded as geometrical in name only, and by a sort of analogy. In its actual application it has little more than a superficial resemblance to Euclid's, as I shall try to show below.

3. Deduction

From the point of view of present-day Empiricism Spinoza is criticized for attempting to set out a comprehensive theory of the world and man as a purely deductive system. Such a task, according to modern logical theory, is in the nature of the case impossible, because purely deductive logic is analytic (and therefore in essence tautological). It can accordingly give no factual information about the world, which can be acquired only from experience and by induction. A deductive system is one in which rules are given for analyticity, for the construction of analytic sentences and for the derivation, by transformation, of other sentences from those conforming to the given rules. These derived sentences will, in consequence, themselves be analytic. Nothing so derived can give us new information about actual facts, and the logical system so constructed can do no more than reveal the logical relations between formulae which it contains and between them and others derivable from them by the transformation rules prescribed.[20]

The rules themselves as well as any definitions and axioms which may be required are formulated quite arbitrarily for none have been found which can be called self-evident and which might not, in another system, be derivable from other axioms. Accordingly, no logical system can be constructed which is ideal or absolute. There are many possible alternative systems, and which of them we use will depend purely on convenience, as most suitable for our subject matter or the purpose we have in hand.[21] It will be clear that this doctrine involves a purely instrumental conception of logic.

Spinoza, in contrast, regarded his definitions as necessary and unalterable. They were, for him, what have been called "real" definitions, as

[19] For the contrary view see, Stuart Hampshire, *Spinoza* (London, 1956), pp. 89-91; R. McKeon, *The Philosophy of Spinoza*, (New York, 1928).

[20] Cf. P. F. Strawson, *Introduction to Logical Theory*, (London, 1952), pp. 58ff.

[21] Cf. Hubbeling, *Spinoza*, (Baarn 1966), p. 44.

opposed to merely stipulative definitions.[22] That is to say, each was supposed to state succinctly what was the actual essence of the thing defined in such a way that all its properties could be deduced from it.[23] His axioms he regarded as indubitably true, such that once presented to the mind they could not reasonably be denied. In short they are offered as self-evidently true. From such definitions and axioms he believed it possible in principle to deduce theorems describing everything in the universe; in particular the correct definition of God, as we have seen, was deemed capable of generating this result.

Quite apart from modern beliefs about God, the twentieth century logician would deny the legitimacy of any of the above claims. Definitions stating actual essence from which all properties can be deduced would be pronounced impossible, unless all the properties of the thing "defined" were already known empirically, and then the definition would be the same as an exhaustive description. That again would be regarded as impossible (at any rate in practice) because it would involve listing an infinite number of experienceable characters. If it were possible, nothing new could then be deduced from the definition.

So far from self-evidently true, many modern philosophers would find the majority of Spinoza's axioms dubious, and some of them even false. If they considered any of them acceptable it would be only when they were tautologous, or else on empirical grounds. But Spinoza rejected "experience" as a source of reliable knowledge. What we learn by experience, he thought, was only the accidental characteristics of things, or, at best, was accepted without clear understanding, and so was true for us only contingently. To know something, in the proper sense of the term "know," was to grasp its necessary relations to everything else, that is, to apprehend its logical relations to the entire system of Nature.[24] The modern empiricist, on the other hand, denies that there are any logical relations between distinct matters of fact,[25] so that Spinoza's requirements for true knowledge he would consider absurd.

These differences are, in the main, consequences of the traditional conflict between Empiricism and Rationalism (of which Spinoza is an eminent representative). But to think of Spinoza simply as a typical rationalist is to underestimate his philosophical importance and to misunderstand his philosophy. The true greatness of Spinoza's thought results

---

[22] Cf. *Ep.* IX.
[23] Cf. *TdIE.*, XIII, 95, 96. (*V.V.L.* I, p. 29).
[24] See p. 33-39 below for explanation and discussion of the use of this term.
[25] Cf. A. J. Ayer, *The Problem of Knowledge,* (Harmondsworth, 1956), p. 29, for instance.

from his ability to rise above this traditional dispute and to offer a doctrine which, in effect, reconciles the differences between the traditional
approaches. The points of conflict listed above follow, for the most part,
from accepting and assuming that Spinoza held a notion of deductive
thinking as something wholly independent of experience, as beginning
from and moving constantly within pure abstraction, and as operating
according to purely formal rules with purely formal concepts.

To some extent, and so far as he followed Descartes, Spinoza did entertain a notion of deductive reasoning which began from simple premisses
and moved step by step, each clear and distinct, to an assured conclusion.[26]
But this is by no means the whole of his views of right thinking and sound
knowledge. It is typical rather of his earlier and relatively immature
thought; and even so, he insists at the same time that abstractions are to
be eschewed.[27] Abstractions, he averred, were mere constructions of the
mind and corresponded to nothing real in Nature. For the most part they
are simply verbal and are liable to be a source of confusion rather than
sound knowledge. On the other hand, he refuses to rely solely upon experience because he holds (like Aristotle) that the full understanding of
any thing or event depends upon a knowledge of its cause, and the finite
things and events of common experience depend on a series of causes
extending back to infinity, which cannot, therefore, be comprehended.
But he does not reject experience altogether, and often appeals to it to
confirm conclusions which he has reached by deductive argument.[28]

On the other hand, he believed that there were certain "fixed and
eternal things," which (he thought he could demonstrate) were the ultimate grounds, and which determined the necessary laws of being of all
mutable and finite entities. If we direct our attention to these, he believed,
we could grasp them adequately and so attain to complete knowledge.
These "eternal things," though individuals, are ubiquitous in their influence and power, and so function for us as universals "or genera of the
definitions of changeable particular things and the proximate causes of
all things." [29] These "eternal things" are of profound importance in
Spinoza's philosophy. We shall see anon that they are the infinite and
eternal essence of God, his attributes and their infinite modes, and we
shall examine the part they play in Spinoza's system. The point to which

---

[26] Cf. *TdIE.*, VIII, 65.
[27] *TdIE.*, XIII, 97-99.
V, vi, S.
[28] Cf. *T.Th.P.*, V. XIX; *T.P.*, I, 3; II, 6; *Ethics* I, App.; II, xviii, S; III, ii, S.;
V. vi, S.
[29] *TdIE.*, XIV, 101 (*V.V.L.*, I, p. 31).

I wish to draw attention here is that though they are not abstractions, and are said to be individuals (*singularia*), yet they are universal.

The idea of God can never be abstract. God is not a category or a class or the common property of a collection of similar things. He is inclusive of all being, and the idea of him is the ground of all ideas and the source of all understanding. It is therefore the most concrete of all ideas. His attributes are the ways in which his essence is conceived and they are similarly both all-embracing, each in its special kind, and concrete. The same is true of the infinite modes. We shall have more to say in later chapters of all these matters. What we must observe at this point is that they correspond very closely to what Hegel and later philosophers called "concrete universals" (i.e. comprehensive, systematically organized realities), and they are the foundation and source of Spinoza's deductive system. It is from them that everything else follows necessarily. It is through them, and only through them, that finite things can be conceived.[30]

Now, as we shall discover, these "eternal things" are concrete systematic totalities made up of distinguishable (but not separable) finite parts (or "modes"), so inter-related that their existence, order of occurrence and individual characters are all intimately interdependent. If then we can discover the laws, or principles, of their mutual relations, we can read off from a knowledge of one part of the system what must obtain in any other. Deduction, therefore, will be possible from particular facts, in conjunction with the laws of their interconnexion, to other particular facts; or from the systematic character of the whole to the consequent nature of the parts. This is a different conception of deductive reasoning from that assumed by both sides in the dispute between traditional Empiricism and Rationalism.

In the first place, it is reasoning which proceeds from concrete facts to other concrete facts – not from abstractly "universal" premises. It therefore involves experience in so far as the concrete facts which serve as first premises are implicit in any experience whatsoever (a point later taken up and developed by Kant). In the second place, the reasoning proceeds by developing systematic connexions between facts which are determined by universal and necessary laws inherent in the all-inclusive structure of reality – the structure which is the absolute presupposition of the method. It is therefore properly called deductive reasoning.

That this is Spinoza's conception of the best method will become pro-

---

[30] *Ibid.*

gressively more apparent as we proceed. One example may, however, be cited as evidence. In the *TdIE.* (VII, 41),[31] after he has explained that reflection upon the idea of the most perfect being will yield the most perfect method, he writes:

"Add to this the fact that an idea is objectively in the same situation as its *ideatum* is in reality. If, therefore, there was anything in Nature which had no inter-connexions (*commercii*) with other things, then, if its objective essence were also given, which ought in every way to agree with its formal essence, it too would have no connexions with other ideas; that is, we could deduce (*poterimus concludere*) nothing from it. On the other hand, those things that have inter-connexion with other things, as do all things that exist in Nature, are intelligible (*intelligentur*), and their objective essences also have the same inter-connexion, that is, other ideas are deduced from them, which again have inter-connexion with others, and so instruments for proceeding further accumulate (*crescunt*)."

Deduction, therefore, is neither a process from simple idea to simple idea (as in Descartes), nor a succession of transformations of formulae, or sentences, as in modern logic, but is the tracing out of connexions within a concrete system, of inter-related facts.

Professor Hubbeling maintains that there is, in Spinoza's philosophy, a pervasive tension between his deductive thinking and his nominalism;[32] but if we understand the character of Spinoza's deductive thinking aright, we see that there is no real conflict. Nominalism is the doctrine that general or universal properties common to a number of particular things (e.g. triangularity, hardness, blueness, etc.) have no real existence in nature, but are simply words or names referring to the innumerable particular occurrences of the quality named. It is a doctrine characteristic of empiricist philosophies and it is therefore surprising to find it advocated by a rationalist like Spinoza. He certainly does maintain that nothing in reality corresponds to general terms, and, in one place, he even denies reality to relations,[33] calling them things of the mind (*entia rationis*), as opposed to real things (*entia realia*). But Spinoza's nominalism is simply the obverse of his protest against abstractions.

Traditional logic teaches that deduction proceeds from a universal (or general) statement to another universal, or to a particular statement, while induction proceeds from the particular to the general. Spinoza rejects both of these methods of reasoning, induction because of its

---

[31] *V.V.L.*, I, p. 13.
[32] Cf. *Spinoza's Methodology*, Ch. I, § 4.
[33] *K.V.*, I, x. (*V.V.L.*, IV, p. 35).

uncertainty [34] and formal invalidity, and "deduction" from general ideas because general (or abstract) ideas are, for him, mere fictions and are, in his opinion, thoroughly unreliable. So he insists that "it is never permissible for us, as long as we are concerned with inquiry into things, to conclude anything from abstractions, and we must take the greatest care not to confuse those things which are only in the understanding with those which are in reality (*in re*). "But" (he continues) "the best conclusions will be drawn from some particular affirmative essence, or from a true and legitimate definition." [35] Again, he claims (at the end of the following section) that ideas are more clear and distinct the more they are specialized, or articulated, whereas we might well have expected him (as he had done earlier) to allege that the simpler and less differentiated the idea the clearer and more distinct it would be. The earlier statement about simple ideas [36] is obviously due to the lingering influence of Descartes, but that influence was already on the wane and the passage at *TdIE.* XIII, 98 [37] is the more typically Spinoza's view.

These passages make it clear beyond reasonable doubt that Spinoza's conception of deduction was the development in thought of the systematic implications in any particular fact of its inter-relations with other facts consequent upon the immanence in them of the structure of the whole to which they belong. Alternatively, it is the following out in thought of the self-differentiation of the whole required by its structural principle or the dynamic principles of its self-development. All this we shall find is borne out by Spinoza's teaching concerning the nature and power of God in their bearing upon finite things; and it is in close conformity with his assertion (the reasons for which we shall examine in a later chapter) that the order and connexion of ideas is the same as the order and connexion of things.

The method which genuine, reputable and developed science has used at least since Galileo and up to the present day, is precisely this kind of deduction: the development of an immanent system implicit in the observable facts. It is what Newton referred to in his *Principia* as "deduction from phenomena." That science seeks to discover and develop a rational system, in the light of which the observable facts become intelligible, was repeatedly affirmed by Einstein. "Certain it is," he wrote,

---

[34] Cf. *TdIE.*, IV, 19 et seq. (*V.V.L.*, I, pp. 7-8), V, 27 and n. (*V.V.L.*, I, p. 9); *K.V.*, II, i (*V.V.L.*, IV, p. 39); *Eth.* II, xi, S. 2; *Ep.* X.
[35] *TdIE.*, XII, 93, *V.V.L.*, I, pp. 28-29.
[36] *TdIE.*, VIII, 65.
[37] *V.V.L.*, I, p. 30.

"that a conviction akin to religious feeling, of the rationality or intelligibility of the world, lies behind all scientific work of a higher order." [38] And again: "The supreme task of the physicist is to arrive at those universal elementary laws from which the cosmos can be built up by pure deduction." [39] Other modern physicists have given similar testimony to the scientific aim of constructing a coherent system in which every particular fact is seen as interdependent with every other and all are deducible from a single principle. This was the clearly pronounced view of Sir Arthur Eddington and, on the basis of a different cosmological theory, has been reaffirmed by D. W. Sciama, while similar or compatible views have been expressed by Louis de Broglie and W. Heisenberg.[40]

Only if one adhered to the view that deduction must and can only be purely formal and analytic would it be true, as Professor Hubbeling alleges,[41] that Spinoza in his deductive method "should have worked with *universalia*" (i.e. *abstracta*). This, if it were the case, would indeed conflict with Spinoza's nominalism. But if we realize that his nominalism is the result precisely of his opposition to abstract reasoning from general ideas, and that his deduction is the development of a "concrete universal," we see that there is no inconsistency in his thinking and that the postulation of "fixed and eternal things," which are *singularia* (individuals) yet nevertheless universal in import, is no contradiction.[42] The apparent contradiction to which Hubbeling refers, between *Ethics,* II, x, and xi, C, (in the first of which it is stated that the nature (*esse*) of substance does not pertain to the essence of man, and in the second that the infinite intellect of God constitutes the essence of the human mind), appears as an inconsistency only if the text is misunderstood. It is one thing to say that the human mind is part of, and is constituted by, the infinite intellect of God, and quite another to say that the human mind is a substance. The denial of the latter is not *ipso facto* a denial of the former. But of these matters I shall treat in the succeeding chapters.

---

[38] *The World as I See It.* (London, 1935), p. 131.
[39] *Op. cit.,* p. 125.
[40] Cf. A. Eddington, *The Expanding Universe* (Cambridge, 1933), pp. 104-5 and 120; D. W. Sciama, *The Unity of the Universe* (New York, 1961); L. de Broglie, *The Revolution in Physics* (London, 1954), p. 205: "The fundamental postulates ... are justified by the possibility of founding on them a coherent theory, compatible with all the experimental facts." W. Heisenberg, *Physics and Philosophy* (London, 1959), p. 69, and *Philosophical Problems of Nuclear Science* (London, 1952), p. 105.
[41] *Op. cit.,* p. 30.
[42] Cf. *op. cit.,* p. 22.

4. Geometry and Metaphysics

To what extent, we may now consider, is Spinoza's geometrical method the same as Euclid's? Clearly it has some resemblance in form. Spinoza begins (as does Euclid) with axioms and definitions, he then formulates propositions which he proceeds to prove, using the axioms and definitions as premisses. One may agree with Caird that geometry, like other special sciences, is based on fundamental assumptions which are not questioned in the science, and that philosophy ought not to accept any unquestioned presuppositions; and one may concede that Spinoza never explicitly acknowledges this obligation. Yet he does not in fact make initial assumptions which are not supported by argument at some stage. The fundamental, and perhaps the sole presupposition of his system is the necessary existence of an infinite, eternal and all inclusive Substance, which is God, or Nature. Nevertheless, he devotes the first fifteen propositions and their proofs, corollaries and scholia (explanatory notes) to the establishment of this foundation. Of the proposition stating the existence of God alone (*Ethics* I, xi) he offers no less than three separate proofs (yet others are given in the *Short Treatise*) and appends a long explanatory scholium.

That Spinoza conceived God as having extension among his attributes is true; but it does not follow that he thought of substance purely in quantitative terms, as Hubbeling maintains. God is not only extended but is also a "thinking thing," and Spinoza did not believe that thought was subject to quantitative categories. In fact, he explicitly denied that it was so. What is extended, or corporeal, must be conceived, according to his teaching, only through extension, and what is thought, or idea, must (can only) be conceived in terms of thought and can never be explained in terms of extension (nor *vice versa*). Specifically, in *TdIE* we find the statement: "A circle is one thing, the idea of a circle another. For the idea of a circle is not something having a periphery and a centre, as a circle has, nor is the idea of a body a body itself . . ." [43] If Spinoza ever fell into the error of conceiving infinity only in quantitative terms it was not because he adopted the geometrical method. Nor was it for that reason that he adopted the method. It is, on the contrary, highly doubtful whether he was guilty, as his critics allege, of this particular confusion of thought. He certainly warns his readers against it, continually emphasizes the importance of distinguishing the imagination of the infinite and of extension

---

[43] *TdIE,* VI, 33 (*V.V.L.,* I, p. 11).

from the conception of them,[44] and inveighs against the errors of attributing imaginative figments to the nature of God.[45]

A comparison of Euclid's proofs with those of the *Ethics* reveals a very noticeable difference. Euclid states his proposition: for instance, "The angles at the base of an isosceles triangle are equal," and then proceeds as follows:

> Let ABC be a triangle such that AB = AC.
> From A drop a bisector of ∠ BAC meeting AC in D.
> In the Δs ABD and ADC, AB = AC,
>   AD is common,
>   ∠DAB = ∠CAD . . , and so on.

Now consider Spinoza's proof of Prop. liii in Part III of the *Ethics*:

> "When the mind contemplates itself and its power of acting it is pleased; and the more so the more distinctly it imagines itself and its power of acting. Man does not know himself except through the modifications (*affectiones*) of his body and the ideas of them (by Props. 19 and 23, Pt. II). Therefore when it happens that the mind is able to contemplate itself, by that very fact it is supposed to pass over to a greater perfection, that is (by Schol. Prop. 11 of this Pt.) to be affected by pleasure, and the more so, the more distinctly it is able to imagine itself and its power of action. Q.E.D."

There is really little similarity in this form of reasoning to that of Euclid. What Spinoza gives us is a straightforward argument to the effect that because self-awareness is of itself evidence of the mind's power of action, and because the awareness of our own power is pleasing to us (as he had shown in Prop. xi), the more distinctly we become aware of our own capacity for action the better are we pleased. There is no use here of equalities of quantities disclosed by the construction of diagrams, or anything of that sort. Both Euclid and Spinoza use (as Hubbeling has pointed out) *modus ponens*,[46] but there is nothing peculiarly geometrical or mathematical about that. Spinoza's reasoning is nothing more than a philosophical argument rather inconveniently arranged in quasi-geometrical form.

It is, moreover, virtually certain that Spinoza regarded the geometrical order primarily as a method of exposition. He could not have believed that, by its own form, it guaranteed the truth of its conclusions, for he

---

[44] Cf. *Ethics,* I, xv. S. and *Ep.* XII.
[45] Cf. *K.V.* I, vii; *Ethics,* I, App.
[46] *Spinoza,* p. 40: e.g., if p then q; but p, therefore q.

demonstrated a large part of Descartes's philosophy geometrically and specially directed his editor (Ludovicus Meyer) to state in the preface that he, Spinoza, did not agree with many of the conclusions so reached. But clearly he did believe that this form of exposition made for rigour, accuracy and closeness of argument, for it obliges the writer to justify every statement he makes by reference to something already accepted as true on adequate grounds. Moreover, it is quite impersonal and draws its conclusions from reasons openly stated and acceptable to any unprejudiced reader. Nobody is therefore entitled to reject a conclusion except on grounds similarly demonstrable. It was as objective and dispassionate a method of exposition as Spinoza could devise for the presentation of his views,[47] and this, for him was of paramount importance. His search was for a truth universally valid for others as much as for himself, not subject to whim or prejudice, and satisfactory, not because it was pleasing (it was to be no mere wish-fulfilment – though it would be the more gratifying because it was true) but because it was what the intellect, purified from confused imaginings, demanded. Undoubtedly, he did believe, with Descartes and others before (and after) him, that Mathematics provided the model of rigorous and reliable reasoning. It was the paradigm of scientific thinking, and so he adopted it as a standard – not, however, of truth, so much as of attitude to truth or objectivity of outlook.

The essential character of the mind was, for him, revealed in the intellect's demand for systematic thinking. Such thinking was the proper and untrammelled activity of the mind, and as such it was self-justifying and adequate. "It belongs to the nature of a thinking thing, as is evident on its face, to form true or adequate thoughts." [48] The standard of such truth and adequacy is the idea of the most perfect being, for the objective (ideal) essence of anything is the same as its real (or formal) essence; and that is the idea of an absolutely complete and comprehensive system – the idea of the universe as a systematic whole. From that everything must follow in necessary sequence. The correct method must, therefore, be a deductive system deriving all subsidiary truths in necessary order from this ultimate truth; and this is the method which Spinoza adopts.

---

[47] Cf. L. Roth, *Spinoza* (London, 1945), p. 37, and *Descartes, Spinoza and Maimonides* (Oxford, 1924), Ch. II.
[48] *TdIE.* 73 (*V.V.L.* I, p. 23). The implications of this assertion will be considered in Ch. V, below.

PART II

GOD

CHAPTER III

THE ABSURDITY OF ATHEISM

1. Is Spinoza an Atheist?

There is perhaps no great philosopher who presents us, with as much confidence and assurance as Spinoza does, with what have appeared to many commentators, and must appear at first sight to most students, as stark contradictions. Yet they are all deduced with rigorous logic from first principles that Spinoza lays down as indubitable and which a critic would be hard put to controvert with any degree of plausibility. One's first reaction on confronting these apparent conflicts is the conviction that something has gone wrong at some obscure point in the course of the reasoning, but closer examination and more careful consideration of Spinoza's system and his explicit statements will, I believe, show that he remains consistent throughout, at least in most important respects, and that the conflicts in his doctrine are apparent only.

During Spinoza's life-time and for long after he was regarded as an atheist, and to this day there are many who would describe his philosophy as naturalism or pantheism. On the other hand, Novalis described him as "a God-intoxicated man," and, indeed, the conception of God is central and indispensable to his system. The charge of atheism brought against him by his contemporaries was based chiefly on his identification of God with Nature and his denial of the traditional theological attributes to God. The existence of a God as commonly imagined by adherents and exponents of traditional religion he rejects in no uncertain terms. God, for him, is not an all-wise, almighty, compassionate ruler and judge, not a being set apart from a world that he had created of his own free will by deliberate fiat.[1] Further, Spinoza asserts that Extension is an attribute of God, so that along with his other attributes God is a corporeal being. To his contemporaries, both Jewish and Christian, this was the rankest heresy.

[1] Cf. *K.V.*, I, vii; *Ethics*, I, xvii, S., xxxiii, S. 2., App.; II, iii, S.

Nevertheless, the existence of God is for Spinoza not only absolutely indubitable, but is the sole, indispensable and universal ground of everything, so that nothing in his philosophy can be properly understood without reference to God and the idea of God (the two are, in fact, not separable). As he himself repeatedly asserts, nothing can either be or be conceived apart from God. If atheism is the denial of the existence of any God, it is an accusation that cannot, with any vestige of plausibility be levelled against Spinoza, and the charge can only be made to seem justifiable on the ground that his conception of God was inadequate or false. If God is identified with Nature then it would appear that strictly speaking only Nature exists and there is no presiding deity transcending the natural world. So the accusation of atheism gains colour from the same line of thought as the charge of pantheism and naturalism. In fact, it is for the same reason that he is called an atheist as that he is called pantheist or naturalist. But whether the accusation is just is quite another matter, and certainly Spinoza himself regarded it as a gross misinterpretation.[2]

Much depends on the way in which the key terms are being used, and we must consider first what is meant by pantheism, or by naturalism. The pantheist is the man who deifies phenomenal nature, the world as we experience it, while the naturalist is one who regards phenomenal nature as the final and sole reality. They are in agreement in that both would deny the existence of any *super*-natural, purely spiritual God, and of an immaterial human soul. Spinoza's position, we shall find, has something in common with both of them but can be identified with neither. Again, we must consider the use of the term "Nature," which, in its turn, determines the meaning of "super-natural." As commonly used, and as defined in the dictionary, the word means (i) the innate or intrinsic properties of anything or its specific character, (ii) the totality of the phenomena of the material world, (iii) the creative and regulative laws which determine these phenomena, or (iv) a vaguely personal conception of them. With the first of these meanings we are not here concerned, for in this usage the term is common to Spinoza with philosophers of many different persuasions. But where the naturalist and the pantheist might use the term in any or all of the last three senses, Spinoza gives it a far wider connotation and would reject the fourth meaning altogether. Spinoza regarded phenomenal nature, what appears of the world to us through sense-perception, as for the most part the product of illusion and error. He would certainly not have identified it with God or have deified it in its phenomenal form, although he would have maintained that it

[2] Cf. *Ep.* XLIII.

was a "part" [3] of God misconceived by us through our ignorance of its true place in the whole. Personification of nature in this phenomenal sense is just a typical example of the sort of error and phantasy resulting from such misconception. Creative and regulative laws of Nature he did recognize as divine laws, but their scope is not, in Spinoza's theory, restricted to the material world as we know it empirically. It embraces the infinite whole of reality, which far transcends empirical (or phenomenal) nature. As will presently appear, "Nature" is a term used by Spinoza to cover the totality of the real, which is far more than the physical world that we experience through the senses.

The identification of Nature with God, if Nature means the whole of reality, physical, mental and whatever other form there may be, is then not pantheism, as that is usually understood; nor is it naturalism, for reasons which we shall develop further below. The Greek word πᾶν, however, means "all," so if "pantheism" is taken literally, as meaning the belief that God is the whole of reality, the term is appropriate to Spinoza's philosophy.

2. The Conception of God

In actuality, Spinoza developed his conception of God from that current among the philosophers and theologians of his time, which they had inherited from the Judeo-Christian tradition; but he made the conception self-consistent and purified it of incompatible and imaginative adjuncts. According to that tradition, God was the creative and sustaining source of the world and of man; in short, of all existence. His knowledge and power were infinite. He was the ground and original cause of everything and of all events. He was perfect in all respects and subject to no defect or limitation. God was in an unqualified sense the supreme being, subject neither for his existence nor for his intrinsic nature to any other.

Such a being, therefore, must be substantial – that is, fundamentally real, that of which everything else might be predicated, but which could not be predicated of (or adjectival to) anything else. God, therefore, must be Substance (οὐσία), the ultimate reality. Further, as God is the original cause and creative source of all things, he cannot himself be an effect, but must be self-caused (*causa sui*). As perfect and subject to no defect or limitation, he must be self-complete and infinite. It follows that he can exclude nothing, for if there were anything excluded by (outside) God, he would be limited by whatever he excluded. It would be an other to

---

[3] We shall find later that the term "part," as applied to God, needs significant qualification.

him, something he could not encompass, and so a limitation upon his
power and comprehensiveness. He could not then be infinite, and so
could not be God. Accordingly, God must be all-encompassing; he must
be all reality. Nothing can be outside (without) God, but, on the contrary,
in God everything has its being and without him nothing can either be or
be conceived.

Because God is of necessity absolutely complete and all-comprehensive,
Spinoza, like Descartes and the mediaevals before him, maintains that
God includes in himself all positive predicates and excludes all negation.
For doing so he has been criticized by Hegelian commentators who allege
that, while his famous dictum, *"determinatio est negatio,"* [4] is an important truth, Spinoza failed to recognize the equally important truth of
its converse *"negatio est determinatio."* All determination or limitation
is indeed negation, but without determination no precise definition is
possible and all negation is significant in that it defines and makes determinate what it limits. Accordingly, say the critics, Spinoza's Substance
absorbs all differences and obliterates them. It contains no negation and
so possesses no definiteness, but becomes a blank indefinite unity without
internal differentiation.

To me it seems that no grosser misunderstanding of Spinoza could be
entertained than this. As I shall try presently to show, Spinoza very definitely conceived God's unity as infinitely differentiated in at least two
different levels of reality, first into infinite attributes and secondly into
infinite modes. Nor are these distinctions cancelled out or eliminated by
their union in God's infinite nature. Spinoza's recognition that negation
and determination are the same thing seen from opposite view-points is
as clear as Hegel's. He realizes, therefore, that all finite entities involve
both. They are finite because they are defined, determined or negated
by other finite entities which are extraneous to them and limit them from
without. This is true even of the attributes of substance each of which is
infinite in its own kind; for each excludes the others, which are of different kinds.

But outside of God there is nothing. He is not of a kind, not a class
delimited by other classes. There is nothing to limit or determine Substance from without. Therefore Spinoza denies determination of God
for *determinatio est negatio.* God is determined, not by an other, but only
by himself, only by his own nature: he is *causa sui,* cause of himself; he
determines himself. In another sense, however, he includes all determinations, for all distinctions are *within* his essence, between his attributes

[4] Cf. *Ep.* L, *Ethics* I, viii, S. 1.

and modes. They negate one another, but nothing can negate God, and his wholeness negates their negation. It does so in two ways; first, because it completes them and fulfils their deficiency, and, secondly, because it is immanent in each and all of them. Their distinctions and mutual exclusions are intelligible only in relation to, and in the light of, the totality of Substance, in and through which alone they are and can be conceived.

Spinoza's Substance, therefore, is precisely what Hegel conceived his Absolute to be, the negation of all negation or absolute negativity; but Spinoza expresses this by saying that God excludes (i.e. negates) all negation – because he includes and renders intelligible all distinctions; not because he absorbs and obliterates them in blank undifferentiated uniformity, but because only their mutual inter-relation within the absolute whole makes them what they essentially are.

Accordingly, although there is a sense in which the infinity of God is opposed to, and contrasted with, the finiteness of his modes, they are not utterly opposed or separable; because the latter are adjectival to the former they are *its* differentiations and apart from it could be nothing. Only in God can finite things be themselves and only through God's nature (or essence) can they be adequately understood. It is equally true that the complete understanding of God is possible only by a complete knowledge of the infinite universe in and through which his nature is expressed. For Spinoza, this complete knowledge is the infinite idea of God, the object of his infinite intellect. Man can approach it only tentatively and only so far as his knowing proceeds from an adequate conception of one of God's attributes to an adequate knowledge of particular things.[5]

Further, if God is infinite and perfect there is nothing that he lacks and nothing he could be conceived to desire. Hence, it could only be a derogation of his self-completeness to maintain that he created a world other than and separate from himself and to fulfil his wishes, or in order to harbour man, who might, by his service and praise, satisfy God's vanity.[6] In this sense God could not have created the world out of nothing, as a craftsman might create a building out of some material. The world must in some way be the expression or manifestation of God's very being, of his creative power in action. So Spinoza identifies God's power with his essence and the exercise of his power with the created world.[7] If, then, we call the totality of being "Nature," God and Nature

[5] Cf. *Ethics* II, xl, S. 2.
[6] Cf. *Ethics,* I, App.
[7] *Natura Naturans* and *Natura Naturata.* Cf. *K.V.,* I, viii, and *Ethics,* I, xxix, S., and p. 48 ff, below.

are identical, for there can be no reality which is not in God and which his power (as cause of all things) does not sustain.

On the other hand, it follows equally necessarily from all this that God cannot be a finite individual like man, and we must not attribute human characteristics to him.[8] Though traditionally we refer to "him," as a person we must not misunderstand the personal pronoun to refer to anything like human personality, even if of super-human dimensions. God is not a super-man, and if we speak of the divine intellect, we must realize that it is not an intellect like our own, but (as Spinoza says) resembles ours no more than the Dog-star resembles the animal that barks.[9] The same applies to God's will (if the term is at all appropriate) and we may not imagine God as a ruler of the world, like a human king, nor of his laws as in any way similar to royal decrees. Any anthropomorphic idea of God is inadmissible. To attribute "personality" to him is to use words which we cannot comprehend. In *Cogitata Metaphysica,* II, viii, Spinoza writes: "We do not lack the word ("personality," that is) which the theologians use indiscriminately to explain the matter [i.e. the inter-relation of God's will, intellect and essence]: but though we know the word, we do not know its meaning, nor can we form any clear and distinct conception of it." It follows that it is wholly inept to describe God as all-knowing, merciful, wise, or supremely good in the sense in which we understand these terms when applied to human beings.[10] We shall see that the notion of goodness, in particular, has special limitations in Spinoza's view, discussion of which will occupy us later.

Accordingly, Spinoza defines God thus (*Ethics,* I, Def. VI.): "By God I understand a being absolutely infinite, that is, a substance consisting of infinite attributes, each of which expresses infinite and eternal essence. *"Explanation*: I say absolutely infinite, not however infinite in its kind. For of whatever is infinite only in its kind we can deny infinite attributes; but to the essence of what is absolutely infinite pertains whatever expresses essence and it involves no negation." From this definition, the most important of all those given in the *Ethics,* follows everything that Spinoza asserts of the divine nature – in fact, his entire system is built upon it. Let us, therefore, spend a little time explaining the terms in which it is couched.

By attribute Spinoza means, as he states in the fourth definition of Part I in the *Ethics,* "what the intellect perceives as constituting the

[8] Cf. *Ethics,* I, viii, S. 2; *Epp.* **XXI, LIV.**
[9] *Ethics,* I, xvii, S.
[10] Cf. *K.V.,* I, vii.

essence of a substance." The essence of anything is *what* it is, as opposed
to its bare existence – that it is. So what the intellect perceives something
to be – or, as we say, "what it is like" – expresses its essence. Accordingly,
the more complete and perfect anything is, or as Spinoza sometimes puts
it, the more reality it has (a phrase taken over from Descartes), the more
attributes it will have. An infinite, or absolutely perfect being, therefore,
must have infinite attributes.[11] "Perfect," again, as used by Spinoza,
means, more often and more properly, complete (*perficio* = I bring to
completion) rather than "supremely good," and though there are contexts
in which the latter meaning is given to the word it is only and always
with carefully explained qualifications.[12] It follows that everything whatsoever that expresses essence will belong to an infinite being. God's attributes, therefore, will be the innumerable ways in which his inexhaustible
essence can be expressed or conceived, and each of them will be infinite
and eternal in its own kind. But as each is infinite and eternal only in its
kind, it is limited to its kind alone, whereas God, the absolutely infinite
is subject to no limitation – no negation – whatsoever, and comprises
accordingly, infinite attributes. Two of these attributes, those known to
man, are Extension and Thought; the rest, though we must affirm them
of the absolutely infinite, we are incapable of comprehending (for reasons
which will be given in what follows). Before we go further, however, we
must face the question which at this stage will inevitably be pressed by
the incredulous critic. On what grounds are we to believe that there is
any such absolutely infinite being as Spinoza has defined. Does God, so
conceived, exist?

3. The Existence of God

Strictly speaking, if God is defined and conceived as Spinoza requires,
no proof of his existence is needed, because the existence of God is then
the inescapable presupposition of the existence of any and every thing,
and the indispensable presumption of all thinking and of all truth. God's
non-existence cannot even be supposed without self-contradiction, for by
that or any other supposal the existence of God would be implied. However, as this is not easily apparent to every reader, and as Spinoza is careful to postulate nothing which he does not at some stage justify and support by rational argument, he offers not one but several proofs of God's
existence, in which what we have just maintained is brought out and

[11] Cf. *Ep*. IX.
[12] See below, Ch. VII, § 3.

made clear.[13] In all, there are eleven different proofs [14] in Spinoza's writings, excluding those that are quoted or explained in his correspondence, but, of these, three are set out in the *Principia Philosophiae Cartesianae* and are proofs given by Descartes, two of them actually quoted verbatim from the second reply to Objections.[15] These I shall therefore ignore, for Spinoza did not accept everything that he reported of Descartes, and what, in these proofs, he approved he repeated in his own.

The ontological form of proof was the one that appealed most to Spinoza: i.e. that which states, in effect, that the necessary existence of God, *qua* perfect being, is self-evident – for otherwise he would not be God (or perfect). The *Short Treatise* opens with this proof stated as follows:

"Everything that we clearly and distinctly understand as belonging to the nature of a thing that we can also assert of it with truth. But that existence belongs to the nature of God we can clearly and distinctly understand. Ergo . . ." [16]

In short, existence is involved in the essence of God – i.e. what we clearly and distinctly understand as belonging to his nature (as a perfect and infinite being). But the same conclusion can be reached by *reductio ad absurdum* and this form of proof we find in the *Ethics* (I. Prop. xi): "Conceive, if it is possible, that God does not exist. Then his essence does not involve existence. But this is absurd (by Prop. vii)"; i.e., God exists, because no alternative is thinkable.

But these are not arguments like Anselm's – that what exists only in the intellect is not that than which no greater is conceivable (not God), hence to assert that that than which no greater can be conceived does not exist is to contradict oneself. Nor are they arguments like Descartes's – that the being that includes all perfections *ipso facto* includes existence. In these "proofs" Spinoza does no more than assert God's existence as self-evident: we clearly and distinctly conceive that God exists thus we may truly assert that he does. It would be absurd to deny it, because, if the denial were true, God's essence would not involve existence. And Spinoza is right to state the matter thus, if the Ontological Proof is to be accepted,

---

[13] Many of these proofs are set out in geometrical order, and they are thus in themselves clear evidence against the allegation that Spinoza's method licensed him to make unquestioned assumptions in the manner of the special sciences.

[14] Cf. H. G. Hubbeling, *Spinoza's Methodology*, Appendix I. Nine of these proofs are set out formally as proofs of God's existence: *K.V.* I, i contains three, *P.P.C.* I, Props. v, vi, vii, give three more, and *Ethics*, I, xi, has three more. But *Ethics*, I, vii is also, in effect, a proof of God's existence (the most fundamental) and the Scholium to Prop. xi contains yet another stated informally.

[15] Cf. *P.P.C.* I, Props. v, vi, vii, and Haldane & Ross, II, pp. 52-59.

[16] Cf. *P.P.C.* I, Prop. v.

for what it amounts to is precisely that the existence of God, rightly conceived, cannot be denied without self-contradiction. But those who deny the validity of the ontological argument maintain that it is not sufficient to conceive God as perfect, or as that than which nothing greater can be conceived, or as necessarily existing. However, we *conceive* God, they say, his existence does not necessarily follow. That essence ever could involve existence is just what they dispute. The force and validity of this contention will engage us presently.

Spinoza, in any case, is not content to leave the matter merely as self-evident. He offers further arguments, some of which are in principle the same as those of Descartes. In fact, the establishment of the existence of God in the *Ethics* is an extremely detailed and carefully worked out series of arguments, beginning with precise definitions of terms, of which the first is the most significant for the proof of God's existence:

"By cause of itself (*causa sui*) I understand that the essence of which involves existence; or that the nature of which cannot be conceived without existence."

It is cause of itself because nothing other than its own nature (or essence) is needed for it to exist.

Substance is then defined (Def. II) as "that which is in itself and is conceived through itself; that is, the conception of which does not need the conception of anything else from which it must be formed."

Of the other definitions we need notice here only that of attribute, as "that which the intellect perceives of substance as constituting its essence." We shall have to discuss this notion at more length in the sequel, but we must observe at the outset that for Spinoza an attribute is not a mere property, but is the full essence of its subject (the substance to which it belongs), or how that subject is conceived. God, we have already seen, is defined as an absolutely infinite being or substance "constituted by infinite attributes of which each expresses infinite and eternal essence" in its own kind. Having prepared the ground with these definitions, Spinoza proceeds, by carefully connected steps to prove that substance exists of necessity, that it is necessarily infinite and that there is no other substance than the one, infinite, necessarily existing substance which is God.[17]

The main steps of this argument are: (i) Two substances, because each is conceivable only through itself and needs the conception of nothing

[17] Cf. *Ethics* I, Defs. I, III, IV and VI, Props. v, vi, vii, viii, ix, xi and Schol., xiv; *K.V.* I, ii; *Ep.* XXXV.

else, have no attribute in common. The essence of each, how its "what" is conceived, is completely self-dependent and thus can have nothing in common with any other (if there be any other) substance. (ii) It follows that one substance cannot produce another, for if it could it would have something in common with that which it produced (something of the cause must pass into and be identical with its effect or else the causal relation cannot be asserted).[18] Moreover, an effect, to be conceived adequately, must be conceived through its cause and not through itself alone. (iii) Therefore, substance cannot be caused extraneously but is *causa sui* and exists of necessity, because nothing besides its own nature (or essence) is needed for it to exist – its essence involves existence. (iv) As substance can have no common attribute with any other, it cannot be limited by any other, for every attribute is infinite in its own kind and any limitation would have to be by something of the same kind, or something with the same attribute. In other words, if a substance were limited by another substance, it would have to be conceived as so limited, or in relation to the other; that is, it would not be conceived through itself alone but through another as well; and as its attributes are the ways in which its essence is conceived, it would have at least one attribute in common with the other – which has already been disproved. (v) Being infinite, substance must have an infinity of attributes (see p. 39 above); and (vi) is therefore God, the absolutely infinite substance, existing necessarily and besides which there can be no other, (vii) for all possible attributes, none of which can be shared with any other substance, must belong to the absolutely infinite, so that no other substance can exist with any attribute whatsoever.

God exists of necessity because he is substance, and substance exists of necessity because it is cause of itself, and it is cause of itself because it is conceived through itself. Only what is infinite and whole, complete in itself and dependent on nothing beyond itself, can be conceived truly through itself alone. For the complete and adequate conception of anything requires that it be conceived through its cause. Finite things, therefore, cannot be adequately conceived through themselves but only through their causes, and if they are to exist, their causes must exist. If the cause is finite the same will apply to it. But what can truly be conceived only through itself is *ipso facto* its own cause, and so cannot fail to exist in virtue of its own self-complete nature. "If anybody were to say, there-

---

[18] It was because he could not discover this identical element that Hume denied necessary connexion between cause and effect and reduced the relation to constant conjunction.

fore," Spinoza comments "that he has a clear and distinct, that is, a true, idea of substance, and nevertheless doubts whether such substance exists, it would indeed be the same as if he said that he had a true idea and doubted nevertheless whether it were false." (*Ethics* I, viii, S 2).

Other proofs of God's existence, which I have not already quoted or summarized, are as follows. For the existence or non-existence of anything there must be a cause or reason, and if no cause or reason for the non-existence of anything can be shown it must exist of necessity. In the case of God, a cause precluding his existence would either be in some other substance, or in himself. It could not be in any other substance, for no other substance could have a common attribute with God, and what have nothing whatsoever in common cannot be related, positively or negatively, as cause and effect. That is to say, neither can be the cause of existence or an obstacle to the existence of the other. But in himself God can contain no impediment to his own existence, because he is by definition and nature (in essence) infinitely perfect and the only intrinsic impediment to his existence would be a contradiction in his essence. There can thus be no cause whatever preventing God's existence and he must accordingly exist of necessity.

This argument anticipates and meets the objection raised by Leibniz to the Ontological Proof, that it is valid only if it can first be shown that the conception of God (an infinite and perfect being) is not self-contradictory. Spinoza asserts that it would be absurd to allege of a perfect and infinite being that it could contain so gross an imperfection as self-contradiction. And, *prima facie* at least, this contention would seem justified. But modern writers have alleged the contrary. They argue that necessary existence is itself a contradiction in terms, so that if the essence of an infinite and perfect being necessarily involved existence it would contradict itself.[19] But the view that necessary existence is a self-contradiction implies the belief that all existence is purely contingent, an assumption that is not supported by any evidence; or else it depends upon the view that all necessity is logical necessity, and that logical necessity applies only to tautological statements which can assert nothing about existence. Neither of these positions is defensible and both are utterly foreign to Spinoza. The former I shall examine below; the latter, that logically necessary statements are factually uninformative, even if true in contemporary logic, does not carry with it the conclusion that there is no other kind of necessity.[20]

[19] Cf. J. N. Findlay, "Can God's Existence be Disproved," in *New Essays in Philosophical Theology*, Ed. Anthony Flew (London, 1955).

[20] Cf. J. J. C. Smart, "The Existence of God" in *op. cit.*, p. 40; and my *Hypothesis and Perception*, (London, 1970), p. 340.

One might argue against Spinoza that even if there is no cause preventing the existence of God, it does not follow that there is any cause for his existence. But then the same reasoning would apply over again. A cause of God's existence would have to be either extrinsic or intrinsic to his nature. It could not be extrinsic, for the reason already stated above, therefore it would have to be intrinsic. In that case God is *causa sui,* that is, he exists of necessity, or unconditionally.

Another of Spinoza's proofs identifies existence with power (as Plato does in the *Sophist*), and argues that if finite things exist, the infinite must necessarily exist because otherwise the finite would have more power (of existence) than the infinite, which is absurd. This dynamic conception of being is one we shall find repeatedly of significance in Spinoza's system, both in understanding his conception of God's attributes and in interpreting his psychological and ethical theories.

In the Scholium to Prop. xi (*Ethics* I) there is still another argument for God's existence. It is, in effect similar to the version of the Ontological Proof that is given by Descartes,[21] demonstrating the necessary existence of God from the fact that his essence involves all possible perfections and can thus not exclude existence. "Whatever perfection a substance may have," writes Spinoza, "is due to no external cause, therefore its existence must follow from its nature alone, which is nothing else than its essence. Perfection, therefore, does not remove existence from a thing, but on the contrary posits existence; imperfection, on the other hand takes it away; and thus there is nothing of the existence of which we can be more certain than of the existence of an absolutely infinite or perfect being, that is, of God." Spinoza's statement, however, lays stress upon the fact that existence depends on the amount of perfection possessed by the entity concerned and does not treat it merely as one perfection among others. Strictly, the argument is that God exists more surely than less perfect things because his perfection is the very ground of existence, not because existence is something additional to other perfections possessed independently. His perfection and his existence are really identical; he exists because he is perfect and not *vice versa*. It is in this sense most truly that God is *causa sui*.[22]

Spinoza goes on to show (*Ethics* I, xv) that God is all-comprehensive, that "whatever is, is in God, and nothing can be or be conceived without him."

---

[21] Cf. *Meditation* V. The proof which Descartes gives in *Meditation* III is repeated by Spinoza both in *P.P.C.* and *K.V.*

[22] Cf. *Ep.* ix.

That God is the whole, is really the heart of the matter, and is the foundation of all the traditional arguments for the divine being. The existence of reality cannot be denied without self-stultification, for the alternative, if it were an intelligible alternative, is to assert that nothing exists.[23] But that is self-refuting, because whoever asserts it must exist in order to deny existence. But is this all we require? Does it follow from the fact that something exists (at least he who asserts or denies), that the totality of existence is an infinite being? Does it follow that, because something happens to exist, anything must exist of necessity? Let us deal with the last question first.

If all existence is merely contingent it must be conceivable that nothing might exist; but this cannot be conceived, first because the conception would have to be a thought, which implies existence of a thinker, and secondly because the object of the thought would have to be nothing, and that can be the object of no thought – to think of nothing is not to think. It is therefore unthinkable that nothing should exist. To argue that, whether or not *we* can think it, it might nevertheless be the case, is simply to contradict oneself again, for it is tantamount to asserting that, even though it is unthinkable we may nevertheless think (presume) it. The only conceivable possibility is that something exists.[24] And it must exist *of necessity,* for to allege that it exists only contingently implies the impossible – that is, that it is possible for nothing to exist at all. But need this necessarily existing something be an infinite being? To this question Spinoza's answer is conclusive. If it were merely finite, it would be limited by something other than itself, and this other would also exist of necessity.[25] This again, or both entities taken together, if finite, would imply something else, and so on *ad infinitum.* We are committed, therefore, either to an infinite series of finite existences, which is one form of infinite existence, or if we reject that as endlessly finite, to the postulation of a complete and all-embracing whole of existence, in which all finites are grounded and which is infinite because complete and absolutely comprehensive, beyond and without which nothing is or can be conceived. So we reach the conception of Spinoza's *Deus-sive-Substantia* (God-or-Substance), the necessarily existing infinite being.

Thus it becomes apparent that an infinite being exists of necessity because its existence is involved in its essence, which is the ontological

---

[23] Cf. *Ethics* I, xi, third Dem.: "either nothing exists, or a being absolutely infinite necessarily exists."

[24] Cf. Joachim, *Study,* pp. 50-55.

[25] Cf. *Ethics* I, viii, dem. If one finite exists of necessity, it necessarily implies the existence of another finite.

argument (the *a priori* proof of God's existence). Further, it is by the same token apparent that if anything finite exists an infinite being must necessarily exist, which is the traditional form of the cosmological argument – or what Spinoza calls the *a posteriori* proof of God's existence.[26] The third traditional proof, the teleological, is also implicit in the above exposition, and we shall have more to say later on its teleological character; for if the infinite being is conceived as the whole through which alone all finites can be or be understood, then (it will become clearer as we proceed) the whole must be viewed as an explanatory principle, or order, evidence of which will be immanent in all its parts. Thus every finite existent will manifest some partial degree of perfection implying a fulfilment or completion in a supreme or superlative perfection. Spinoza does not state explicitly any form of teleological argument for the existence of God. In fact, in several contexts he rejects emphatically what is in effect its major premiss. We shall see, however, that in spite of his explicit avowals, the *vis argumenti*, or nerve of the argument, is implicit in his whole theory, and that his thought is teleological despite his own and his commentators' assertions to the contrary.

4. Dismissal of the Indictment

A philosopher who spends so much space and careful argument to establish the absurdity of any form of denial of God's existence can hardly be accused of atheism with any justice. Spinoza insists time out of number that nothing can either be or be conceived without God. Atheism therefore would be not just the denial of the existence of one being (God) among others, but the denial of all possible being and any intelligible knowledge. It thus becomes the same as extreme scepticism, which, Spinoza argues, is an impossible position to hold. The standard of all truth is truth itself and to have a true idea is to know that one knows; but the idea which in itself is most concrete and self-assuring is the idea of the whole, the most perfect being, and to deny that would make it impossible to assert anything.

"If after this there is perchance any sceptic, who still remains doubtful of the first truth itself and of everything we may deduce in accordance with the standard of the first truth, he speaks, surely, contrary to his own awareness, or else we must confess that there are men either mentally blind from birth or because of some prejudice, that is, some external accident; for neither are they aware of themselves. If they affirm anything, or doubt, they do not know that they doubt or affirm: they say

[26] Cf. *K.V.* I, i; *Ethics,* I, xi, S.

they know nothing, and of this itself, that they know nothing, they profess ignorance; nor do they say so absolutely, for they fear to admit that they exist since they know nothing. Having reached this point they must needs be silent lest perchance they suppose what has some savour of truth." [27]

The sceptic is he who doubts "the first truth itself" (*ipsa prima veritas*) and that is the existence of the most perfect being, or God; but the consistent sceptic can only be dumb (*obmutescere*). Thus is atheism silenced, for there is nothing consistent with it that can be affirmed.

Those who accuse Spinoza of atheism, however, are those who do not conceive God as the whole of reality, but precisely as one being among others, though the greatest and best of all. But Spinoza shows incontrovertably that such a notion is not of an infinite or absolutely perfect God but of a finite deity presiding over a world by which he is limited. The limitation, moreover, would infect his power and his knowledge, as well as his existence; for the world, once created would have its own nature independent of God (except so far as he was its presumed first cause) and its laws would then continue to act independently of his (supposedly) free will. He could then act in the world only by interfering with those laws, that is, by performing miracles, and that would be to contradict his own original act of creation. Further, man's free will, if free in the sense of undetermined, must equally be independent of God's and must impose a limit upon God's knowledge. For if God knows man's acts before they are performed they must in some way be determined. This form of Deism Spinoza certainly does reject, and he shows it to involve insuperable contradictions. The intractable problems of mediaeval theology largely derive from it, and he avoids them by making the conception of God, as *ens perfectissimum,* self-consistent – that is, by acknowledging its implication of absolute wholeness and all-inclusiveness. So far from atheism, this is theism made intelligible, without the need *in extremis,* when problems become insoluble, to appeal to human frailty and the inscrutability of the divine nature.

---

[27] *TdIE.,* VII, 47.

CHAPTER IV

GOD'S CREATIVITY

God-or-Substance-or-Nature is the totality of the real, infinite in the sense of absolutely complete, self-contained, self-caused and self-maintaining. Its eternal essence is expressed in infinite attributes each inexhaustible and illimitable in its own kind, but limited wholly to its own kind. Under each of these attributes there follow from the infinite power (or essence) of God interminable series of modes, some infinite in themselves and the rest finite, singular things. The infinite modes are the immediate consequences of God's essence as expressed in his attributes; they follow from his nature, Spinoza insists, in the same way as the properties of a triangle follow from its definition; that is, they are logical consequences of God's eternal essence. But his essence is the same as his power, so they are consequences, likewise, or effects, of God's causal efficacy. This two-fold character of God's creative potency involves some obscurity and needs explanation, to provide which will be the main object of the present chapter.

1. Natura Naturans and Natura Naturata

What Spinoza understands by *Natura Naturans* [1] is God, conceived in and through himself, that is, the infinite and eternal attributes expressing his essence. It is God conceived as free cause, as active, or as creative potency – "Nature naturing," nature producing, issuing as the existing universe. The created or elaborated system of the universe he calls *Natura Naturata,* "nature natured," "everything which follows necessarily from the divine nature or from each of God's attributes; that is, all the modes of God's attributes considered as things which are in God, and without God can neither be nor be conceived." [2]

In the demonstration of the 15th Proposition of the first Part of the

---

[1] *Ethics* I, xxix, S: cf. *K.V.* I, viii.
[2] *Ibid.,* and *Ethics* I, xv.

Ethics, the statement appears: "Besides substances and modes there is nothing." [3] They exhaust reality. Does this mean that God's attributes are nothing real, for they are defined as *what the intellect perceives* of substance as constituting its essence? Are they then only ways of thinking or are they real differentiations within God's essence? There has been much controversy over this point, which has been the more complicated because of Spinoza's contention that the attributes of God are infinite in number. Some have alleged that the attributes are purely subjective ways of conceiving the essence of substance, mere *entia rationis*, like all other universal ideas to which nothing corresponds in reality. Others reject this subjective interpretation and maintain that the attributes are "*extra intellectum*" (outside of the intellect), real features of substance itself. [4] I cannot enter here fully into the details of this controversy, but I shall deal with it just so far as it bears upon the vexed question of the diversification of the unity of substance, which is virtually identical with the question of the nature of God's causality.

Caird argues [5] that Spinoza failed to explain the diversity of the world by any principle intrinsic to the nature of substance. The unity of God, he says, remains ultimately blank, without means of explaining the infinite diversity that, according to Spinoza, follows necessarily from it. Accordingly, (so Caird contends) Spinoza uses the finite human intellect as an extraneous source of diversity. The attributes are the ways in which it perceives the essence of substance. Caird then criticizes Spinoza for committing a paralogism; for the human intellect (as we shall find) is only a finite mode in one of God's attributes – that of Thought – and so could not possibly be the source of the attributes themselves. Nor could the source be the infinite intellect of God, for that too is only a mode of Thought, though an infinite one, and so cannot be the source of the attributes of which Thought is only one. Joachim rejects the subjective-objective dichotomy and alleges that Spinoza did so too. The attributes, Joachim says, are genuine features of the real for Spinoza, but as the real is eminently knowable, they are the ways in which it is known. " 'Attribute' is neither the Reality apart from knowledge, nor knowledge apart from Reality; but that which is known or knowable of Reality." [6] Yet

---

[3] Cf. *Ethics* I, vi. C. and *Ep.* IV.
[4] Cf. Gabriel Huan, *Le Dieu de Spinoza*, (Arras, 1913), Ch. III, with the numerous references given. Also, John Caird, *Spinoza*, pp. 146-153; Joachim, *Study*, pp. 22-27; H. A. Wolfson, *The Philosophy of Spinoza* (Harvard, 1934), Vol. I, p. 146; G. H. R. Parkinson, *Spinoza's Theory of Knowledge* (Oxford, 1954), pp. 84 f.; Hubbeling. *Spinoza*, p. 61 n, and *Spinoza's Methodology*, pp. 42 f.; J. E. Erdmann, *A History of Philosophy* (Trans. W. S. Hough, London, 1892), Vol. II, pp. 67 ff.
[5] *Spinoza*, Ch. VIII.
[6] *Study*, pp. 22 and 27.

Joachim himself, in other contexts, accuses Spinoza of failure to provide a principle of differentiation intrinsic to God,[7] so that interpretation must oscillate between blank unity and inexhaustibly concrete diversity without ever finding a satisfactory principle of reconciliation. I believe this criticism to be a misjudgement (it is shared by many besides those I have quoted, Hegel not the least), and I shall attempt to deal with it as I proceed.

As to the attributes, there is little doubt that Spinoza intended no subjectivist implication in his definition of them. He was far too acute to fall into the kind of logical blunder attributed to him by Caird. The attributes constitute the very essence of substance, but essence is *what* a thing is, and what it is, is how it is conceived, or conceivable (so far Joachim is right), and therefore Spinoza defines attribute as the essence of substance as perceived by the intellect. It was, however, far from his intention to suggest that attributes were *entia rationis*, or ways of thinking. The clue to the solution of this problem is the passage already quoted from *TdIE.*,[8] he speaks of "fixed and eternal things" according to which all particular things occur and are ordered and without which the mutable things can neither be nor be conceived. These fixed and eternal things, he says, although they are individuals (*singularia*), yet are ubiquitous and most extensive (*latissima*) in power, and are therefore like universals or the genera of the definitions of single entities and they are the proximate causes of all things.

I believe that when he wrote of these "fixed and eternal things," Spinoza had in mind the attributes of God and the infinite modes which follow immediately from them [9] – more probably the latter. This is one of the more obscure topics in his philosophy, but there are, I think, sufficient indications in the text to enable us to form a tolerably clear idea of what he meant. As the eternal things are individuals and not *abstracta,* they must be actual realities and no mere *entia rationis*; and as they serve us as if they were universals or *prima genera*,[10] they must be very high in the hierarchy of being.

2. *Attributes and Modes*

In order to understand the relation between God's attributes and his modes we must remind ourselves first of Spinoza's identification of per-

---

[7] *Op. cit.,* Book I, Appendix.
[8] P. 23 above.
[9] See below, p. 55.
[10] "... *erunt nobis tanquam universalia sive genera ...*" *TdIE.,* XIV, 101.

fection, or reality, with power (*potentia*). The more perfection a thing has, the more power of existence it exerts. And God, who has infinite perfection, and exists of necessity for that reason, has infinite power. His essence, existence and power are, therefore, all one and the same. But we have just noted that God's essence, which is expressed by his attributes, is what Spinoza understands by *Natura Naturans,* and that this is the dynamic aspect of substance, God conceived as free cause (a phrase we shall examine below). The attributes, therefore, being the ways in which God's essence is expressed are, by the same token, ways in which God's power is exercised.[11] This exercise of power issues in the production of infinite modes, or differentiations of being. "From the necessity of the divine nature, infinite things, in infinite modes (that is, everything that can fall under the infinite intellect) must follow" (*Ethics* I, xvi) . . . "Hence it follows that God is the efficient cause of all things which fall under [i.e. are conceived by] the infinite intellect" (*ibid.* Corol. 1); "that God is absolutely first cause" (*ibid.* Corol. 3).[12]

The modes in each attribute, as will presently become plain, constitute a complete system, infinite in its own kind, and this system is both actual and individual, as well, in its kind, as universal or all-embracing. It is therefore at once *singulare* and *universale,* concretely universal. The attribute itself is nothing over and above the system of modes which belong to it, but *qua* system of modes it is part of *Natura Naturata,* whereas *qua* attribute, or form of God's potency, it is an aspect of *Natura Naturans.* As such, while it is no mere abstraction nor *ens rationis* – not just a way of thinking (whether ours or God's – except so far as God's intellect and his power are identical), it is pure potency and is distinguished (though inseparable) from the modes in which that potency issues. Once again, we find Spinoza's rationalism consistent with his nominalism, his rejection of abstraction in keeping with his concrete systematic thinking,[13] and it is now plain why he says that besides substance and its modes nothing else exists; for the attributes of substance are its powers, not the variations or modes of its existence.

The attributes, then, are the real and operative forms of God's potency, and each is "co-extensive" with substance (using the term "co-extensive" figuratively, for Extension is one only among infinite attributes). The whole range of the infinite variety that issues modally from God's infinite nature is covered by each attribute, for substance is one and is single, and

[11] Cf. G. Huan, *op. cit.,* Ch. III, ii.
[12] Spinoza identifies God's intellect with his will, or power; thus it is the same to say that God conceives a thing as to say that he creates it. Cf. *Ethics* I, xvii, S.
[13] Cf. p. 27 above.

the attributes in which its power is expressed are forms or aspects of it inseparable in reality though distinguishable in kind. Every mode (or modification) of any attribute, therefore, is identical in substance with a corresponding mode in every other attribute; so that, as Spinoza repeatedly tells us, the order and connexion of modes in one attribute (e.g. ideas) is the same as the order and connexion of modes in any other (e.g. bodies).

It is because each attribute covers the whole range of God's infinitude, except so far as that is expressed through other attributes, that Spinoza is able to speak of the eternal things as the ultimate genera for the definitions of mutable things, though they are by no means generalizations or abstract ideas. Each attribute, therefore, is infinite in its own kind with the infinity of substance, but substance is infinite absolutely, and so its potency is exercised in infinite ways; that is, in infinite attributes. Logical as this conclusion seems it is a source of great difficulty, to the discussion of which I shall return. What I wish to emphasize here is that the attributes are *distinctions* within the nature, or essence, of substance they are not divisions of substance. "No attribute of substance," Spinoza says, "can be truly conceived from which it would follow that substance could be divided." [14] For that would mean either that substance could be destroyed by being dissipated into many finites, or that many substances could be derived from one, both of which alternatives have already been shown to be absurd. Spinoza is here rejecting Descartes's view that though, strictly speaking, God is the only substance, we may legitimately speak of created substances, such as the extended world and the thinking souls of men.[15]

Just as Spinoza insists that substance is indivisible and is not divided by, or among, its attributes, so he insists that no attribute is divisible in its own kind. Extension, he declares, is indivisible and so is Thought, though we imagine them as divisible when (as we commonly do) we think confusedly; for "whole" and "part" are not realities but only *entia rationis*. If clearly and distinctly conceived by the intellect, attributes are understood to be absolutely indivisible.[16] The argument is that the infinite does not consist of parts, for the parts would, by their nature (being mutually exclusive), be finite and could not then, by aggregation, no matter how many there were, constitute an infinite whole. Extension,

---

[14] *Ethics* I, xii.

[15] At an early stage of his thinking, Joachim points out, Spinoza tended more towards this position of Descartes than in his mature thought. Cf. Joachim, *Study*, pp. 18. 21: Descartes. *Principia Philosophiae* I, li. *et seq.*, and Spinoza, *Ep.* IX.

[16] Cf. *K.V.* I, ii; *Ethics* I, xii, xiii, C and S, xv, S; *Epp.* XII, XXXV, XXXVI.

for instance, is infinite and everywhere the same, and is continuous with itself, thus it cannot be augmented or reduced in quantity (as it could if it consisted of parts). It cannot be increased, for nothing can be added to what is already infinite in extent; it cannot be reduced in quantity because that would imply a limit and something beyond it; but there is nothing other than extension which could limit or "extend" beyond extension itself. If one could divide it, the parts would be separable, but there is nothing that could separate them except extension itself, which would thus remain continuously indivisible. Again, if divisible into parts, each part would be independent of the rest, and could be and be understood without the rest, so one might be destroyed without affecting the others. But this is impossible in extension as such, of which no part is intelligible without extension as a whole and none can be destroyed. Any "part" of space is a system of spatial relations, and any spatial relation between points involves and implies similar relations to other points, and these again to others, and so on *ad infinitum*. Thus every "part" is conceivable only in relation to all the rest. For the same reason, if *per impossibile* any part were eliminated the whole would, by that very fact, be annihilated. It is only when we consider things as modes of extension (or bodies) that they appear divisible and are said to consist of parts.

Spinoza develops these arguments almost exclusively with respect to Extension, because his critics had declared him at fault for alleging that God could have extension as an attribute, and thus might be divisible. They argued that because extension was divisible it could not be infinite. But Spinoza seeks to turn their argument against themselves by showing that extension because indivisible must be conceived as infinite.[17] The same, moreover, must apply to all the attributes, but nobody seriously contends that Thought is divisible into separable parts, though there are obviously differences distinguishable within it. Spinoza, however, does not deny the possibility of distinctions within the substance and its attributes, and commentators misinterpret him when they allege that he does. In fact, the very arguments we have been summarizing show that while he denies the possibility of separable parts, he not only allows but asserts the presence of distinctions.

It must surely be obvious that Spinoza, while excluding partition did not exclude distinction within substance. That which has infinite attributes, in each of which infinite modes issue from the boundless potency of substance is indeed infinitely diversified and variegated. Both in the *Ethics* (*loc. cit.*) and in the *Short Treatise* he says that, conceived as sub-

---

[17] Cf. *Ethics* I, xv, S.

stance, extension (or space) cannot be divided, but if conceived as "variously affected" (*materiam diversimodo affectam*), "then its parts are distinguished modally only, but not in reality" (*Ethics, loc. cit.*).[18] Modes, accordingly, are distinguishable differentiations (affections or modifications) of substance, analogous, one might suggest, to the allotropic forms of carbon, or sulphur, in all of which the "substance" is the same; [19] and when we regard substance as so modally diversified, we tend to think of it imaginatively as divisible into parts. But the category of whole and parts is only an aid to the imagination and is inapplicable to substance as rightly conceived. The modal differentiations, however, are not themselves the product of our imagination. They are real in that and so far as they follow necessarily from the infinite nature of God.

Commentators like Caird and Joachim criticize Spinoza for providing no principle of self-differentiation in the nature of substance which will adequately explain how the infinite unity of God issues in the infinite variety of his attributes and modes, so that his readers are left with the impression, consequent upon a number of explicit statements, that we shall attend to later, that in God all diversity vanishes, and that both attributes and modes are mere appearance, the product of finite human thought and imagination. That this was Spinoza's *intention* is obviously not the case, nor do these two commentators allege that it was. In fact, the inference that the modal variety is a product of human imagination is too gross an error to be entertained. For it involves an obvious *hysteron proteron* – a reversal of the true order of things, as Spinoza conceived it. The human mind, for him, is itself a finite mode of Thought, and could not possibly be the source and origin of the whole modal system. Neither could Spinoza have committed so palpable a blunder, nor do all the commentators, though sometimes they almost seem to be suggesting it. Nevertheless, the question how the unity of substance can differentiate itself as required by Spinoza's theory, is a difficult one and must be faced. It concerns primarily the nature of God's causality, but before we deal with it directly, some account must be given of the modes of substance and the order in which they are said to follow from the infinite essence.

---

[18] The passage in *K.V.* (*V.V.L.*, IV., p. 13) runs, "If then I divide water, I divide only the modes of the substance not the substance itself, which mode, whether water or something else, is always the same." He appends a note: "Dividing the water, then, I do not divide the substance but only the modes of substance; which substance, although variously modified (*verscheidendlijk gewijzigd zijnde*), is always the same."

[19] We must not, however, confuse our common use of "substance" with Spinoza's.

3. Modes, Infinite and Finite

Mode is defined as *"substantiae affectiones,"* the affections or modifications of substance, "or that which is in another, through which it is also conceived" (*Ethics* I, Def. v.). That in which modes are is substance, and they are conceived through substance, as the chemist can understand what a diamond is only when he knows that it is a form of carbon. Modes, in short, are the various ways in which substance manifests its power of existing.

Spinoza says that infinite things follow in infinite ways (*infinitis modis*) from the divine nature (*Ethics* I, xvi): and what they follow from immediately is the attribute to which they belong. Really every thing (*res*) is in all the attributes, so that to every mode in each attribute there is a counterpart in every other. Considering any one attribute, however, as expressing the essence of substance in one way, it is infinite and eternal in its own kind, and Spinoza asserts, in Prop. xxi of *Ethics* I, that whatever follows from "the absolute nature" of any attribute must itself be infinite and eternal. It cannot be finite, for that would imply limitation by some other finite entity, which would also be constituted by the same attribute. In that case we have the absurd consequence that the absolute or entire nature of the attribute would both constitute, as well as not constitute (negate or limit), the thing supposed to follow immediately from it. Accordingly, any mode that is the immediate consequence of the attribute as such, must be an infinite mode. Again, whatever follows from such an infinite mode will have to be infinite also.

Finite modes follow in a different fashion, as is set out in Prop. xxxviii of *Ethics* I. The proximate cause of a finite mode is always another finite mode, and of that another, *ad infinitum*. As Spinoza puts it, it must follow from an attribute of God so far as that is modified by another finite mode. The crucial questions are: how do the infinite modes follow from the essence of substance (or God)? How is an attribute modified by finite modes? And how are these two different kinds of modification related to each other?

These are among the more obscure points in Spinoza's philosophy, for he tells us little that throws light upon these questions. Something pertinent, however, may be gleaned from what he says about Extension and its infinite modes, so I shall turn to that first; though even here he usually dismisses the subject as belonging more properly to a treatise on natural science, which (he tells his correspondent, Tschirnhaus) he has not yet systematically worked out. (*Ep.* LX). Descartes had identified matter with extension and had alleged that God introduced a fixed and definitive quantity of motion into it. But Spinoza rejected Descartes's view, although he retained certain features of it.[20] For him, as we know, Extension is an attribute of God, that is, an aspect of his power or creativity, and so will involve a dynamic principle. The first infinite mode of Extension, he says (*K.V.*, II, xix, *V.V.L.*, IV, p. 72), is Motion and Rest,[21] by which alone bodies are differentiated – for they do not differ in extension.[22] As we have seen Extension is not divisible *qua* substance, but modal distinctions can be made within it. As motion and rest is the sole principle of discrimination between simple bodies (for diversity of size is a subsequent relation pertaining only to composite bodies, as appears from their definition), primary bodies appear to consist solely of a certain proportion of motion and rest; and composite bodies are made up of these, their individuality being maintained by the constancy of the proportion of motion and rest in the whole, which is communicated to one another by the simpler parts.[23] This overall proportion may be maintained despite variations in the motions of the simpler parts. Extension, we have maintained, is conceived by Spinoza as a form of God's activity and this evinces itself in space as motion and rest in the varying proportions which constitute bodies. Would the suggestion be excessively speculative that this doctrine is analogous to the teaching of contemporary physics, in which energy is described as curvature or contortion of space, and a special combination of fields of force (e.g. in the atomic nucleus) constitutes matter – what Eddington called a fold or pleat in space-time? [24]

When primary bodies combine and transmit to one another a constant proportion of motion and rest they constitute composite bodies, which again may combine into a larger physical whole in which a constant proportion of motion and rest is still maintained, and so on, until the entire physical universe is encompassed. "And if we continue thus *in infinitum,*" Spinoza puts it, "we may easily conceive that the whole of Nature is one individual, whose parts, that is all bodies, vary in infinite ways without any alteration of the whole individual." [25] This total individual Spinoza refers to elsewhere (e.g. *Ep.* LXIV) as *"facies totius universi,"* the "face"

---

[20] Cf. *P.P.C.* II, ii *et seq.,* and *Epp.* LXXXI and LXXXIII; also Joachim, *Study* pp. 82-85.

[21] Cf. also *K.V.* I, ii, *V.V.L.,* IV, p. 12 n. In *K.V.* I, ix, however, he speaks only of Motion.

[22] Cf. *Eth.* II, Lem. I and Axiom II (following Prop. xiii).

[23] Cf. *Ethics* II, Def. following Axiom II, *loc. cit.*

[24] Cf. A. Wolf, in *Proceedings of the Aristotelian Society,* 1926-7, p. 186.

[25] *Loc. cit.,* Lem. vii, S. Cf. also *Ep.* XXXII, where Spinoza explains and illustrates the doctrine at greater length, and pp. 65-67 below.

(or *Gestalt*) of the whole universe,[26] and he offers it as an example of an infinite mode in the attribute of Extension subsequent to motion and rest.

In the attribute of Thought there should be a similar sequence, but Spinoza nowhere sets it out as fully or as clearly as he does the infinite modes of Extension. In the same letter answering Tschirnhaus' questions, to which reference has been made above (*Ep.* LXIV), he gives as an example of an infinite mode of Thought *"intellectus absolute infinitus,"* the absolutely infinite intellect, which would be the intellect of God, and the content of which would be (presumably) the whole of reality, the *infinita idea Dei.* God, therefore, as Joachim points out, is, for Spinoza, self-conscious, a fact which does not easily comport with the common accusation against Spinoza's doctrine that he conceived God as impersonal and purely naturalistically. The infinite idea of God, however, as it should include not only the idea of the *facies totius universi,* so far as that is only a mode of Extension, but also ideas of all other infinite attributes, gives rise to special difficulties about which I shall have more to say below. Now we may return to the question of God's causality and can try to understand how his unity is differentiated, first into the attributes and, secondly, how the attributes specify themselves into infinite and subsequently into finite modes. We must then determine what the relation is between these two orders.

4. The Causality of God

First and foremost, God is free cause because he is *causa sui* and cannot be determined to action by anything other than himself (for there is no other). But this is not the place to discuss the nature of freedom, which is reserved for a later chapter. Secondly, God is the immanent, not the transient cause, of all things. This is, again, because there is nothing outside and beyond God into which his causal efficacy could pass over. Everything that is, is in God, so he is cause of all things in the same way as he is cause of himself.[27] But his causation of infinite modes is immediate; they follow directly either from God or from one of his attributes (which is virtually the same thing); whereas finite modes follow from God's attributes only mediately, through the infinite modes. Both alike are, and are conceivable, only in and through God, but there is a qualified sense in which God is the "remote" cause of finite modes, though he is the proximate cause of the infinite modes – remote, that is, not as separate or disconnected from finite things, but only in the sense that the essence

---

[26] Not to be confused with *communis ordo naturae,* for which see pp. 98-103 below.
[27] Cf. *Ethics,* I, xviii.

and existence of finite things are mediated by those of the infinite and eternal things.[28]

These two types of causality seem, at first sight, to be mutually incompatible, for while the infinite modes follow directly from God's nature, each finite mode, as we have seen, requires another, prior, finite mode as its cause, and that another, and so on to infinity. These finite entities follow from God only so far as his nature is "affected" (or qualified) by another finite mode. This relationship between finite cause and finite effect is transient causation, and though God's nature is essential to every mode, both cause and effect, and is immanent in all, by traversing the infinite series backwards one never reaches the infinite whole, which is alleged to be immanent in every item of the infinite series.

The difficulty is enhanced by Spinoza's frequent insistence that all things follow necessarily from God's nature, in the same way as it follows from the nature of a triangle that its three angles are equal to two right angles.[29] Necessary logical implications of this kind have traditionally been called eternal truths, and Spinoza asserts that all things that follow from God's nature in this way, are eternal truths: "You ask me," he wrote to de Vries "whether even things and the modifications (*affectiones*) of things are eternal truths. I say, Certainly." (*Ep.* X.). That this should be the case does not seem inappropriate to the infinite modes, for they are eternal, as God's essence and existence are eternal. But it seems hardly appropriate to finite things, which, by their very nature are limited in time and space (the finite modes of Extension, in particular). Such finite things are usually contrasted with eternal truths as contingent. But Spinoza denies that anything at all in Nature is contingent and nothing can be said to be so "except with respect to imperfection of our knowledge." [30] Nevertheless, finite things differ from the infinite and eternal things in being determined always by finite causes which never take us back to the eternal things themselves however far we trace the causal chains; yet they involve the causality of God and his attributes without which they can neither be nor be conceived. How is this apparently double causality of God to be understood?

5. *Interpretations, Comment and Criticism*

Some commentators have been tempted, because of the apparent incompatibility of the two types of causation, to explain away the finite

---

[28] Cf. *Ethics* I, xxviii, S, and *TdIE*, XIV, 99-101 quoted above, p. 23.
[29] Cf. *Ethics* I, xvii, S; II, xlix, S; *Epp.* LVI, LXXV; and Joachim, *Study*, p. 60.
[30] Cf. *Ethics* I, xxix and xxxiii, S. 1.

series, which seem clearly to involve temporality, as the product of human imagination, as appearance, which is at best misleading and at worst sheerly illusory; for are not these finite causal chains precisely what we think of as contingent events, and does not Spinoza explicitly say that they seem so to us simply because of the deficiency of our knowledge? If this deficiency could be made good they would appear in their true light as eternal truths, following necessarily from God's infinite perfection.[31] Their temporal character would disappear and they would be seen as fixed and necessary factors in a fixed and unchanging system of Nature. Joachim (who is in general agreement on this matter with Caird) goes even further and contends that, despite Spinoza's evident wish to retain concreteness in the nature of God, if we take him at his word we must regard the temporal series as mere appearance, which, when seen *sub specie aeternitatis,* disappears altogether, leaving only the infinite modes, and that even they reduce one to another – the face of the entire universe to motion and rest, and that to pure extension – leaving us with a multiplicity of attributes in no way explicable in terms of any principle of differentiation inherent in the unity of God.[32]

There seem to me to be cogent reasons why this criticism ought not to be accepted. If it were valid against Spinoza it would be equally valid against modern physical theory; for according to that bodies are made up of atoms, and atoms of elementary particles, some united in the nucleus as a complex field of forces, and others (electrons) "orbiting" round the nucleus as standing waves of energy. All of these particles are equivalent to definite quantities of energy determinable by Einstein's equation: $E = mc^2$ and are, in certain circumstances, convertible into radiation. Thus in the final analysis all matter turns out to be energy; and, according to the General Theory of Relativity, energy is resoluble into space-time curvature, and we are left with a single continuum, which, though actually differentiated, contains no obvious intrinsic principle of differentiation. For space-time curvature is said to be determined by the distribution of matter, and that fact, if no other principle of differentiation is identifiable, simply commits us to a circle – space-time into which curvature is introduced by matter, which, as a complex of fields, is itself but a singularity (or fold) in space-time – and this circle is not self-explanatory. Spinoza's position, we shall find is in better case.

The text, moreover, gives ample evidence, which, of course, Joachim

<hr />

[31] Cf. Joachim, *Study,* p. 227; and H. F. Hallet, *Benedict de Spinoza* (London, 1957), p. 48.
[32] Cf. *Study,* Bk. I. Appendix.

acknowledges,[33] that Spinoza quite definitely regarded attributes and modes as real existent differentations of the unity of Substance, and not mere appearances to consciousness. The latter hypothesis, as has been argued above, would be ridiculous, not only because it would attribute the apparent differences, as an illusion, to one (or several) of themselves, but because Spinoza quite definitely and plainly asserts that each mode of consciousness answers to some mode in every attribute,[34] and that the attribute of Thought is but one among an infinite variety. This infinite multiplicity, therefore, cannot be a mere product of thinking. He must certainly have been aware of any implication that all this variety was merely a phantasmagoria pertaining to finite modes in a single attribute, and he would have attempted to correct or explain away any such suggestion. But clearly it never entered his mind. He maintains (even if commentators have difficulty in finding the explanation) that infinite things in infinite ways must *of necessity* follow from the fulness of the divine nature (*Ethics* I, xvi), and that God's attributes are expressed in certain determinate ways, i.e. modes, which are particular things, which are (and are nothing but) determinations of God's attributes (*Ethics* I, xxv, C.).

All this is demonstrated in the first Part of the *Ethics,* which is devoted explicitly to the exposition of the fundamental nature of the real; it is intended to be a demonstration of the strictest cogency and truth and it was Spinoza's most strenuous effort to express the highest (metaphysical) form of knowledge. To suggest, therefore, that the modal differentiation of the real depends solely on imaginative thinking, the nature and explanation of which is expounded only in Part II and is meant to be logically posterior to what has been established in Part I, would be little short of ludicrous. When William van Blyenberg asked Spinoza to explain why he denied that the thinking substance was the same as the human soul, along with various subsequent ethical points, Spinoza declined on the ground that "as everybody knows, Ethics must be based upon Metaphysics and Physics." [35] The differentiation of Substance into attributes and modes is primarily what Metaphysics is about and so must be both fundamental and prior to the nature of the human mind and any of its products.

Other commentators interpret Spinoza as advocating a more naturalistic doctrine. What has to be explained is the apparently double causation by God of eternal things and of finite temporal changes. The

[33] *Op. cit.,* Bk. I, Ch. I.
[34] *Ethics,* II, vii, S.
[35] *Epp.* XXIV and XXVII.

eternal things are taken to include the essences of finite things, while the temporal are their existence in space and time, their coming to be and passing away. As Spinoza says, in the Scholium to the corollary of Proposition X of *Ethics* II, "Certainly, everybody must concede that nothing can be or be conceived without God. For it is admitted by all that God is the sole cause of all things both of their essence and of their existence; that is, that God is cause of things not only *secundum fieri* (of their coming to be), as they say, but also *secundum esse* (of their being)." And Spinoza certainly maintains that essences (even of finite things) are eternal and exist eternally in God – a doctrine the significant consequences of which will engage us at a later stage. It has been suggested that God's causation of temporal existents, their coming into being, changing and decaying is, as Spinoza asserts, the natural causation of one event by a prior event and of that by yet another *ad infinitum*; but the assertion that all things are in God and that he is the immanent cause of all that is or occurs, as well as the description of the causal series as the determination of each finite mode by God, not as infinite, but as constituting another finite mode,[36] are interpreted as meaning that the causal chains follow universal laws of nature. Hence any finite event will be deducible from the nature of God, as expressed in these universal laws, along with some prior event (or events), what modern philosophers call "initial conditions." Spinoza equates God with Nature, so this interpretation is held to be both feasible and compatible with God's causation of eternal essences.[37]

The eternal essences of things can (according to Spinoza) be deduced, from the definition of a divine attribute and from nothing else. That this is his view may be inferred, not only from what has already been quoted, but also from his reply to Tschirnhaus' question how particular things (e.g. bodies) can be deduced from the nature of Extension alone.[38] He replies that this is impossible if Extension is conceived, as Descartes conceived it; that is, as matter. "It ought to be defined necessarily by an attribute which expresses eternal and infinite essence" (*Ep*. LXXXIII). Presumably then, if so defined, the conception of Extension alone is sufficient to engender all particular extended things, and all can be deduced from such definition. This is taken to mean that from the definition of the attribute, the essences of the various figures can be deduced as the

---

[36] Cf. *Ethics* I, xxxviii, dem.
[37] Cf. A. J. Watt, "The Causality of God in Spinoza's Philosophy," *Canadian Journal of Philosophy,* II, 2, 1972, and Stuart Hampshire, *Spinoza* (1956 edn.) pp. 34 ff.
[38] Cf. *Epp*. LXXX - LXXXIII.

properties of a circle or of a triangle can be deduced from their definitions. This may be done quite independently of the actual existence of any particular finite things. For instance, from the nature of a circle it can be deduced that the rectangles formed from the segments of all chords intersecting in a single point are equal in area, and of these an infinite number may be drawn, though none of them need actually exist (Cf. *Ethics* II, viii, S.). In short, one may deduce the *possibility* of existence of any one of these rectangles from the conception of a circle; and so, from the conception of one of God's attributes, one may deduce the possibility of existence, since one may deduce the essence (or nature), of any of its modes. Thus Spinoza's doctrine becomes a purely naturalistic one in which God and Nature are synonymous and all "supernatural" causes (whether of essence or existence) are excluded.[39]

This interpretation is appealing and has much to recommend it, but still fails to do justice to Spinoza's thought. Undoubtedly Spinoza wished to exclude supernatural causes, for the very word expressed an impossibility in his view. What is *super*-natural must be beyond and outside Nature, and, for Spinoza, God-or-Nature included everything there is or ever could be. There could, therefore, be nothing whatever beyond it. But, as we have already seen, "nature" may be taken in two senses, either as phenomenal nature, as the world of common experience, or as the true and essential nature of the whole universe. The first of these Spinoza calls *communis ordo naturae,* the common order of nature, and this he regards as largely a texture of error and illusion concocted by the imagination.[40] The second is *Natura Naturans* issuing as *Natura Naturata.* It is the last which follows necessarily and is deducible immediately from the essence of God.

Again, it is true that Spinoza speaks of the laws of nature as "the eternal decrees of God" (Cf. *Ethics* II, xlix, S.), but he did not understand by this the laws of nature as empirical generalizations – very much to the contrary. Empirical generalizations were, for Spinoza, like all abstractions, mere aids to the imagination; and of the empirical method, "by which we conclude one thing from another," he says "by such a method one may perceive nothing ever in natural things except accidental properties which are never clearly understood without prior knowledge of their essences." [41] Consequently, when he maintains both that finite modes proceed from God's nature and yet follow finite causes

[39] Cf. Hampshire, *loc. cit.*
[40] Cf. *Ethics* II, xxix, C and S, XXX, dem., and V, xxix, S.
[41] *TdIE.,* IV, 21 and V, 27.

in an infinite sequence, he certainly does not mean that we can infer temporal events from other temporal events ("one thing from another") according to empirical laws.

Further, the eternal essences of things which follow necessarily from the definition of God's attributes, must not be understood as generic concepts, for such concepts are mere abstractions. Nor can it be the case that what is deduced is the mere possibility of their existence; for, as nothing in nature is merely contingent, possibility, Spinoza tells us, is either determined by reason of the essence itself (in which case the thing would be *causa sui*, or God, and nothing finite), or else by the causes of the thing in question. But, in the case of finite things, these causes would be other finites and so we are thrown back to the type of God's causality that involves infinite series of finite causes.[42]

What Spinoza means by "essence" I have already attempted to indicate. It is no abstract concept like "animality" or "humanity" but is precisely and exactly *what* the individual thing is. In *Ethics* II, Definition II, he writes: "To the essence of any thing, I say, that pertains which, if given, the thing is necessarily posited, and if taken away the thing is necessarily removed; or that without which the thing neither can be nor be conceived and *vice versa* what cannot be nor be conceived without the thing." It is not easy to understand this definition unless one bears in mind what Spinoza says elsewhere and especially his statement in the Scholium of Proposition vii of this Part – a statement to which we shall have to revert – that a thing and its idea are one and the same in substance. Similarly, in the unfinished *Treatise on the Improvement of the Intellect,* he maintains in effect that the objective essence and the formal essence of a thing – the true idea and the reality – are one and the same.[43] Thus the essence of a thing is just precisely what constitutes the thing, so that without it the thing neither is nor can be conceived, and *vice versa*. Hence what must follow necessarily from the attribute of God must be the actuality of the thing, in some sense at least – its essence which cannot be or be conceived without the thing, as the thing cannot without the essence. Each is the necessary condition of the other (not, however, without God, the sufficient condition).

---

[42] Cf. *Ethics* I, xxix and xxxiii, S.

[43] *TdIE.,* VI, 35: *"Hinc patet, quod certitudo nihil sit praeter ipsam essentiam objectivam; id est, modus, quo sentimus essentiam formalem, est ipsa certitudo."* "Hence it is plain that certitude is nothing other than the objective essence itself; that is, the way in which we are aware of the formal essence is itself certitude."

6. Solution of the Problem

Accordingly, we need a better interpretation of God's causality than
we have hitherto found if we are to do justice to Spinoza's theory. In the
first place God is conceived and defined as infinite substance, and what is
infinite has, by that very fact infinite attributes. The more reality a thing
has the more attributes it must possess,[44] therefore an infinite being must
be infinitely differentiated. What Spinoza is in effect maintaining is that
blank, undifferentiated unity is incompatible with infinity. The blank unity
of which some critics complain simply would not be God. In two places,[45]
Spinoza asserts that to say that God is one, is really only a manner of
speaking because what is one, is one of many, or one of a class (even if the
class has only one member). But God is not a class concept and is not one
of many. When we say that there is one God only we are not counting,
but merely denying that there can be anything other than God. The
proper description is that God is the whole, beyond which there is nothing
and within which everything. The principle of differentiation, therefore,
of God's "unity" is his very infinity, his necessary all-inclusiveness. There
can be no whole which is not diversified.

Certainly Spinoza denies that substance is divisible and objects to the
use, with reference to it, of the category of whole and parts. But that is
only if and so far as the parts of a whole are thought of as prior to it, or,
in other words, if the whole is regarded as an aggregate of its parts.[46]
We have already seen that Spinoza not only admitted but required the
existence of distinctions within substance, as well as within each attribute,
and we shall see presently that he conceived the most fundamental reals
as constituted by an infinite variety of distinguishable, though inseparable, elements.

If God's infinity necessarily implies his possession of infinite attributes,
it is quite natural and consistent to identify Extension and Thought as
two of these. Spinoza shows reasons why we cannot follow Descartes in
calling them created substances, reasons implicit in Descartes's own
theory and admitted by him. They are not *causa sui* and do not exist
solely by virtue of their own essence. But if they are not substances then
(as we read in *Ethics* I, x, S and xiv, C 2) they must be attributes of substance, and, as an infinity of attributes follow necessarily from the infinite
nature of substance, these two must necessarily be among them. Thus we
can account for the differentiation of God into attributes by recognizing

that, being infinite, he has infinite power of existence which (for the same reason) must manifest itself in infinite ways. Any such ways of expressing God's essence, or power, known to us, must, therefore, be among his infinite attributes.

Each attribute then specifies itself according to its special nature, Thought is an activity, and is always so conceived by Spinoza. He protests repeatedly against regarding ideas as passive and inert pictures.[47] And this activity in its proper and original form is intellect – the absolutely infinite intellect of God – the product of which is the idea of the universe, or God's idea of himself – *infinita idea Dei*. These are the infinite modes of Thought and how they specify themselves into finite modes Spinoza does not explain; but as the principle of specification, whatever it is, must be the same for each attribute, what he says about Extension may give us a clue.

Like Thought, Extension is a dynamic principle and no inert mass.[48] It is one of God's creative powers. Consequently there follows from it immediately motion-and-rest, or energy. We may, as suggested above, conceive this relationship between motion-and-rest and extension on the analogy of the modern conception of the relation of energy (or field) to space-time. Spinoza's view anticipates that of Leibniz, who also objected to the Cartesian notion of extension as inert, and postulated, in consequence, the existence of *vis viva* (living force) as characteristic of substances, and therefore inherent in all bodies. Motion-and-rest is, as it were, Extension manifesting itself as activity. The degree of motion or the proportion of motion and rest in any region differentiates it from other regions and so gives rise to the differences between "bodies." [49] Now simple bodies, distinguished only by the degree of motion-and-rest that constitutes them, may combine into complex bodies the persistent individuality of which consists purely in the constancy of the proportion of motion-and-rest transmitted from one to another of its simple constituents, and these again may combine into more complex bodies. So bodies may become to any degree complex and, like the human body, may retain their identity in spite of internal changes and the movement of parts in relation to one another.[50]

In the 32nd. Epistle, Spinoza gives the example of the blood as a single body composed of several fluids. It is a most instructive example, for it throws light on Spinoza's conception of the category of whole and

---

[47] Cf. *Ethics* II, Def. III, Exp., xlix, S.
[48] Cf. *Ep.* LXXXI.
[49] Cf. *Ethics* II, Axioms I & II and Lemma i following Prop. xiii.
[50] Cf. *Ethics, loc. cit.*, Def., and Lemm. iv - vii (*V.V.L.* I, pp. 86-88).

part, which, as we saw, he regards in at least one of its uses as inadequate to substance. That was the sense in which the whole was thought of (or imagined) as an aggregate of separable parts, and was therefore conceived through its parts, which were regarded as prior to its composition out of them. Here, however, he says:

"By coherence of parts, therefore, I understand nothing other than that the laws, or nature of one part adapt themselves to the laws or nature of another so as to conflict with one another as little as possible. With respect to whole and parts, I consider things as parts of some whole in so far as their natures accommodate themselves to one another so that they are as far as possible in mutual agreement."

He then gives the example of the blood consisting of chyle, lymph and other ingredients, each of which we may consider as distinct yet which are regulated in their behaviour, so as to combine into one composite fluid, the proportions of each to each being determined by the whole. If we were to imagine a minute creature ("a worm") living in the blood and able to perceive the difference between the particles of the different constituents, "it could not know," Spinoza writes, "how all the parts are controlled (*moderantur*) by the universal nature of the blood, and are forced, as the nature of the blood requires, to accommodate themselves to one another so as to harmonize according to a certain proportion (*ratione*) among themselves." So we, living in the material world, imagine the variety of things as mutually separate and independent and may well be unaware of the ways in which their mutual relations are regulated by the nature of the larger whole to which they belong.

What he says in the Scholium already quoted,[51] he explains more fully here:

". . . all the bodies of nature can and should be conceived as we have here conceived the blood: for all bodies are surrounded by others and are mutually determined to exist and act in a definite and determined relationship (*ratione*), preserving always together the same proportion of motion and rest, that is, in the entire universe. Hence it follows that every body, so far as it exists modified in a certain way, must be considered as part of the whole universe, as in harmony with its totality and as coherent with the rest; and, as the nature of the universe is not, like the nature of blood, limited, but is absolutely infinite, therefore its parts are modified in infinite ways (*modis*) by this nature of infinite power, and compelled to suffer infinite changes. But, with respect to substance, I consider that each part has a closer union with its whole. For . . . as I have tried to show, since it is of the nature of

[51] *Ethics* II, Lem. vii, S; see p. 56 above.

substance to be infinite, it follows that each part pertains to the nature of corporeal substance, and cannot be or be conceived without it."

Thus it is clear that the nature and pattern of the whole determines the nature and activity of the parts and the changes which occur within it. But the whole, in this case (as we learned from the Scholium to Lemma vii in Part II of the *Ethics*), is the face of the whole universe (*facies totius universi*), and this is an infinite mode of Extension. That remains eternally one and the same while (as is said in the letter) it forces its innumerable parts to undergo infinite changes, and *ipso facto*, since they are all various proportions of motion and rest, moulds and modifies them in infinite ways. It is in this manner that the infinite mode gives rise to, and regulates the occurrence of, finite bodies (the finite modes of extension) and so God's infinite power is transmitted through the infinite modes of his attribute to finite things.

It is now a relatively simple matter to infer how the infinite idea of God determines the particular nature of finite ideas – the ideas of finite things – and why they can neither be nor be conceived without it. The idea of God is the ground and source of all ideas, the norm of all truth and the criterion of validity of all thinking, just as the face of the whole universe is the ground and source of all events in the physical world.

So it is that God's causality is immanent in all things, for the principle of the totality is determinant of every detail within it. It specifies itself first as the infinite modes, each of which is a concrete universal, a dynamic and systematic whole, governing the variations and interplay of its own activities. The immanent causality of God issues, therefore, without hiatus or contradiction, in infinite modes, in eternal essences as these are dictated by the nature of the whole, and in the constant flux of changes among particular finites. At the same time it is compatible with the successive causation of each finite mode by a preceding finite event, for the total (unchanging) structure, or *Gestalt*, of the whole universe both requires and is itself unaffected by the internal changes.

This can be illustrated by three analogous examples: (i) a candle flame in calm air retains its shape and colour in spite of a continuous flux of particles through it, each of which is continuously changing its state. (ii) Similarly, the form of a living organism remains the same throughout constant changes and exchanges of its constituent material. (iii) But an even more apt example from the biological sphere is the ontogenetic process of development of a complex organism, like a mammal, from fertilized ovum to adult. This is a succession of changes, all determined by the specific character of the developing organism which remains the same throughout. The successive phases are adapted to one another (as Spinoza says) as the complete system requires, yet each is produced directly by its predecessor as proximate cause. The organism as a whole and its vital energy is immanent cause of every change and of the form and character of each part, yet every change and every detail of the constituent organs is brought into being by an immediately prior condition which is its transient cause. The causality of God in Spinoza's theory is to be conceived as operating similarly, except, of course, that Nature as a whole undergoes no process of growth, maturation and decline. It is more like what biologists call a biocoenosis, or an eco-system; that is, an ecological unit such as a pond, a lake, or an ocean, a forest, a continent, or the entire planet, in which the life and maintenance of every individual and species rests upon the mutually interdependent relations and mutually regulating influences of one species upon another, as well as of surrounding non-organic substances. Populations in such a system keep one another in check and balance one another to mutual advantage, plant life oxygenates the atmosphere benefiting animal life, both of these fertilize the soil sustaining vegetable cover, which in turn holds and regulates the seepage and flow of water in the earth. A thousand and one such mutual influences, cyclical in their interplay, maintain a constancy of environmental conditions favourable to the continuous change and unceasing flow of living activity within the system.

Another analogy from contemporary science is Eddington's conception of the physical universe as a four-dimensional hypersphere. He considered this as a single system of energy applying the principles of quantum mechanics to determine the disposition of matter in a series of energy levels regarded as the eigenvibrations of the whole of space – standing waves, represented mathematically by the surface harmonics of the hypersphere. The occupancy of any energy state then follows from the successive saturation of the primary levels defined as multiples of Planck's constant h in accordance with the Exclusion Principle of Pauli. From this basis (corresponding, we might say, to the *facies totius universi* in Spinoza's system) Eddington was able to calculate the "proper masses" or energies of elementary particles, the gravitational potential, and the behaviour of particles under the influence of electrical forces, as well as the physical constants otherwise determined experimentally. Thus particular physical events, which cause one another successively in the transient process of nature are determined ultimately by the shape and structure of the whole universe which is itself a constant system in a state of dynamic equilibrium constituted by those events.

7. Residual Difficulties

In spite of the consistency and coherence of Spinoza's reasoning two major problems remain unsolved and perhaps, on his principles, insoluble. In his own life-time these difficulties were raised in questions asked by his correspondent, von Tschirnhaus, but his answers are cryptic and obscure.[52] The questions are, first, why it is necessary to assign infinite attributes to God, though only two, Extension and Thought, are known to us; secondly, if there are infinite attributes in each of which the modes correspond to those in every other, why is it that we do not know all of them – or, at least, more than two – since the attribute of thought should comprehend them all. Thirdly, even if we are unable to comprehend more attributes than two, God must know all of them; consequently the attribute of Thought must be different from, and more comprehensive than, any of the others.

Spinoza's answer to the first question is clear and cogent enough, but his replies to the other two leave much to be desired. We must attribute an infinity of attributes to God because God is infinite absolutely, and nothing less exists by virtue of its own essence alone. Attributes are mutually exclusive and there is more than one of them, thus they cannot be infinite absolutely, but only each in its own kind, and they can be and can be conceived only through God, as his attributes. Spinoza explains to Jan Hudde,[53] that if we were to say that any one attribute could exist by its own sufficiency we should, *a fortiori*, have to assert that there is an absolutely infinite being which must exist of its own sufficiency, for otherwise we should imply that something less than the absolutely infinite had a greater power of existing than what is infinite without qualification. As attributes express essence, what has absolutely infinite essence must have an infinity of attributes.

But human beings are bodies, that is, extended things, and of every mode of extension there is an idea in God's intellect. The idea of the human body, as we shall see in the next chapter, is the human mind. Thus the human mind is aware of its body and, through that, (since bodies are conceivable only through their appropriate attribute) it is aware of Extension. At the same time, since every idea involves an idea of itself (*idea ideae*), the human mind is aware of itself and so of the

[52] Cf. *Epp*. LXIII, LXIV, LXV and LXVI.
[53] *Ep*. XXXV.

attribute of Thought. It is a matter of experience, and Spinoza accepts this as sufficient ground, that we are not directly aware of any other attribute, and it is only by logical inference from our knowledge of God's infinity that an infinity of attributes is postulated.

Trouble arises, however, from Spinoza's insistence that all the attributes are of one and the same substance; so they are all virtually the same *thing* (*res*), and all the modifications of substance are the same in every attribute. Thus each mode is multiplex and is manifested simultaneously in every attribute. It is one and the same thing with an infinite variety of forms.[54] An idea and that of which it is an idea are, therefore, substantially one and the same, as had already been maintained in the Treatise on the Understanding – objective essence is the same thing as formal. It is not strictly the case, therefore, as is commonly alleged, that Spinoza regarded the modes in all the attributes as running parallel, although he does say that the order and connexion of ideas is the same as the order and connexion of things. It is the same, because ideas and extended things are identical in substance. There are not two (or infinitely many) parallel series of modes. There is only one series, issuing from God's infinite essence; but it can be "explained" in terms of any of the infinite variety of attributes – though by us only in terms of thought or of extension.

If this is the case, however, any idea should be identical in substance with a corresponding mode in *every* attribute and not only in one (Extension). Yet our ideas apparently cannot comprehend other attributes than Extension and Thought. If God's ideas do, as surely they must, comprehend all attributes, then the attribute of Thought, as expressed in God's infinite intellect, must be wider, or more comprehensive, than any other attribute, and must, therefore, be different from any of the others, and related differently to them from the way in which they are related to one another.

When Tschirnhaus raised this difficulty in a letter transmitted to Spinoza by G. H. Schuller (*Ep.* LXIII), and repeated it later in his own hand (*Ep.* LXV), Spinoza replied (*Ep.* LXVI): "In answer to your objection, I say that, although each thing is expressed in infinite modes in the infinite understanding of God, those infinite ideas by which it is expressed cannot constitute one and the same mind of an individual thing (*rei singularis*), but infinite minds; seeing that each of these infinite ideas has no connexion with any other . . ." Presumably, this means that each of the modes of any particular body in other attributes than Ex-

[54] Cf. *Ethics* II, vii, S.

tension has a mind (or idea) of its own; and as I cannot directly experience what is in other people's minds, but only what is in my own, so I cannot experience the ideas of the modes in other attributes than Extension which correspond to the extended bodies of which I can have ideas. But God's intellect comprehends all minds, mine, yours and other people's, as well as the minds (or ideas) of all modes in all attributes.

But this answer will not do. First, because if there is an infinity of singular minds (or ideas) for every mode of substance, and if this infinity is, as it must be, comprehended in God's intellect, then the attribute of thought is, in spite of all Spinoza says, in some sense more comprehensive and "wider" than any other attribute. For every mode in every attribute will have its own idea and all ideas belong to the attribute of Thought. Some commentators have tried to dispel this objection by pointing out that the relation of wider and narrower, or more and less extensiveness, pertains only within one attribute, namely Extension, and cannot be applied to the relations between attributes,[55] which do not exist side by side, nor are they spatially coincident, nor yet could they in any sense overlap. But the difficulty is not so easily avoided, for Spinoza is quite explicit and repeats more than once that the order and connexion of ideas is the same as that of things, which would not be the case if there were an infinity of orders of ideas in the attribute of Thought and only one order of things in each of the other attributes.

Nor is it possible to solve the problem, as some have attempted,[56] by correlating the infinite attributes with the infinite series of *ideae idearum* (ideas of ideas). Spinoza holds that of every idea there is another idea to which the first is related as object, and of the second there is a third, and so on *ad infinitum*.[57] Some of the commentators suggest that this infinite series of ideas corresponds to the infinite plurality of the attributes. The suggestion is, however, quite unacceptable; first, because it would obviously fail to resolve the problem of the apparent discrepancy between each of the other attributes and Thought, which would still have to span the entire infinity; and, secondly because it is a palpable misinterpretation of Spinoza's doctrine of *idea ideae*.

Spinoza meant by *idea ideae* something quite different from a set of ideas of the same mode in different attributes. We shall discuss the meaning of the phrase at more length in a later chapter and shall see that it does not involve other attributes than Thought and Extension, and

---

[55] Cf. Joachim, *Study*, p. 136; Huan, *op. cit.*, Ch. IV, § vii.
[56] Windelband and Batuscheck. Cf. Huan, *op. cit.*, Ch. IV. § viii.
[57] Cf. *TdIE.*, vi, 33-34, and *Ethics* II, xxi., S.

that it does not give rise to the same sort of asymmetry between the attribute of Thought and other attributes as does Spinoza's reply to Tschirnhaus. *Idea* and *ideatum* (what it is the idea of), we are clearly told by Spinoza, are one and the same thing, thus the idea of an idea will equally be the same thing as the idea which is its object, and thus identical in substance with the body of which it is the idea.[58] So the series of ideas of ideas does not involve a series of distinguishable modes in more attributes than one. For ideas are not pictures but are acts of thought or consciousness and to be aware that one is aware is no more than to be aware more fully and clearly of the object of one's awareness.

Secondly, this substantial identity of *idea* and *ideatum* deepens the problem of the infinite multiplicity of the attributes. For if my idea of my body is substantially the same thing as my body, it ought equally to be substantially identical with my body in every attribute there is, not only as a mode of Extension but also as a mode in all other attributes. But in that case I should be conscious of the other attributes as I am of Extension, which I am not, and which Spinoza admits to be impossible, or at least empirically false. Moreover, if it were possible, all attributes would be conceivable through the same system of ideas, and that Spinoza denies. Each attribute, he says, can be conceived only through itself, and this is the reason why he maintains that the ideas of modes in different attributes have no connexion one with another. Yet even this contention leads to difficulty, for it ought to affect the relation between Thought and Extension. They are different attributes and if each can be conceived only through itself either our ideas of extended things should have no connexion with our ideas of mental events, or extended things should be as unknowable to us as the modes of all other attributes. The second alternative is obviously false and Spinoza maintains that all our ideas are ideas of particular modes of extension (our bodies) and that all mental events are the awareness of bodily events.

As the doctrine is set out there seems to be no solution to these problems and, while Spinoza's arguments appear cogent, paradox persists. In short, the doctrine cannot be sustained; but to discover the error involved and to say how it might be corrected is no easy matter. Perhaps the most fruitful course would be to trace back its history – at least to Descartes – and to consider the reason for ascribing attributes to God in the way that Spinoza does.

One may, of course, use the term "attribute" in a wide sense which does not involve Spinoza's doctrine; that is, one may use it as roughly

[58] Cf. *Ethics* II, xxi.

synonymous with "property." Spinoza, however, distinguishes these two terms sharply. A property, for him, is what follows necessarily from the essence of a thing, whereas an attribute is the essence itself of God "as perceived by the intellect." This is a very special and technical usage, and it is notable that Spinoza speaks of attributes only with reference to God and never with reference to finite entities. His argument that the more reality a thing has the more attributes must be assigned to it would have held equally well of properties, so we may suspect that he had a further and a special reason for asserting that Extension and Thought were attributes of God. Once he did so, it would follow naturally that, being infinite, God must have an infinity of attributes. Why, then, does Spinoza regard Extension and Thought as attributes in the first place?

Descartes had maintained that Extension and Thought were created substances, because he regarded them as distinct from God, and as produced by God in definitive acts of free will. Spinoza denies both these contentions for weighty reasons, some of which have already been mentioned. For Descartes, then the world was an extended manifold created by God and substantial so far as it depended on nothing except God for its existence. Extension, however, includes nothing of thought or consciousness and cannot account for its existence. In fact, Descartes was convinced that while we know indubitably the existence of thought in our own self-consciousness, the existence of the extended material world remains doubtful until we can prove it from premises one of which is the existence of the thinking thing (*res cogitans*). The thinking thing, therefore, exists in its own right and not posterior to the existence of extended things (*res extensae*). Not wholly in its own right, however, because it is evidently imperfect, suffering from doubt, ignorance and illusion; hence it cannot be cause of itself – or it would make itself perfect and supply its own deficiencies. It must, therefore, and can only be dependent for its existence upon a perfect being which is *causa sui*.[59] Accordingly, that which thinks must also be a created substance. Subsequently, Descartes had the problem on his hands of discovering an intelligible relation between the two created substances, especially their union in human personality, a problem he never satisfactorily solved.

Spinoza's theory may, perhaps, be better intelligible if seen as an attempt to avoid the impasse which Descartes created. Substance, he agrees, is that which exists in and of itself and is conceived through itself – in short, is *causa sui,* and so perfect (absolutely complete). Hence there can be but one substance, which is God. The human mind or soul, there-

[59] Cf. Descartes, *Meditations* III.

fore, is not a substance and can be no more than a mode, or "part," of
God. Thought, however, embraces all things and God must be aware of
all things, for all things are in him, including man's consciousness. Hence
the infinite intellect must be God's intellect, must pertain peculiarly to
God. Similarly, the extended world is all inclusive, save that it excludes
thought, so that too must pertain to God; not as a created other-being,
for God, being perfect lacks nothing and so has no reason to create what
he does not already include. In fact, he could not, for that would imply
an augmentation of the already infinite and complete. This, we shall find
Spinoza arguing, is no limitation on God's power, for he can do whatever is conceivable without self-contradiction. To create an augmentation
to himself, however, would be a self-contradiction and is inconceivable.
It would imply a limitation and an imperfection in God, not an expression of his omnipotence. Extension and thought, therefore, are assigned to God as attributes expressing his eternal essence, the emanation,
so to speak of his omnipotence.

As God is one, however, and as substance is indivisible, Spinoza asserts
that Thought and Extension are identical in substance, and this enables
him to solve Descartes's problem of the relation between man's body and
his soul, as we shall shortly see; but it involved him at the same time in
the problem of the infinity of the attributes. How, if at all, could he have
escaped this latter difficulty?

Clearly, if substance is self-complete and infinite, either we must say
that it has infinite attributes (as Spinoza does), or we must say that it
has only one, which is its absolutely infinite self-completeness. We might
then maintain that the unity of substance is differentiated, as it must be,
into an infinite variety of modes and that these constitute a hierarchy or
developing series progressively increasing in what Spinoza describes as
"degree of reality." Extension and thought might then be complementary
aspects of all modes in varying degrees of complexity, with human
mentality relatively high in the scale. There would then be no question
of their separability or of each aspect being conceivable only through
itself. They would be interdependent in just the way that Spinoza repre-
sents them and conceivable in and through the complete system of
Nature, or God, as he requires. We shall find much in Spinoza's teaching
to support this kind of theory, but he seems to have been diverted from
advocating it explicitly in this form by the lingering influence of Descartes. In the following chapters I shall try to show that a position of this
kind is implicit in Spinoza's teaching and that it runs counter to many
of the salient features of the more common interpretations.

PART III

MAN

CHAPTER V

BODY AND MIND

1. The Material World

In his very brief, yet very significant discussion of the nature of physical bodies, Spinoza describes a hierarchy, or a series continuously increasing in degree of complexity. The simplest bodies are distinguished from one another only by their state of motion, but any contiguous group, which transmit to one another a constant proportion of motion and rest, may be regarded as a single individual; and a group of such groups, on similar conditions, constitutes a more complex unity. The series continues indefinitely until the physical universe is seen as one single whole governed by a principle of organization which determines the proportion of motion and rest transmitted from one to another of its internally distinguishable parts.

A complex body may retain its individuality despite constant internal changes, even of material content, so long as the common pattern of motion and rest is preserved, and its constituent parts may change position with relation to one another without altering its individual identity if these movements do not disturb the prevailing relations of the physical movement transmitted from one part to another, or the total proportion of motion and rest characterizing the body as a whole.[1]

Spinoza also asserts that all things are besouled, or beminded (*animata*); for there is in God an idea of every body, and the idea of a body Spinoza identifies as its mind or soul. But just as bodies differ in degree, so do their minds, for the *idea* and its *ideatum* are one and the same thing in substance.[2] "We cannot however, deny that ideas differ from one another, as do the objects themselves, and that one is more excellent than

---

[1] Cf. *Ethics* II, Def. and Lemm. iv-xii, S, following Prop. xiii.

[2] Cf. *Ethics* II, vii, S. "*Sic etiam modus extensionis, et idea illius modi una eademque est res, sed duobus modis expressa...*" "So also a mode of extension and the idea of that mode is one and the same thing, but expressed in two ways."

another, and contains more reality, just as the object of one idea is more excellent and contains more reality than the object of another." [3] Bodies with their minds, or beminded physical things, thus constitute a scale of increasing degrees of "excellence" or reality, a fact to which Spinoza alludes at the end of the Appendix to Part I of the *Ethics* when he says that "God ... did not lack material for the creation of all things, from the highest to the lowest gradation of perfection."

As the physical world is fundamentally motion-and-rest, there is evidently constant movement and change among bodies, and it is quite naturally conceivable that simple bodies constantly combine and separate, as well as the more complex ones which the combination of simple atoms brings into being. Among physical processes, therefore, we must presume that some kind of evolution takes place from the simpler to the more complicated physical entities, with a parallel development of mental capacity. For the "mind" of a simple body must be extremely rudimentary, and even that of a more complex thing, like, say, a stone, would be nugatory by comparison with the mind of a body as complex as a living organism. And the important fundamental difference is described as one of degree of reality, excellence or perfection, a concept which will become clearer in the sequel.

In the Scholium to Prop. xiii of *Ethics* II, Spinoza proceeds:

"This I say in general, the more any body is better adapted than others for doing and suffering many things at the same time, the more capable is its mind than others of perceiving many things at the same time; and the more the actions of one body are dependent solely upon itself and the less other bodies take part (*concurrunt*) with it in its action, the more is its mind capable of understanding distinctly."

Now a body the actions of which are more dependent upon itself with less cooperation from other bodies external to it is, to that extent, more like an organism, or, we may say, is more organic in its constitution. A living organism is a body so constituted that it tends to adapt either its environment to itself or itself to the environment so as to be less dependent on external changes for the maintenance of its own integrity (as Spinoza might say, for the maintenance of a constant proportion among its parts of motion and rest). Plants by transpiration cool the surrounding air and so mitigate changes of atmospheric temperature which might be injurious to them. Some exude substances into the soil favourable to the multiplication of bacteria upon which the plant itself depends for the absorption and chemical transformation of its foodstuffs. Again, some

[3] *Ethics* II, xiii, S.

organisms incorporate favourable environmental conditions into their own make-up. For instance, the saline content of mammalian blood is the same as what has been calculated to be that of the pristine ocean in which aquatic creatures lived from which mammals evolved. Biologists consequently often refer to the state of the blood and other internal factors in the organism as "the internal environment." Similarly, warm-blooded animals regulate their own internal temperature so as to be less susceptible to the effects of external changes. In short, organic activity is such as to depend more upon the nature and economy of the organic body itself than upon the "concurrence" (as Spinoza calls it) of external bodies.

Although Spinoza was not aware of all the biological facts which are at our disposal today, it is clear that he understood "in general" the principal difference between inorganic and organic bodies. If, then we accept Spinoza's doctrine of the substantial identity [4] of body and mind, it is quite proper and natural to conclude that the more highly developed a body is organically, as a living thing, the more capable it will be of feeling and perceiving its surroundings; and as we ascend the scale of organic efficiency and complexity, the greater will be the mental capacity of the organism, the more will it be intelligent, or capable of distinct understanding.

About the physical world and the processes which go on within it Spinoza tells us all too little. "If I had intended expressly to deal with matter or body," [5] he says, "I should have had to explain and demonstrate these matters more at length, but I have already said that I have another intention, and I have referred to these things only because I can easily deduce from them what I have set out to demonstrate." (*Ethics* II, *Lem*. vii, S). It seems reasonably clear that he did intend to write a book on the subject for he refers, in the unfinished *Tractatus de Intellectus Emendatione,* to empirical science as something to be dealt with more at length elsewhere,[6] and in a late letter to von Tschirnhaus he remarks wistfully that he has not yet set out these matters in the proper order (*Ep.* LXXXIII). So we are left to infer what we can from the short section in *Ethics* II that comes between the thirteenth and the fourteenth Propositions.

Here I must leave the matter until after I have dealt further with Spinoza's theories of man, his knowledge and his welfare; for, as the distinction between less and more complex bodies as well as between their

[4] See § 3 below.
[5] *Opera Posthuma* has simply "*de corpore*" but in *Nagelaten Schriften* we find "*van de stoffe of lighaam.*"
[6] *TdIE.*, XIV, 103.

ideas, is said to be their degree of reality, excellence, or perfection, Spinoza's views on good and evil and what constitutes excellence become pertinent. Also, if, and to the extent that, there is change and movement in the physical world, we must understand how Spinoza looked upon time, quantity and measure. There are contexts in which he says that all these notions (including good and evil) are mere "ways of thinking," *entia rationis,* or aids to the intellect, so we shall not be able to discuss them properly until we have examined Spinoza's theories of knowledge and value.

2. Mind as Felt Body

„The first thing that constitutes the being of the human mind, is nothing else than the idea of some individual thing actually existing" (*Ethics* II, xi). And "the object of the idea constituting the human mind is a body, or a certain mode of Extension actually existing and nothing else" (*Ethics* II, xiii).

First, we must remember (and Spinoza has just reminded us in Prop. ix) that the idea of an individual thing actually existing has God for its cause, not in so far as he is considered as infinite, but in so far as he is considered as affected by another idea of an actually existing individual thing, of which God is also the cause so far as he is affected by a third, and so on *ad infinitum.* At the same time in God's infinite intellect there are adequate ideas of all things which he conceives (i.e. creates).[7] We shall find, therefore, that the dual character of God's causality leads to a duality in the ideas of things in the human mind evident in the distinction between inadequate ideas and adequate or true ideas – a distinction which will shortly engage our attention.

Next, we must attend carefully to the statement expressed in Proposition xiii, quoted above. The mind, we are told, is constituted by the idea of an actually existing body, and nothing else. Bodies, we have learnt, are more and less complex, and the human body is a highly complex mode, or combination of modes, of Extension. The idea of such a body will, accordingly, be similarly complex, for of every body there is an idea which is identical with it in substance and all things are beminded (*animata*) although in different degrees. This should make it clear that what Spinoza means by the idea of the body is the body's awareness of itself. An idea he insists is no merely passive or inert replica of its *ideatum.* It is an activity of consciousness, a word which, perhaps better than "thought,"

---

[7] Cf. above, p. 51.

translates Spinoza's (and, incidentally, Descartes's) term "*cogitatio*." The human mind, then, is said to be the consciousness of the body, while it actually exists, and nothing else.

The statement is at first surprising, for we commonly think of our minds as aware of our environment and not of our bodies alone. We have ideas of innumerable bodies, not only one, although we identify ourselves only with one of them. And that is precisely Spinoza's point. There is only one body which we *feel* (*sentimus*), each of us as himself, and when one speaks or thinks of oneself as "feeling" other bodies (e.g. tactually), it is only when and because one experiences a specific sensation in some part of one's own body. All our awareness, whether of ourselves or of surrounding objects, therefore, is mediated by our own bodies, and our immediate ideas of other things are strictly speaking sensations, or, in Spinoza's terminology, "ideas," of their effects upon our own bodies, either through direct contact or some indirect influence. The human mind, therefore, is primarily and fundamentally nothing other than the human body, as felt. "From this not only do we understand that the mind is united to the body," Spinoza writes, "but also what should be understood by the union of mind and body." (*Ibid.* S).[8]

The reason why it requires special reflection to recognize this fact, that all our awareness is primarily of our own bodies, is that for the most part we project our sensations outside of ourselves and ignore that aspect of them that apprises us of our bodies unless it indicates malfunctioning. Our sense organs are to us transparent like the glass of a pair of spectacles which is not apparent to the person looking through them, though it is nevertheless the medium of his viewing. Only if the glass becomes dirty or scratched is it noticed. So with our bodies, we are aware of them immediately in pain or the aberration of any normal function, but if every part is healthy and functions normally, we become aware of our bodies only so far as we observe them in the way we do other bodies. I can see my own limbs as I see external bodies, and I feel one when it comes into contact with another, as I do when I touch a book or a pencil; and when I do so I tend to objectify, or externalize, at least part of myself. The feet that I see are "down there," and the hands are "in front of me," and when I feel my knee with my hand I ignore or suppress the tactual sensation of the hand that the sense registers in favour of that of the knee which the hand registers. But both are actually felt and one becomes

---

[8] Cf., for the elucidation and elaboration of this position, H. F. Hallet, "On a Reputed Equivoque in Spinoza," *Review of Metaphysics*, III, 1949. Cf. also R. G. Collingwood, *The New Leviathan* (Oxford, 1942), Part I, i-v.

plainly aware of the former if, for any reason, the hand becomes numbed, or cold, or sticky. The essential point, however, is that every sensation is an awareness of a state of the body, or of some part of it, and our knowledge of external objects is all derivative from such awareness.

3. Substantial Identity

Spinoza's theory of body-mind relation is in effect an identity theory, and not, as is usually held, a theory of parallelism. Body and mind are one thing viewed in two alternative ways: as a mode of extension or as a mode of thought. But the view differs from some contemporary forms of identity theory which assert that the distinction is no more than that between two different languages with an identical referent. Spinoza does, in his letter to de Vries (*Ep.* IX), illustrate the difference between the attributes by the possibility of referring to the same thing by two different names (the third Patriarch is called Jacob, in virtue of his grasping his brother's heel at birth, and Israel because chosen of God), and of defining the same thing in Geometry (e.g. a plane) in two different ways. But the attributes, we have seen, are real differentiations in Nature, they are not merely different ways of referring in speech to God's unity. They cannot be only *entia rationis*; for the human mind, which makes the linguistic reference and invents (or abstracts) the ways of thinking, is posterior, and not prior, to differentiation in God between attributes. Thus ideas, as well as bodies, are actual modes (*affectiones*) or variations of God's existence.

Another modern view of body-mind relation is the neural-identity theory, according to which consciousness is identical with neural activity and sensations are the same as brain-states. This, again, is not (though it is like) Spinoza's theory. Ideas are not modes of Extension in any sense, although the mode of extension which is the *ideatum* of any idea is substantially the same thing. The difficulty which besets the modern theory is that of understanding in what precise sense such diverse phenomena as, on the one hand, an electrical discharge in a neurone, or in a series of neurones and nerve fibres, and, on the other, a feeling of pain, or a sensation of warmth, can be identical.[9] Spinoza's answer to this question is that one is the consciousness of the other, or the way in which the other becomes aware of its existence. But Spinoza does not (at least, not explicitly) identify consciousness with neural states. The mind is the

---

[9] Cf. my *Foundations of Metaphysics in Science* (London, 1965), pp. 299-303; and "The Neural Identity Theory and the Person" in *The International Philosophical Quarterly*, IV, 4, 1966.

idea of the body as a whole, not only of the nervous system; and, no doubt, different physiological activities are reflected in it by differences in idea, but the awareness of the body that constitutes the mind is not a clear and distinct idea of the body and its internal processes, but (at any rate, in the first instance) a confused idea.[10] Perhaps the best interpretation of the doctrine would be in terms of the example already quoted from *Ep*. XXXII, although intended there to illustrate a different point. As the blood may be considered a single "body," though composed of several perpetually varying parts, so may the body as a whole, including all its diverse cycles of physiological change. It is this whole of which the idea is the mind or consciousness, related to it very much as Aristotle maintained, as form to matter.

Now, the form of a complex entity is not another entity, separable even in thought, from its matter, though the distinction between them can be recognized. They are merely two ways of regarding the same entity. So for Spinoza, the idea of the body (or the mind) is not a separate entity from the body, but is just another way of regarding the same thing. We must not, however, fall into the error committed by Sir Frederick Pollock, and shared with him by many contemporary philosophers who advocate the neural-identity theory. It is not sufficient to say that there is only one set of facts but two alternative descriptions of them, one such as a physiologist would give and the other such as the subject of the experience would give in whose body the physiological facts are occurring.[11] What I describe as the experience of a bright flash, the physiologist may describe as the stimulation of a certain portion of my brain by an electrical impulse (or in some other appropriate way). But the physiologist can do so only so far as he observes my body (or another subject to which he regards me as similar) and its neural activity as public external objects. When I describe the flash I am not observing my own brain and neural activity in any way at all; I am much more likely to be observing something totally different, say, a thunderstorm. What I see is not a neural discharge. If we are to identify what I describe with what the physiologist describes, we must still explain how they come to be identical (for we have no evidence that they are except simultaneity of occurrence). Nobody would wish to suggest that what I see when I observe a thunderstorm (for example, a lightning flash) is identical with a neural discharge in my brain. It is only the experiencing of it, not the meteorological event, that is supposed to be identical with the physiological

[10] Cf. *Ethics* II, xxvii and xxviii.
[11] Cf. Pollock, *Spinoza, his life and Philosophy* (London, 1899), p. 198.

activity; and my describing that experience as it occurs in me is not describing any physiological event at all. To speak of it as if it were suggests that "I" am a homuncule situated somewhere inside my skull, observing what goes on in my brain and describing it as the experience of a flash, which, if it were not absurd, would only involve a recapitulation of the whole problem in relation to the homuncular perception.

Spinoza's theory, is certainly not subject to this criticism, but he treats the matter somewhat obscurely and needs interpretation. The flash (or any other sensation) I experience and might describe is an element in the *cognitio* or consciousness of the body in a certain state. But, if I describe it as directly experienced, I describe it as *idea* in the attribute of Thought; whereas if I describe the state of the body physiologically, I describe it as a mode of extension in terms of motion and rest. Neither description is the actual experience, or the actual neural discharge. It is not merely a matter of describing one set of facts in two different ways, but of one reality manifesting itself in two different forms; and, of course, the description of each form will differ from that of the other. To say that I see a bright flash is not the same as to say that a certain pattern of neural discharge occurs in my brain, but no more is it the same to *say* that I see a bright flash as it is to see it. The difference of attribute is not reducible to a difference of description (although it involves one). The seeing and the neural discharge are the same entity, but that does not make the former a physiological event nor the latter an idea. Neither is reducible to the other. The entity which is both has two forms of being, just as (analogously) a triangle exists as three straight lines on a plane forming three angles, and as a distinctive three-cornered shape; or as blotches of coloured paint on a canvas are the same thing (*res*) as the picture of a landscape.

4. Rejection of Parallelism

None of the three categories into which theories of body-mind relation have traditionally fallen properly fits Spinoza's theory. He is commonly classed as a parallelist following Descartes, but this is a double error for neither was Descartes a parallelist, nor does Spinoza follow him. Descartes espoused an interactionist theory of the body-mind relation but could not make it intelligible to the satisfaction of his immediate followers, who (like Geulinx) modified it into Occasionalism, which is a theory of parallelism. Spinoza, however, explicitly rejected interactionism,[12] but, in spite of his assertion that the order and connexion of ideas is the same

[12] Cf. *Ethics* II, vii, S., III, ii and S.

as the order and connexion of things (*loc cit.*), he is no parallelist. The succession of ideas in the mind is not a series of events separate from but parallel to that of physiological processes. There is only one series of events each of which is both idea and bodily process. I have already sufficiently explained the nature of this identity on the analogy of matter and form. Yet, again, Spinoza's theory is not epiphenomenalism such as is usually characteristic of materialist theories popular in our own day. Epiphenomenalism is the doctrine that consciousness is a product of material causes (physiological events) but has no reciprocal effects upon bodily processes. Spinoza denies causation of any sort between the attributes and their respective modes. Ideas cannot cause motions nor motions ideas. Nevertheless, as we shall presently see, ideas are by no means epiphenomena. They are, or can become, genuine actions of the mind and are identical in substance with bodily acts involving motion conducive to the health and preservation of the bodily organism.

5. *Alleged ambiguity of "idea"*

Pollock complains that Spinoza used the word "idea" ambiguously to mean both concept (our more usual sense of the word) and also the counterpart of a physical thing or physiological process,[13] and that he failed to make the necessary distinction between these two senses. But Spinoza was making no mere inadvertent confusion; his double usage is deliberate. For "idea" in the sense of "concept" means an abstract idea, which can be entertained only by a developed mind such as man's. But man's mind is defined as the "idea" (in the other sense – the counterpart in Thought) of his body. The body is highly complex and so, accordingly, is its idea or mind, and an abstract idea or concept, of something other than the body, would thus be a "part," or one of the complexities, or differentiations within the idea of the body. Spinoza held that abstract ideas corresponded to nothing real or actually existent. He was a nominalist, as we have seen. Such ideas, he maintained, were no more than convenient devices for description and classification – part of the technique of a certain level of thinking peculiar to man.[14] They are and can be entertained only by conscious beings, and consciousness (*cogitatio*) is always idea as counterpart of body. Abstract "ideas," in fact ideas of any kind, are all and must all be rooted in this immediate awareness of the body, which forms the basis of all kinds and grades of knowledge. All my ideas are thus "parts" of the idea of my body, and Spinoza finds no

---

[13] Cf. *Spinoza*, Chs. IV and IX.
[14] Cf. *Ethics* II, xl, S. 1 and 2.

reason to make any distinction other than that between adequate and inadequate ideas.

Another misconception to be avoided concerns the relation of *idea* to *ideatum*. My body is the *ideatum* of my mind, and every other body has an *idea* of which it is the *ideatum*. But the *ideatum* of my "idea" of Peter's (or some other) body, is some element or process in my own body and (for good reasons which will presently appear) not Peter's body itself. The *idea* of which Peter's body is the *ideatum* is Peter's mind; [15] and if some less complex body is the object of the *idea*, the same is true; but the "minds" of bodies less complex than living bodies are so rudimentary as to be hardly, if at all, worthy of the name.

As every idea in any single mind is a differentiation within the idea of its body, there is no question, for Spinoza, of any consciousness independent of sensation. In this he is in agreement with the Empiricists, although he builds a very different theory of knowledge on this foundation. Sensation, the idea of a body actually existing, is the indispensable condition of all knowledge, but it is not its source.[16] That ultimately is the infinite power of God and his immanent causality. The true source of all knowledge is the idea of God immanent in all minds. In the Second Dialogue of the *Short Treatise*, Spinoza makes Theophilus explain to Erasmus that, although our idea of God is caused solely and immediately by God himself – if only because God can be conceived adequately only through himself – yet the condition of our having the idea of God is the existence in Nature of a body, the idea of which is a mind.[17] In the same way, in order to let light into a room we open a window, but the window is not the cause of the light, only its condition. The simile is especially instructive, for as the window admits light which reveals objects other than itself, so the sensation, or awareness, of the body reveals other bodies, while itself remaining unnoticed. The idea of God, of course, is a special case. It is implicit in every idea because it is the immanent cause of everything. It is, as we shall shortly discover, what makes any idea intelligible. Sensations and sensory awareness are confused ideas, for reasons presently to be explained, and it is only when they can be experienced as they are in God, that is, only when their objects are seen in their complete circle of relationships in Substance, that they become "clear and distinct." The

---

[15] Cf. *Ethics* II, xvii, S.
[16] Cf. Kant, *Kritik der Reinen Vernunft*: "Although all our knowledge begins with experience, yet it does not follow that all of it originates from experience." (Introd., B1).
[17] *K.V., loc. cit., V.V.L.,* IV, p. 21.

confused ideas do not properly speaking constitute knowledge, for which only clear and distinct ideas are adequate.

6. Idea Ideae

As the idea of the body is the mind, so the idea of that idea is the idea of the mind. In *de Intellectus Emendatione* Spinoza explains that every idea is the "objective essence" of its *ideatum,* of which the actuality is the "formal essence." But the idea is a different entity (or mode) from its object (although they are identical in substance), if only because they exist in different attributes. The idea of a circle has no centre or circumference.[18] So, he says, the idea has a formal essence of its own, of which the objective essence is the idea of the idea (*idea ideae*). This is further explained in the *Ethics* (II, xxi, S) as "nothing else than the form of the idea so far as it is considered as a mode of thought and apart from its relation to its object." Its relation to its object, we already know, is substantial identity (or, as Spinoza says in some contexts of adequate ideas, exact correspondence). Apart from this relation, the idea is considered purely as a mode of Thought and is the pure form of the object, as the triangular shape is the pure form of three right lines intersecting in a plane in three separate points. The idea of the idea is then the idea of this form, and that involves an idea of the idea of the idea, and that again another, *ad infinitum.* "Just as if a man knows something, by that very fact he knows that he knows it, and at the same time he knows that he knows that he knows, and so *in infinitum.*" (*Ibid.*).

The precise meaning of this doctrine has been endlessly discussed but it seems plain to me that it is Spinoza's recognition of the essential self-reflectiveness of consciousness. To be fully conscious is *ipso facto* to be self-conscious; and, for Spinoza full or adequate consciousness is always the standard. One might argue, justly, that there are levels of consciousness at which the awareness of self is not yet present. But these low levels, though Spinoza would not have denied their existence, are, for him, levels of confusion and inadequacy which do not properly amount to knowledge. Yet even low levels of consciousness are more than a merely passive reception by the mind and are not just inert depictions of presented objects. The very least involves some sort of contrast between a distinguishable object and a background, and therefore transcends to some extent what is immediately presented. This distinction of "figure" from "ground" is dynamic or active. It is made by the mind cognizing. Spinoza never makes this point quite explicitly, but he does always insist that

[18] *TdIE,* VI, 33.

ideas are activities and not mere pictures and that they involve self-awareness.

The inherent self-reflectiveness of consciousness is what enables us to purify the intellect and progress (as we shall shortly see) from confused and inadequate ideas to clear and true knowledge. This point is made early in the *Tractatus de Intellectus Emendatione*. It is because we can reflect upon what we think, and know that we know, that we can criticize and improve our thinking. *Idea ideae*, therefore, is nothing but the consciousness of one's own thinking, or the idea of one's own mind. Although Spinoza speaks of a series of *ideae idearum* (ideas of ideas) *ad infinitum*, strictly no infinite regress is involved, only an unlimited capacity for reflection or self-knowledge. The object of an idea and the idea of the object are substantially identical. Both are the same essence, one formal and the other objective. Thus the idea of an idea is strictly the same object or entity merely conscious (or more fully conscious) of itself. We have seen what the union of body and mind is – substantial identity – the mind being the body's self-awareness. Now Spinoza tells us that the idea of the mind is united to the mind in the same way as the mind is united with the body (*Ethics* II, xxi). As the mind is the idea or consciousness of the body and is identical with it in substance, so the idea of the mind will be identical with the idea of the body (for it is the idea of that idea). It is merely a heightened awareness of the original *ideatum* and not a new or separate entity, any more than the mind is an other or separate entity than the body. To know that one knows, therefore, does not imply a vicious infinite regress; it implies only that one knows whatever the original object of one's knowledge is more fully, more self-consciously and with keener critical awareness. The doctrine of *idea ideae* is simply the doctrine that *idea* is conscious and thereby self-illuminating. Hence the mind is infinitely capable in principle of progressive self-awareness. There is no question whatever of an infinite series of separate objects, still less of an infinite series of separable minds. This notion of *idea ideae*, therefore, is quite irrelevant to the problems of the infinity of the attributes of God, and cannot be what Spinoza is referring to in *Ep.* LXVI, where he says that the ideas of modes in other attributes than Extension cannot constitute one and the same mind, since each idea of this infinite series has no connexion with any other. *Idea ideae*, the idea of the idea, of the body (and any further degree of reflection) is identical with the body, not with any mode of any other attribute, and does not constitute an infinite series of separate minds, as the letter asserts; for we are plainly told in the proposition cited from *Ethics* II that the idea of the mind is united to the mind in the same way as the mind is united to the body. Commentators like Windelband and Batuscheck, who have tried to maintain that the infinite series of *ideae idearum* corresponds to the infinite series of attributes, are therefore plainly wrong.

No doubt, Spinoza's theory of the infinity of the attributes is untenable and cannot be made self-consistent, and no doubt, to be consistent, he should have maintained that the modes in all attributes were united to one another as the mind is united to the body. His statement in the 66th letter is itself out of harmony with his main teaching, and contradictory even on its face. For he says that each thing is expressed in infinite ways in the infinite intellect of God, and yet that the infinite ideas by which it is expressed cannot constitute one and the same mind of a singular thing.[19] However, if they are all, as they must be, in the infinite intellect of God, they do constitute one and the same mind, not, of course, of one singular finite thing, but the infinite mind of Substance as a whole, which is an infinite individual. Yet again, if the modes in every attribute are identical with those in every other, as the Scholium to Prop. vii of *Ethics* II asserts, to which in the letter reference is made, then the mind of one and the same singular thing should be the idea in the attribute of Thought of all the concomitant modes in every other attribute. But we have been over this ground before.

7. *Passivity and Activity*

One major difference between Spinoza's position and that of an Empiricist, like Locke, is that for Locke "simple ideas of sensation" are the primary elements of knowledge, while for Spinoza what sensation provides, though an indispensable condition of knowing, is strictly speaking not knowledge at all. Although Spinoza refers to sensations, as he does to memory and mental imagery of all kinds, as ideas, he does not really consider them to be ideas in the full and proper sense of the word. Only adequate ideas are deemed worthy of the name if we are to speak with complete accuracy – that is, ideas as they are in God's intellect. Sensuous images, whether what we should call perceptual or imaginary, are all inadequate in Spinoza's view, and in themselves they lack the essential characteristic of knowledge (though it may, in any particular instance, be attached to them), namely, affirmation or denial. Spinoza, in different contexts, vacillates somewhat as to whether sensuous ideas involve af-

---

[19] "... *quamvis unaquaeque res infinitis modis expressa sit in infinito Dei intellectu, illae tamen infinitae ideae, quibus exprimitur, unam eandemque rei singularis Mentem constituere nequent.*"

firmation. At times he asserts firmly that all ideas do involve such affirmation, and at others he concedes that imagination without it is neither true nor false. This wavering is the result of his effort to free himself from the influence of Descartes, whose error in this matter he saw and corrected, while he still clung in some respects to the Cartesian theory. But before we go into further comparisons, let us look more closely at Spinoza's own account of sensuous awareness.

The human mind is the idea of the human body, and is consequently diversified by any and every effect produced in the body by its contact or other interrelations with other bodies. These effects are registered in idea as sensations, and if the body is so modified by its interaction with others that their effects are persistent, the sensations will persist even after the bodily interactions have ceased. It is only in and through the perception of such modifications of the body that the mind becomes aware of the body and of itself.[20] But this awareness is not an adequate idea of the body, or of the mind, or of the component parts of the body, or of the other bodies causing the modifications. All such ideas are confused.[21] The reason that Spinoza gives for this fact is that the ideas of the modifications of the human body involve the nature of the external bodies affecting it as well as that of the human body and its component parts. But adequate ideas (as they are in God) of all of these would include their implications of all their relations to other (prior) causes and effects in Nature. While these are implicit in the modifications produced in the human body, they are not explicitly presented in the immediate sensations, or awarenesses, of them. Spinoza expresses this contrast by saying that the idea in God of the external body, as an individual thing without reference to the human body, involves those of its prior causes, whereas the mere idea of the modification of the human body (i.e. what in the human mind is a sensation) omits these implications (*Ethics* II, xxv. Dem.).

Moreover, the sensation presents the external body as actually present and with qualities many of which really pertain to the nature of the human body rather than that of the external body, yet all are liable to be confused and attributed solely to the presented object. So-called "secondary" qualities are explained in this way. They are qualities, like colour, sound, scent and taste, which we attribute to external objects but which actually depend upon the nature and condition of our own bodies and result from their reactions to the physico-chemical properties of the

[20] *Ethics* II, xxiii.
[21] *Ethics* II, xxiv-xxxi.

objects. Ideas of such qualities are therefore confused ideas, and, like Descartes, Spinoza holds that adequate and reliable knowledge of physical things consists only in clear and distinct ideas. Inadequate ideas are thus in part a confusion or conflation of elements that do not really go together, and in part an omission (or separation) of elements that actually do belong together.

Such ideas are passive in the sense, and to the extent, that they result from the effects upon our bodies of external causes and are not the products solely of our own nature. But we must not think of them as wholly and simply passive, for we have been told from the outset that ideas are actions of the mind (*actiones mentis*), and Spinoza rejects the view of ideas as passive impressions or replicas of external objects.[22]

It is here that we may trace the influence of Descartes (more apparent in the *Short Treatise,* where the intellect is said to be passive),[23] who regarded the senses, along with the common sense and the imagination (*phantasia*) as bodily organs, in which external bodies, through the physiological reactions they caused, produced actual physical changes. The mind (or thinking thing) then perceived these physical changes and passively registered them as percepts, about which it might then judge or not, by an act of will, as to whether they pertained to the nature of the external objects. The affirmation or judgement is an action, but the mere perception is purely passive. So Descartes contends that perception by itself is neither true nor false, but only the judgements that we make about it and that we should never err if we refrained (as we are free to do) from affirming except what we clearly and distinctly perceived.[24]

There is no error in asserting that sensations in themselves are neither true nor false, but the view that perception does not involve judgement and that affirmation and denial are acts of free will additional to the experiences on which they pass judgement is very disputable, and is rejected by Spinoza.

He maintains that if the human body is affected in a manner involving the nature of some external body, the human mind will continue to contemplate that external body as actually existing and present until the body is affected in some further way which excludes the existence of the external body (*Ethics* II, xvii). Thus we can imagine objects not actually present, or even non-existent, as if they were actually present. Such imagination, he says, regarded in itself, contains no error. So far he is

---

[22] Cf. *Ethics* II, Def. III, and xliii, S.
[23] Cf. *K.V.*, II, Ch. XV.
[24] Cf., Descartes, *Rules for the Direction of the Mind,* XII, and *Meditations* IV.

in agreement with Descartes; but he denies that any idea is devoid of affirmation or judgement, and agrees that judgement is what is true or false. This being so there is a sense in which all ideas even imaginary ones are active. Yet Spinoza regards imagination in general not only as error and illusion but as the sole source of error, for the intellect by its very nature frames true ideas. What he means, then, in the Scholium to Prop. xvii, in *Ethics,* Part II, when he says that, regarded in itself "imaginations of the mind contain no error," is simply that the error consists in the oversight or omission of those ideas which exclude the actual existence of the imagined object. If we bore them in mind simultaneously, we could not affirm the existence of the object. Error, therefore, consists, not as Descartes believed, in affirming (by an act of free will) what we do not clearly and distinctly perceive, but in omitting (without noticing that we are doing so) something which really pertains to the idea that we do affirm. It is in virtue of this unrecognized omission that the idea we affirm is confused. Error, for Spinoza, therefore, is mere privation or abstraction – the omission of essential fact or implication – it is nothing positive.

All sensuous awareness is the consciousness of effects on the human body, either present or past, of external causes, and so far it is passive; but, so far as it is an awareness of a fact, for instance, that something actually existing is present to us, it is a judgement, and so active. Its positive content, regarded purely by itself, contains no error, but so far as it omits, disregards or overlooks essential implications, that should modify the judgement, it is false, or misleading. Its error consists in what it leaves out, in its incompleteness or imperfection – in its inadequacy – and that, Spinoza holds, is a characteristic of all sensuous perception, to which, whether of present or absent objects, he gives the general name, *imaginatio.* All ideas on this level, therefore, are both passive and active: passive as ideas of affections of the body, active as judgements; but because they are ideas of effects upon the body of outside causes, and so passive, they are defective and inadequate. To the extent that we are aware of this we are not deceived, and imagination, as a capacity for free imagery, is an advantageous power of the mind: "For if the mind, while it imagined non-existent things are present to it, knew at the same time that those things did not exist, this power of imagining should be attributed to its nature as a virtue not as a defect; especially if this faculty of imagining depended solely on its own nature, that is (by Def. 7 of Part I), if this capacity of the mind to imagine were free." (*Ethics* II, xvii, S.).

But so far as we accept the defective idea as true, we become the victim of error and confusion.

8. *Imaginatio*

Spinoza's account of *imaginatio* in the *Ethics* is in part anticipated by what he says in *de Intellectus Emendatione* about Fictions, Errors and Doubt. "Fictions" or supposals transpire as the mere contemplation of mental images, grouped at random or capriciously without explicit affirmation. It is closely akin to, if at all distinguishable from, reverie or dream, and, taken as such, does not involve error. Falsity, on the other hand, involves assent though its objects are the same as those of supposal, or fictitious ideas. Doubt arises only when we have two or more such confused ideas and nothing in them to dispose us to affirm or deny any one of them. It is a vacillation caused by a conflict of evidence, which cannot occur if we have one idea only before us, but only when some other is presented as well which is incompatible with the first but is not sufficiently clear to enable us to make a decision. A countryman will have no doubt that the sun is about as far away as it looks until somebody tells him that the senses sometimes deceive us. But we cannot doubt about clear and distinct ideas, and once we learn exactly how and why the senses sometimes deceive us we discover the actual state of affairs and have no more room for doubt.

Truth and falsity, however, involve affirmation or assent, but in the case of error, such assent is no proper act of the intellect, for that follows only strict logical principles and affirms only what logical sequence demands, wheras sensuous images come to us in an order which (though in fact it is not really fortuitous but determined and necessary) obscures, for us, the true connexion between, and reasons for, their occurrence. The order of the imagination is haphazard, for not only do its ideas come to us fortuitously but we tend to associate any that happen to occur simultaneously or contiguously, and any that are superficially similar. The order of the imagination, therefore, is what psychologists have come to call "association of ideas," which is not a logical order or one based on necessary causal connexions. If we fully understood these we should not be misled, as we commonly are, by the apparently fortuitous association of ideas, but should grasp both the reasons for the ways in which things appear to us and their true nature and mutual connexions. Our errors, therefore, are simply deficiency of insight and what we do perceive is, in itself, not so much false as fragmentary and mutilated.

If, in this fashion, we fall into error the remedy is simple; all we need do is reflect upon our ideas and deduce from them what, in proper logical order, follows from them, and then discrepancies and consequent contradictions will soon appear; whereas, if the ideas are not false, the deductions will proceed smoothly and without interruption.[25] For instance, if I imagine a centaur – an animal half horse, half man – the mere image is no error so long as I do not affirm that there is or could be any such thing in reality. But if I were inclined to believe that there could be such a creature, I have only to consider carefully what would be its anatomical structure, how its bones and muscles could be connected to one another so that its movements could be co-ordinated, and how its internal organs would have to be organized if vital functions were to be carried out, to realize that it would be a biological impossibility.

Here we encounter two difficulties which are not mutually unconnected. Spinoza, while he usually insists that all ideas involve affirmation or denial, seems here to regard imaginal ideas as merely floating before the mind which contemplates them passively. It "attends" to them in supposal only in the sense of "beholding" or "viewing," for Spinoza generally uses the word "attend" more strictly to refer to examination and analysis of the matter in prospect. But to regard the mind as passive in this way (as Joachim points out [26]) omits consideration of whatever it is that unites the various images (e.g. horse and man), and we are left to assume that it is mere psychological association. However, not only must there be some associative influence, but when the association has been made there is still tacit affirmation involved (for instance, that this presented animal is equine in legs and body, human in head, arms and torso), even though what is affirmed is not that the presented object exists in actuality.

This objection is not very serious, however, because it supports, rather than contradicts Spinoza's conviction that all ideas involve judgment. Indeed, he himself insists on this element of affirmation for, in *Ethics* II, xlix, S, he writes in criticism of the Cartesian view:

---

[25] *TdIE.*, VIII, 61: "... *mens, cum ad rem fictam et sua natura falsam attendit, ut eam pensitet et intelligat, bonoque ordine ex ea deducat, quae sunt deducenda, facile falsitatem patefaciet; et si res ficta sua natura sit vera, cum mens ad eam attendit, ut eam intelligat, et ex ea bono ordine incipit deducere, quae inde sequuntur, feliciter perget sine ulla interruptione ...*"

"When the mind attends to a fictitious object and one false by its own nature, so that it reflects upon and understands it, and deduces from it in proper order what ought to be deduced, its falsity easily becomes apparent; and if the object is true by its own nature, when the mind attends to it, so that it understands it and begins to deduce from it in proper order what follows from it, it proceeds propitiously and without interruption."

[26] Cf. *Spinoza's Tractatus*, p. 145.

"Further, I concede that nobody is deceived so far as he perceives, that is, I admit that imaginations of the mind considered in themselves involve no error; ... but I deny that a man affirms nothing so far as he perceives. For what else is it to perceive a winged horse, than to affirm wings of the horse."

What he seems to be trying to establish is that while all perception involves affirmation, the purely sensuous content of *imaginatio,* regarded virtually as preperceptual, is in itself neither true nor false, but becomes one or the other in becoming the subject matter of a perceptual judgement.

Nevertheless, the human intellect is not like God's and cannot in a single act create what it conceives. The subject matter of the judgement must in some way be passively received from some other source than the human understanding. Here we are faced with a more puzzling question, what could this other source be? Empiricists would take it for granted that the sensuous content of knowledge was the product of external objects acting upon the sense organs and the brain, as Locke does in his *Essay Concerning Human Understanding*; or at least, like Hume, that it consisted of passively received impressions produced by unknown causes. But no such expedient is open to Spinoza. He is too wise to fall into the trap to which Locke fell victim of assuming a relation between knowledge and its object which, by its very nature, must prove to be unknowable,[27] and he maintains unreservedly that there can be no causal relations between modes in different attributes. Physical motion does not and cannot cause ideas, nor ideas movement in bodies. If we seek the cause of an idea it can only be in another idea, and of that in another, *ad infinitum,* while the ultimate and immanent cause of all will be the infinite idea of God. This, then, is the only possible source from which imaginal ideas could be received. But now we are faced with a more serious problem, for in God there is no passivity; the infinite idea is pure intellect and (as will presently transpire) is wholly active. What then is the status of imaginal ideas? Are they in God? – for how could they not be? Yet God can contain no defect or limitation such as is typical and constitutive of *imaginatio*.

Joachim convicts Spinoza of failure to resolve this paradox.[28] He quotes the passage from *Ethics* II, xi, Corol., in which Spinoza says: "When we say that God has this or that idea, not only so far as he consti-

---

[27] Cf. My *Fundamentals of Philosophy,* New York, 1968, London, 1969, Chapters XVI, XVII and XVIII.
[28] Cf. *Spinoza's Tractatus,* pp. 169-173.

tutes the nature of the human mind, but so far as, at the same time as
the human mind, he has also the idea of another thing, then we say that
the human mind perceives a thing partially or inadequately." Joachim
then complains that this fails to explain the occurrence in man's mind of
imaginal ideas; for all ideas in God's mind must be adequate; and our
ideas are no more (nor less) than ideas in God's mind (for our minds are
no more than the ideas in God of our bodies). How then can the fact
that God has two ideas "together" (one so far as he constitutes the human
mind and the other external to that) make either of them inadequate,
whether "together" means juxtaposed or mutually implicated?

But this criticism seems to turn Spinoza's argument upside down, a
mistake almost incredible in a commentator as scholarly and perceptive
as Joachim, who had previously given so clear and admirable account of
this very matter in his *Study of Spinoza's Ethics,* and one whose own
theory of knowledge is so closely akin to Spinoza's.[29] For what Spinoza
contends is that ideas are, or become, inadequate in abstraction and
separation, not in their mutual connexion. "Together" in God's mind
they are adequate; but separated and isolated in our partial thinking they
are falsified. We must consider this doctrine more closely.

Spinoza tells us that inadequate ideas (those characteristic of *imaginatio*) are in God, not in so far as he is infinite, but so far as he is considered as constituting the human mind (that is, so far as he is affected
by another idea of an individual thing);[30] and the idea of the human
body is in God so far as he is affected by many other things, and not
merely so far as he is considered as constituting the human mind. Therefore, the ideas of the affections of the human body in the human mind
are only a fragment of what they are in God, although that fragment is,
of course, also included in God's ideas. An idea in the human mind of
an affection of the human body is divorced from the ideas of other things
which are in fact related to the human body and its affections. When seen
(as in God) in relation to these, the idea is transformed and has new and
different significance – it becomes adequate – but seen as truncated, as
it is in the human mind, it is inadequate and misleading, so that it subjects the human mind to confusion, from which God is necessarily free.
Hence inadequate ideas are no more than fragmentary ideas and though
they are indeed in God, in him they are supplemented and completed in
such a way as to make them fully intelligible and adequate, as well as to

[29] Cf. Joachim, *Study,* pp. 166 ff; and *The Nature of Truth* (Oxford 1906) and
Logical Studies (Oxford, 1948).
[30] Cf. *Ethics* II, ix; xi, C; xx; xxiv; *et seq.*

explain their inadequacy when, in isolation, they constitute human misconceptions.

Descartes tried to absolve God from responsibility for man's shortcomings by saying that God gave man an intellect perfect and infallible
in its clear and distinct perception and a will free and infinite in its
capacity. Man's errors, therefore, are due only to his using his free will to
assent to ideas which he does not clearly and distinctly understand, and
are not due to deficiencies in God's providence. Spinoza rejects the conception of a free will undetermined by any kind of cause, and also the
attribution to it of affirmation and denial. It is the intellect that judges,
and when it does so by its own nature alone, it is, as Descartes averred,
infallible; for it is in the nature of the intellect to frame true ideas.[31] But
when its ideas are partial and torn from their proper context, its judgements are faulty, not because of intrinsic defect either in the intellect or
in the content of the ideas, but because the ideas are of effects in the body
which in part are caused by external bodies, so that the ideas are not due
solely to the nature of the intellect, and because they do not include the
relations to other ideas of other things than the human body which are in
truth essentially related to them. These deficiencies, however, are merely
negative characters or limitations, and God, in the fulness of his being,
excludes all negation and limitation, or better, supplies all deficiencies.
In him, therefore, ideas, which in man are inadequate (and to that extent false), are adequate and commensurate with their true *ideata*.

Having stressed the purely negative character of falsity, Spinoza gives
two examples. Men, he says, commonly believe that they have free will,
but this is because they are conscious of their actions only, but ignorant of
the cause of their actions. They then speak of free will, using words without meaning, for they have not the least understanding of what will is or
how it moves the body. Again, when they see the sun they imagine it is
only 200 ft. away, being ignorant not only of the true distance but also
of the reason for the appearance, which is in fact due to a modification of
their bodies, and not to their ignorance of the sun's real distance.[32]

Joachim objects that there is still something positive in error for which
Spinoza fails to account, namely the belief that the false judgement is
true. There is some justice in the objection and Joachim discusses the
difficulty at length in relation to his own theory of knowledge in *The
Nature of Truth*. But Spinoza contends that all ideas are (or involve)
judgements – implicit assertions or denials – which by their very nature

[31] *TdIE*, IX, 73.
[32] *Ethics* II, xxxv, S.

claim truth.[33] If the ideas are inadequate, the claim is *ipso facto* un-
justified, but if they are adequate the judgement is *ipso facto* true.

Joachim points out that ignorance is not necessarily a cause of error.
If I do not know the causes of my actions I do not necessarily have to
believe that there are no causes and that I am free.[34] But this is not Spinoza's point. He is arguing that my belief that I am free is simply the
result of ignorance, not that this particular ignorance must produce just
this particular error.

In the second example about the sun's distance Joachim also finds a
positive element in the error, namely, the assumption that in vision we
apprehend external bodies in their self-existence as they really are, and
points out that Spinoza virtually admits that fact when he says that "the
sun appears so near to our perception . . . because it is only so far as our
body is affected by the sun that our mind forms an idea of the latter's
size" [35] Spinoza, however, admits that there is a positive element; i.e.
the way in which our body is affected and how the effect is registered as
sensation. But this, he contends, contains no error in itself. The error
consists in the privation, in what is left out,[36] to wit, the conditions under
which the effect is brought about, the laws of optics and perspective
which determine the relative size of retinal images, and the like. Considered in relation to all these, the appearance of the sun no longer de-
ceives us as to its distance, though the positive content of the imaginal
idea has not changed, only the interpretative judgement. The appearance
remains the same even though I know the sun's distance, but when I
understand the reasons for the appearance the error is dispelled.

Imaginatio is the first and lowest of the three kinds or levels into which
Spinoza divides human knowledge. The other two are *ratio* and *scientia
intuitiva*, the nature of which I shall examine shortly.[37] First, let us take
note of the scope and consequences of sensuous knowledge (*imaginatio*),
which accounts for the bulk of human belief and behaviour. I shall then
return to the nature of adequate thinking in section 10 below.

9. *The Common Order of Nature — Time, Measure and Number*

Supposal, error and doubt are all characteristic of *imaginatio*; but it

---

[33] Cf. *Ethics* II, xlix, S.
[34] Cf. Joachim, *Spinoza's Tractatus*, pp. 179ff., and also *Study, loc. cit.*
[35] Cf. *Spinoza's Tractatus*, p. 180f., and *Ethics* II, xxxv, S.
[36] Cf. *Ethics* II, xxxiii and xxxv.
[37] In *TdIE* he lists four: hearsay, vague experience, inference of the essence of one
thing from another, and apprehension of the thing through its own essence, or through
its proximate cause. In *K.V.* he groups the first two of these together as one kind of
knowledge, and calls what is derived from a true belief the second kind, and that of
which we have clear and distinct conception the third kind of knowledge.

is not confined merely to these. It includes everything we should today describe as perceptual or common sense knowledge, that is, all awareness of bodily changes and all ideas acquired through the sense organs. These ideas occur in succession, but not in any logical order, and the knowledge we base on them is what nowadays is called empirical, presenting to us the phenomenal world in space and time. It is the knowledge we acquire when, as Spinoza puts it, "the mind perceives things in the common order of nature," [38] perceptions to which it is determined by external causes, by things encountered fortuitously. Such knowledge is never adequate, for the things encountered and the effects they produce in our bodies are themselves the effects of causes traceable back in infinite series which the mind can never comprehend.

The infinite series of finite causes are real, for an infinity of things in infinite ways follow from the necessity of the divine nature; and they are completely determined by God's nature, through the infinite modes of his attributes, in the manner discussed above, in Ch. IV. But our knowledge of them, as acquired through casual encounters with relatively very few of their effects, is confused and mutilated, so that to us events in the common order of nature appear contingent and corruptible (*Ethics* II, xxxi, C) and we have no adequate knowledge of their duration any more than we have of our own bodies (*Ibid.*, xxx). Events in the common order of nature, therefore, appear random and accidental to us, though in God there is an adequate knowledge of how and why things are disposed (*Ibid.*).

The precise status of the common order of nature in Spinoza's metaphysical system is one of the most difficult points to settle in interpreting his philosophy, because, among other considerations, it obviously involves the succession of events in time, and the nature of time is never clearly and unambiguously placed in Spinoza's system, nor is its relation to eternity at all easy to understand. One might expect time to be an aspect of Extension, which accounts tolerably well for space; but Spinoza does not relate time to space, although motion, which is essential to bodies as modes of Extension, is virtually impossible to conceive without temporal lapse and succession.

In all his discussions of the matter, time and duration seem to be dismissed as largely illusory. Nothing in Nature, we are told, is contingent, and what appears to us to be so is no more than the result of deficiency of our knowledge (*Ethics* I, xxxiii, S 1); and this is further explained as a lack of adequate knowledge of the duration of corruptible things conse-

[38] *Ethics* II, xxix, C and S.

quent upon *imaginatio*. (*Ethics* II, xxxi, C.). In *Epistle* XII (to Ludovicus Meyer), time, measure and number are dismissed as mere aids to the imagination (*auxilia imaginationis*) and the intractable philosophical puzzles connected with them (such as appear in Zeno's paradoxes) are attributed to our imagination (as opposed to intellectual conceiving) of the quantities to which they apply.

Nevertheless, though we can be tolerably sure of one thing, that our perceptual knowledge of phenomenal events and their order of occurrence is confused and largely misleading, we are also told that it is not absolutely false, because it consists of fragments of ideas and of mutilated concepts, which, if completed as they are in God, would be true. But when so corrected it is transformed and, as we shall discover, its temporal character disappears, at least in some respects, perhaps altogether. Further, there can be little doubt that Spinoza regarded the infinite modes as real, and one of them is motion-and-rest. But motion implies time, or at least change, to which temporal transition is essential; so it would seem that time must have some kind of reality. And even in the twelfth letter, where he is apparently explaining time away as a mere *ens rationis*, he says what must to some extent imply the contrary.

There he writes:

"I call the affections of Substance Modes, the definition of which, so far as it is not the definition of Substance itself, cannot involve existence. For which reason, although they exist, we can conceive them as not existing; from which it follows further that we, when we attend only to the essence of modes, but not to the order of the whole of Nature, cannot infer from the fact that they now exist, whether they will exist or not hereafter, or whether they have existed or not hitherto. Whence it clearly appears that we conceive the existence of Substance as differing wholly in kind from the existence of Modes. From this there arises the difference between Eternity and Duration; for we are able to explain the existence of Modes only through Duration, but that of Substance through Eternity, that is, the infinite enjoyment of existence, or (in awkward Latin) *essendi*."

The problem here is that, though modes are modifications of substance and follow necessarily from its nature, their existence is purely durational, and that of Substance purely eternal, so that while the distinction between the two ways of existing is sharply drawn, the connexion and mutual dependence, which is no less inescapable is not elucidated. Moreover, temporal existence is inseparably implicated in the nature of modes in a way that makes it difficult, or rather impossible, to dispose of it as a figment of imagination. It is because finite modes are "contingent" beings that they may exist at one time and not at another (meaning by "contingent" that their essence does not involve existence – this is the sense of the quoted passage). And it is for the same reason that we cannot know, from contemplating either their essence, or the fact that they exist at a particular time, whether or not they exist at any other time. But if this is so, then time is involved in the very notion of finite existence, and only if finite modes are unreal, only if they are the product of imaginal thinking, would time be unreal. That, however, would be a paralogism, for imaginal thinking is a property of human consciousness, which again is a finite mode of Thought, the idea of a finite mode of Extension. The reality and actual existence of finite modes is therefore prior to imaginal thinking and cannot be a merely illusory product of it. Moreover, we already know that infinite things follow necessarily in infinite ways (*modis*) from God's essence and this is clearly meant to include finite modes. Whatever follows necessarily from God's essence must be real. But this very fact raises the crux of the difficulty.

Spinoza repeatedly asserts that the infinite consequences of God's nature follow from it as the properties of a triangle follow from its definition; and, if so, those consequences must be eternal, as God's essence is eternal, as are all essences. He maintains, also, that what follows immediately from the eternal and infinite is itself eternal and infinite. Yet this cannot apply to finite modes. On the other hand, it does apply to motion-and-rest, which is an infinite mode of Extension. Can there be motion in any sense without lapse of time? True, Spinoza argues that the *facies totius universi* remains eternally the same although the bodies within it are compelled perpetually to change, but that very fact implies that change, and so temporal lapse, is involved in an infinite mode.

Dr. Ch. H. van Os understands Spinoza to conceive motion and rest as the mathematician does in kinematics who deduces propositions about the motions of bodies as eternal truths. He is no more concerned with temporal movements than the geometer is concerned with temporally existing figures, and the time in which such motions "occur" is not the time we experience from day to day, but an ideal, eternal time belonging only to his science.[39] But if we take this view we come no nearer to explaining the connexion between the eternity of Substance and the transitory events of every-day experience, while we encounter the further difficulty that the mathematician's concepts are abstractions, whereas Spinoza's "eternal things," as we saw in Ch. II above, are concrete individuals.

[39] Cf. *Tijd, Maat en Getal, Meededelingen van Wege het Spinozahuis,* VII (Leiden, 1946), pp. 11f.

The best solution I can find to this difficult problem is to conceive the system as follows. First, we must regard the infinite series of causes and effects that determine the existence of finite modes as real, and as proceeding necessarily from God's eternal nature. And as the modes are related to one another as cause and effect the series would hardly be conceivable except as successive and temporal. Also, we must regard the *facies totius universi* as a concrete individual, infinite, eternal and unchanging in its total character (or *Gestalt*), but preserving its constant form through and by means of an infinite variety of movements among the bodies that compose the whole. This infinite variety of changes is identical with the infinite series of causes and effects that determine the existence and duration of finite modes. Thus the infinite and eternal unchanging totality is constituted by temporal series of events, all of which are absolutely determined by the nature of the infinite whole, so that no event in the series is contingent.

We come to know the world as so constituted, however, only by the third kind of knowledge (*Scientia Intuitiva*), whereas commonly we are aware of it only through sense-perception and imagination, which present it as a congeries of things and events occurring more or less randomly, a world of contingent and corruptible things. Thus we believe our own actions to be free in our ignorance of their real causes, and we imagine that events which happen to us and around us are fortuitous, or are the arbitrary acts of a capricious God.[40] Further we imagine spatio-temporal objects as divisible into parts, and as separable and mutually independent. So we invent metrical systems which enumerate their parts or quantities in space and time. We also form confused ideas of the common qualities of objects and group them under abstract class concepts the members of which we also enumerate. Thus arise time, as the measure of duration, number, as the tale of separate parts and members of abstractly conceived classes, and measures of quantity, all of them mere aids to the imagination which cannot in any intelligible way be applied to the infinite, but which, when we attempt so to apply them, result in insoluble paradoxes concerning (e.g.) the infinite extendedness of space, the beginning and end of the world, and problems of that sort.[41] It is time and measure as we try to imagine them in application to the reality of substance that are illusory. But the infinite series of causes and effects constituting the common order of nature as it actually occurs is real and a necessary consequence of God's eternal nature.

[40] Cf. *Ethics* I, App.
[41] Cf. *Ep.* XII.

This common order of events is not, however, the same as (although it is constitutive of and dependent upon) the face of the whole universe. That is not, in its eternal form, a changing, passing series, but a determinate individual form analogous to the determinate individuality of a living being which remains constant despite interminable and continuous metabolic change. Still less is the common order of nature, as it appears to us in our sensory experience and our imaginal thinking, to be identified with the real world. The conception of the common order of nature in either of these two ways does not make it in the least identifiable with *Natura Naturata.* Obviously our halting and mutilated imagination of the world, as presented to common sense, is a far cry from the reality; and even the actual series of finite events determined as it is by the eternal laws of nature and, as a whole, constituting the face of the physical universe, is only one infinite mode of one attribute (Extension) and falls far short of the absolute infinity of nature as synonymous with Substance-or-God. Spinoza's God is thus a transcendent deity and is by no means the god of the pantheist as usually understood.

10. Adequate Knowledge

Man is not wholly and inevitably restricted to inadequate ideas, as his ability to give an account of his own shortcomings bears witness. He can by his own effort and endeavour purify his intellect of imaginative errors, discern and follow the correct method of discovery and raise the level of his knowing above that of sense-perception and imagination. Contributory to this development are two important features of the essence of the human mind. One we have already discussed; that is, its capacity for self-reflection. The other is a principle of great significance which Spinoza does not introduce until the Third Part of the *Ethics,* although it has already been adumbrated in the corollary to Proposition xxiv of Part I. There he writes, "God is not only the cause of things' beginning to exist but also of their persevering in existence"; and in the sixth and seventh propositions of the third Part, we learn that as finite modes are nothing but particular determinate ways in which God's power expresses itself, "everything, so far as it is in itself, strives to persist (or persevere) in its own being." This *conatus,* or effort, to preserve itself is nothing more nor less than the actual essence of the thing endeavouring to persist, and in as much as activity originating from the actual essence of a thing is action (as opposed to passion), the *conatus* is always the endeavour of the thing to increase its own power of action. The importance of this principle is more evident in relation to practical life, but neither is its bearing on intellectual activity unimportant, nor is intellectual activity irrelevant to practical. In fact, they are really two aspects of one activity and not two separate activities in more or less intimate relation. For convenience, however, as Spinoza does, we may treat them in succession.

It is not immediately apparent from Spinoza's account of knowledge in the *Ethics* how we progress from *imaginatio* to adequate ideas, but that we can and must be able to do so is obvious, for if we could not we should never become aware of our own errors in *imaginatio*; and how we do so is the professed subject of the unfinished *Treatise on the Improvement of the Intellect*. From that we learned that the proper method was reflection, and we have seen that consciousness in its very nature is self-transcendent and self-reflective – every idea involves *idea ideae*. We are therefore aware of our own ideas and can submit them to examination. Moreover, of every idea the immanent cause is God, thus to be able to think at all is to have in one's mind (at least implicitly) the idea of God. This crucial point demands closer inspection.

To be conscious is to be aware that you are conscious. As Descartes showed (and St. Augustine before him) it is impossible to doubt or to deny one's own consciousness, a point which Spinoza (apart from his restatement of Descartes in *Principia Philosophiae Cartesianae*) felt no need to repeat. He does, however, make it the foundation of his refutation of scepticism.[42] But the consciousness which convinced Descartes of the impossibility of denying his own existence was the consciousness of uncertainty about everything else: in short, of his own deficiency of knowledge, an awareness involved in his certainty of his own existence. But to be aware of one's own deficiency is *ipso facto* to be aware of (to have an idea of) that standard of perfection by which deficiency is recognized as such – to have an idea of a perfect being.[43]

Spinoza does not himself use this argument but he restates it in his geometrical version of Descartes's principles and in that context he dismisses as ludicrous any denial that we have an idea of God in our minds. "There are some," he writes, "who deny that they have any idea of God, whom nevertheless, as they themselves say, they love and worship. And although you were to put before their eyes the definition of God and the attributes of God, you would accomplish nothing; no more, by Hercules, than if you should labour to teach a man born blind the differences of colours. But unless we wish to regard them as a new species of animal

---

[42] Cf. *TdIE*, VII, 47.
[43] Cf. Descartes, *Meditations*, III.

midway between men and brutes, we ought to pay little attention to their words." [44]

Having an idea of a perfect being, we may accordingly reflect upon it and relate all other ideas to it, and this we are told in the *Tractatus* is the proper method of purifying or rectifying the intellect. (*TdIE*, VII, 38). Confused and erroneous ideas are nothing but true and adequate ideas mutilated and fragmented. To correct them we must grasp them as they are in God, in the light of the whole; thus we shall rectify, or purify from error and confusion, our imaginal thinking. How and to what extent, as well as by what method, this can be done is set out in *Ethics* II, xxxviii and the following propositions, which give some account of *ratio* and *scientia intuitiva* (later to be developed in Part V). It is not, however, until we come to the sixth proposition of Part III, that we learn what the motive is that impels the human mind to purify its own power of knowing and to think as required by the second and third kinds of knowledge. It is its inherent *conatus,* or urge, to persevere in its own being and to increase, thereby, its power of acting. For adequate ideas depend upon the intellect alone. They are not simply awarenesses of effects upon the body of external causes. They follow, therefore, from the nature or activity of the human mind itself, and are therefore actions of the mind pure and undiluted. Our power of action is consequently directly proportional to our capacity for framing adequate ideas.

The true essence of the mind is thinking, *cognitio,* and that is an attribute of God; thus Spinoza frequently says that the human mind is a part of God's intellect, or of "the thinking thing." [45] But God thinks only adequately and does not perceive sensuously or imagine. Therefore, the real essence of the human mind is intellect, of which the true nature is to frame adequate ideas. This appears in all Spinoza's treatment of the mind both in the *Tractatus* and in the *Ethics,* as well as in his letters. In the *Treatise* the doctrine is explicit,[46] and in *Ethics* IV, xxvi, it is evident in his statement that "whatever we attempt by reason is nothing else than to understand; nor does the mind judge anything as useful to itself, so far as it uses reason, other than what conduces to understanding"; for its *conatus* is to persevere in its own essence (*ibid.,* Dem.); and to understand, to think clearly and distinctly, or to frame true ideas, is what constitutes its essence.

---

[44] *P.P.C.* I, vi, S.
[45] Cf. *Ethics* II, Ax. 2, xi and C; *Ep.* XXXII. Descartes designates the human mind *res cogitans,* but, for Spinoza, that phrase applies primarily to the infinite intellect of God.
[46] *TdIE,* IX, 73.

Again, when he is asked by Blyenbergh whether to a mind which did not by nature find villainy repugnant there would be any reason for virtue, he replies that such a nature would be self-contradictory, for what makes us men is "the knowledge of God and ourselves" (*Dei et sui ipsius cognitio*) [47] which, as we shall see, is the essence of virtue.

It is of the nature of intellect to frame adequate ideas and so the inadequate arise only in the first kind of knowledge (*imaginatio*): "If it is of the nature of a thinking being, as is obvious on its face, to frame true or adequate thoughts, it is certain that inadequate ideas arise in us only because we are part of some thinking being certain of whose thoughts, some in whole and some in part only, constitute our minds." [48] The inadequate ideas are those which we have "in part only," and they are imaginal. So we are told, in *Ethics* II, xli, that the first kind of knowledge is the one and only cause of falsity. But such ideas as we have complete, as they are in God, are and must be adequate. (*Ethics* II, xxxiv).

(a) *Ratio*. Such adequate ideas are obtainable in two ways. First, any idea of what is common to all things and is equally in the whole and in the part, is adequate, for it must be adequate in God so far as he has the idea of the human body and its modifications, as well as ideas of other bodies by which the human body is affected. Therefore it must be adequate in God so far as he constitutes the human mind. Of whatever is common to all bodies with the human body and is equally in every part and in the whole, the idea will be in the human mind as it is in God, and will accordingly be adequate. (*Ethics* II, xxxviii). But, Spinoza tells us, such common properties do not constitute the essence of any single thing. What such common properties are is an important question, for they certainly are not the common properties on which we base our general ideas, such as "humanity," or "lapidity," or universals like "man," "horse," "dog," etc. We are expressly told, in the first Scholium to the fortieth proposition of *Ethics* II, that such general terms are the result of the confusion of numerous images of individual things when we experience too many to retain them all separately. In such circumstances, we remember only salient features which have struck us and which are common to all the images, and so we form class concepts and use them to apply to the individuals concerned. Thus some people define man as an animal of erect stature, others as one who laughs, others as a featherless biped and yet others as a rational animal; "for which reason it is not

---

[47] *Epp.* XXII and XXIII. In the Dutch version: "*de Kennis van God, en sigh selve, dat is, het voornaamste, dat ons mensen maakt.*" (*V.V.L.* III, p. 104).
[48] *TdIE.*, IX, 73.

surprising that so many controversies should arise among philosophers who wish to explain natural objects solely through the images of things." (*Ibid.*). Obviously, this is the work of *imaginatio*.

The common properties of which we can form adequate ideas, therefore, must pertain to those "eternal things" mentioned at the end of the fragment on *The Improvement of the Intellect*, and these we identified as the attributes of substance and the infinite modes.[49] Thus the spatial properties of all bodies which are common to the whole of Extension are clearly and distinctly conceivable, and everything that follows from them by strict deduction. The same would be true of numerical properties. Hence would arise the mathematical sciences all of whose propositions are certain and the reasonings of which are rigorous and precise. But nothing deduced in mathematics constitutes the essence of any singular, finite entity, thus it would answer exactly to what Spinoza calls *ratio*, the knowledge of the second kind.

This knowledge of the second kind might be identified with "science," but if so care must be taken to include only the mathematical sciences, for the empirical sciences, to which we refer today by that name, Spinoza would not have admitted, except so far as they were mathematized. Theoretical physics possibly might qualify, but very little else. He never wrote the disquisition on inductive reasoning and empirical methods which he promised in a footnote to the Treatise on the Intellect, so we do not know precisely how he would have classed the inductive sciences, but we can be fairly sure that they would rank below *ratio* and would probably be relegated to the sphere of *imaginatio*. For the adequate knowledge of concrete entities and their mutual relations the only form of knowledge he found suitable was the third kind, about which there is more to follow.

There are two characteristics of mathematical science (*ratio*) of which note must be taken before we pass on. First, it contemplates nothing as contingent but everything as necessary. And, secondly, it perceives things "under a certain form of eternity," [50] because it perceives them as necessary and as they are in God, and thus as pertaining to his eternal nature, and apart from all relation to time. Mathematical truths are eternal truths. Temporal predicates do not apply to them. They neither come to be nor pass away.

(b) *Scientia Intuitiva.* The second way of obtaining adequate ideas and the best of all is, in Spinoza's list, the third kind of knowing, "In-

---

[49] P. 23, above.
[50] *Ethics* II, xliv, and C 2: "*sub quadam aeternitatis specie.*"

tuitive Knowledge." This is defined in the *Ethics* (II, xl. S 2) as knowledge which "proceeds from an adequate idea of the formal essence of certain attributes of God to an adequate knowledge of the essence of things." It is, in fact, a knowledge of the essence of things as a consequence of God's nature. It is a knowledge of things in their complete determining relationships within Nature as a whole. By this knowledge we see things as they are in God.

Why, we may ask, does Spinoza call the third kind of knowledge intuitive? Intuition is usually associated either with the immediacy of sense or with unreasoned and irrational inspiration, foreboding or inexplicable revelation. Perhaps, for this reason, Spinoza is often said to be a mystic, or at least give way to mysticism in the last resort. But by intuitive knowledge Spinoza is far from intending anything irrational, or inscrutable. The knowledge is "immediate" only in the sense that we are conscious of it all, in all its articulations, at once and without transition. In it we grasp the object concretely and whole.

In the *Short Treatise,* Spinoza says that in this kind of knowledge the mind feels or enjoys (*"door een gevoelen en genieten"*) the thing itself,[51] and he sheds some, if rather diffused, light on it in his favourite illustration of the three kinds of knowledge – not really a very helpful one, but one which he repeats in several places.[52] This is the example of the fourth proportional. Given three numbers, (i) a merchant will find the fourth proportional by multiplying the first and the third and dividing by the second, because he has learnt the rule of three by hearsay and follows it blindly without demonstration. (ii) A scholar may prove the rule by Euclid's theorem; but (iii) a skilled mathematician, who understands the nature of proportion will see by direct insight what the fourth number is, especially when the numbers are small. As an illustration of the first two kinds of knowledge the example serves tolerably well, but the distinction between the second and the third is not so clear. It seems that the point Spinoza wishes to make is that with a thorough understanding of the principles involved and a sufficiently deep insight into the relations obtaining, it is possible to grasp the nexus of the matter in a single apprehension (*uno intuitu*). This single intuition is not inarticulate but in itself contains the insight into the whole systematic structure of the matter under survey. In *scientia intuitiva* it is an insight into the nature of Substance and its attributes, in particular the attribute appropriate to the thing under

---

[51] *K.V.,* II, Ch. II.
[52] *Ethics* II, *loc. cit.; TdIE,* IV, 23; *K.V.,* II, Ch. I.

scrutiny, in the light of which, and in its proper place in the total system, the object is clearly and distinctly understood.

Scientia intuitiva then is the concrete knowledge of things in their total setting. To be fully achieved it would require a complete knowledge of Substance, and this belongs only to the infinite intellect of God. But Spinoza was convinced that, short of such complete knowledge, man was capable of "clear and distinct ideas" of God and his attributes, by which he seems to have meant a firm and indubitable understanding of the holistic nature of the universe, from which everything else in his philosophical system follows by necessary inference. In the *Short Treatise* he writes: "I do not say that we must know him [God] as he is . . . but it is enough that we know him in some sense." (II, xxii). In the *Ethics* he argues that every body, in fact every single thing that exists in actuality, necessarily involves the infinite essence of God (II, xlv.), and therefore, because ideas of what is common to all things, both whole and part, are adequate, our conception (*cognitio*) of God's eternal and infinite essence, which every idea must involve, is "adequate and perfect" (II, xlvi and xlvii). Consequently, in reply to Albert Burgh, who, having become a convert to Catholicism, asked him, "How do you know that your Philosophy is the best among all those which have ever been taught in the world, are taught even now, or ever will be taught?" (*Ep.* LXVII), he is able to write: "I do not presume that I have found the best Philosophy, but I know that I understand (*intelligere*) the true one. If you ask how I know this, I shall answer, in the same way as you know that the three angles of a triangle are equal to two right angles." (*Ep.* LXXVI).

If then we have adequate and perfect ideas of God and his attributes we can proceed from these to adequate ideas of things as essentially related to them and to one another in the system of nature. This is how *scientia intuitiva* is defined. It is a grasp of the universal immanent in the particular and of the particular in its setting within the infinite whole. Such knowledge obviously is not the result of the collection of particular instances and of inductive generalizations from these. It is philosophical knowledge, not empirical science. It is the fruit of that synoptic capacity which Plato found to be characteristic of the true dialectician,[53] a capacity which is certainly possessed by some men, if not by all, and at least to some extent, even though, as Spinoza asserts in later Parts of the *Ethics*, we can never free ourselves wholly from *imaginatio*, nor ever become entirely free from the passions.

[53] Cf. *Republic* VII, 537c.

CHAPTER VI

PASSION AND ACTION

1. Affects

We observed that the passivity of our sensuous awareness was not pure passivity, but that some degree of mental activity was also involved. Similarly, the passivity of the body in registering the effects of external causes is not pure passivity and involves some degree of bodily activity. Not only secondary qualities among our ideas express the nature of our own body as much as, or more than, that of the external bodies which cause those changes in our own of which the ideas are sensations. We also and concomitantly experience emotions which are similarly ideas of the results of interactions between our own and other bodies.

An "affect," or emotion, (*affectus*) Spinoza defines as a state (*affectio*) of the body by which its power of acting is increased or diminished, assisted or restrained, along with the idea of that state.[1] We act when something either within or outside us is accomplished of which we are the "adequate cause" – that is, what is done follows from our nature and is clearly and distinctly explicable through that alone. On the other hand, when something is brought about either within or without us of which we are only a partial (inadequate) cause, we suffer (*patimur*), or are subject to passion (*ibid*. Defs. I and II). An affect or emotion, therefore, may be an action as well as a passion depending upon whether or not its adequate cause is our nature alone.

2. Conatus

The proximate source of emotions, the motivation of affective behaviour and of action alike, is the *conatus in suo esse perseverandi* (the urge to persist in its own being). We have learnt that the *conatus* is identical with the essence of the thing concerned and this identification

[1] Cf. *Ethics* III, Def. III. Care must be taken not to confuse *affectus* with *affectio*. See Joachim, *Study*, p. 201.

becomes intelligible if we examine carefully the implications of Spinoza's definition of essence (*Ethics* II, Def. II). He says that what pertains to the essence of a thing is that which, if given, the thing is necessarily given, and if removed the thing is necessarily removed; or alternatively, that without which the thing can neither be nor be conceived and which without the thing can neither be nor be conceived. In other words, the essence of a thing is the thing itself, is *what* it is, what makes its existence possible and what it is conceived as being. Essence, however, does not (except solely in the case of Substance) necessarily involve existence, in spite of what the definition appears to say. Spinoza is quite clear and quite emphatic that the essences of finite things do not necessarily involve their existence, and what he is asserting here is only that what pertains to a thing's essence is the necessary condition of its existence, if and when it is "given."

The existence of a finite thing is determined by causes extraneous to its own essence, except in so far as an adequate definition of it (which expresses its essence) includes its proximate cause. Hence, nothing pertaining to its essence can militate against its existence and it follows that "in so far as it is in itself, it endeavours to persist in its own being" (*Ethics* III, vi). For essence is nothing static: such persistence in its own being is no mere inert endurance but involves *conatus* or *nisus* – striving.

The existence of a finite thing depends upon an infinite series of causes which flow ultimately from the nature of substance; and we have seen that the essence, existence and power of substance are all one and the same. God's essence is his existence and his existence is his power which is the efficient and immanent cause of all things. The dynamic acting in any finite cause is, therefore, the power of God himself, mediated only by the intervening finite causes all of which derive their efficacy originally from the divine omnipotence. The infinite modes, which follow immediately from the attributes expressing the eternal and infinite essence of substance, determine (or compel) [2] the endless changes among finite things that are one after another (*invicem*) the causes which bring other finite things into existence and destroy them. So the efficacy of finite causes is really the power of God acting in and through them. But, so far as the essence of any finite thing is concerned, in itself alone, this power tends purely to the persistence of that thing in existence and can be counteracted only by similar but opposing forces exerted by other things. Thus the *conatus,* or urge, to persist in its own being is at the

---

[2] *Ep.* XXXII, *V.V.L.,* III, p. 121.

same time the essence of the thing concerned *qua* power of God working in and through it.

In the human body, (as in everything else) this urge is the impulse to action, and being a *nisus* to persist in its own being (which *is* its power of acting) it is equally an impulse to increase that power. So we shall find that the *conatus* to self-preservation is at the same time an endeavour towards self-improvement. But what pertains to the body is expressed in the mind by a feeling or "idea," and the mental aspect of the *conatus* of the human body – the way it is felt – is called "will," or "appetite" (when related at the same time to mind and body), or "desire" (when man is conscious of it).[3]

Spinoza says that between appetite (*appetitus*) and desire (*cupiditas*) there is no difference, apart from the fact that the latter term usually refers to men and to the fact that they are conscious of their appetites. In the explanation of the first definition of the affects (at the end of Part III in the *Ethics*) he says that whether a man is conscious of it or not the appetite remains the same. Joachim objects that this makes the consciousness a mere epiphenomenon, for the efficacy of the *conatus* remains the same as that of the appetite and is unchanged by our becoming aware of it. (See *Study* II, App. 5, p. 227ff.) If this interpretation is correct it constitutes an inconsistency in Spinoza, for, as I shall argue below, man's capacity to overcome the passions is the same as his ability to improve his knowledge (from *imaginatio* to *ratio* and beyond) which depends upon his self-reflective consciousness, involved in the doctrine of *idea ideae*. Here again, Joachim criticizes Spinoza's account of *idea ideae,* as an empty reduplication. To me, however, it seems that both these interpretations are too unsympathetic. Of *idea ideae* I have already spoken, and there is much more to it than mere reduplication. Nor is it necessary to understand Spinoza to mean that appetite is in no way modified by our consciousness of it. *Qua* impulse, as the effort to persist in our own being, it is the same whether or not we think of it as pertaining to body or to mind, for body and mind are one. In the same way, for Spinoza, appetite and desire are one. It does not follow that self-consciousness makes no difference to its efficacy. The whole of Spinoza's doctrine tends to affirm the contrary.

Appetite refers primarily to the body and less complex bodies than men's have appetite of which the idea or "consciousness" is insignificant. Even in the lower animals it is only instinctive impulse of which the consciousness must be extremely confused and dim. Man, however, is aware

[3] *Ethics* III, ix, S.

of his appetites and urges (though not of their causes) and so, particularly when we have this self-awareness in mind, we may speak of desire. That consciousness makes no difference means only that the bodily aspect remains appetite or *conatus* whatever the degree of consciousness, but it can hardly mean that desire in man is no different from the instinctive impulses of brutes.[4] Spinoza explains in detail and with some care (as we shall later see) how man's subjection to passion can be overcome and his passions may be transformed into actions, by no other means than through his reflective self-consciousness, his awareness of his desires and discovery of their causes in the relations between his own and other bodies.

The *conatus* whether of body or mind operates both in the reaction to causes from without and in impulses, or actions, of which the human being is the sole, or adequate, cause; thus "the mind, both so far as it has clear and distinct ideas and so far as it has confused ideas, endeavours to persist in its own being, for an indefinite time, and it is conscious of this its own endeavour" (*Ethics* III, ix). So far as it has clear and distinct ideas it acts, but so far as it has inadequate and confused ideas it suffers passions. (*Ethics* III, iii); for adequate ideas are the work of our intellect acting according its own true nature alone, whereas inadequate ideas are of effects caused in part by influences external to our own nature.

3. Primary and Secondary Affects

Frustration of the conatus such as diminishes the power of action of mind and body results in the affect of *tristitia*. This word, which is usually translated "sadness" or "sorrow," is used by Spinoza more in the sense of "pain," but he clearly wishes also to include the notion of dejection which goes with the feeling of reduced competence and frustrated effort. He defines *tristitia* as the transition from a greater to a lesser perfection, and uses the latin word *"dolor"* to mean sorrow or grief.

The opposite of *tristitia* is *laetitia,* which, again, means "pleasure" rather than "joy" (for which Spinoza uses *"gaudium"*), and is defined as the transition from a lesser to a greater perfection (*Ethics* III, Definitions of the Affects II and III). Pleasure results from successful striving issuing in the increase of the power of action while pain is the consequence of frustration.

These two affects are primaries from which all others are derivative according to the objects toward, and the circumstances in, which they are

---

[4] Cf. *Ethics* III, lvii, S: "Hence it follows that the affects of animals, which are called irrational . . ., differ as much from human affects as their nature differs from human nature."

felt. *Cupiditas* or desire is usually classed with them as one of the primary affects,[5] but *cupiditas* is strictly the feeling or awareness of the *conatus* itself. It is the feeling of one's active capacity and is always either pleasant or painful according as it is being successfully exercised, and so augmenting, or is suffering diminution and restraint due to external causes. Desire (*cupiditas*), therefore, is essentially related to pleasure and pain, the former being attendant upon success and the latter upon failure. But it would be wrong to imagine that pleasure or the avoidance of pain was the object of desire, for that would imply that pleasure and pain were prior to desire, whereas the contrary is the case. Desire is a prior condition of the experience of either pleasure or pain and not *vice versa*. Though Spinoza was strongly influenced by Thomas Hobbes, he is no hedonist, and his theory of pleasure and pain is much nearer to that of Aristotle.[6]

We must notice in passing that Spinoza describes the increase in the power of action as a transition to greater perfection, and its diminution as transition to lesser perfection. Presently we shall have to discuss Spinoza's theory of good and evil, so that the introduction here of an evaluative term is important. We must remember, also, that perfection is equated with reality and reality with power, a synonymity that will prove very significant at a later stage of our exposition.

Accompanied by the idea of their external causes these two primary affects, pleasure and pain, become love and hatred respectively. "Love (*amor*) is nothing else than pleasure (*laetitia*) accompanied by the idea of an external cause; and hatred (*odium*) nothing other than pain (*tristitia*) accompanied by the idea of an external cause" (*Ethics* III, xiii, S.) The rest of the affects, by and large, are simply complications of these we have already mentioned, resulting from the conditions in which, and the kinds of objects by which, they are excited.

The mind endeavours to imagine and think of whatever increases its own and its body's power of action, and, *per contra*, to imagine and think of whatever will exclude the existence of that which decreases that power. For the power of action of both body and mind is really one and the same, and the desire to augment it is no more than the mental aspect – the consciousness – of the endeavour to persist in one's own being, both bodily and mental.[7] Thus whatever increases or assists the power of action is

[5] Cf. Joachim, *Study*, Bk. II, ch. III, § 5; and Hallet, *Benedict de Spinoza*, Ch. VIII. Spinoza himself speaks of "the three primary affects, desire, pleasure and pain" (*Ethics* III, lix, S.), but what he says elsewhere bears out my interpretation. Cf. Def. I of the Affects.

[6] Cf. Thomas Hobbes, *Leviathan*, Ch. VI, and Aristotle, *Nicomachean Ethics*, Bk. X, 1-5.

[7] Cf. *Ethics* III, xi, xii and xiii.

loved, and whatever diminishes that power is hated. Likewise, we seek to preserve in existence and to augment the power of existing and acting of anything we love; but we seek to destroy, to remove, or to decrease the power of action of whatever we hate.

Just as the images of two objects experienced together tend to become associated so that the presence or imagination of either arouses the imagination of the other, so the emotions they arouse tend to be associated and the thought of one is liable to evoke both emotions at once. Similarly, when an object to which we should normally be indifferent has a property similar to one possessed by an object we love or hate, it tends to evoke in us the same emotion and we come to love or hate it for no other reason. Moreover, any object which is associated with one which we love or hate tends to arouse in us the same feeling. Consequently, conflicts and vacillation will arise whenever an object usually exciting love becomes associated with one which excites hatred or acquires a property similar to one possessed by such an object, or if one which usually excites hatred becomes associated with or acquires a property similar to that of one which is loved. It is sufficient (and very frequently the case) that we merely imagine a similarity or an association between objects for us to be affected in this way, whether or not the objects are actually alike or actually have the connexion that we imagine. So arises wavering of the mind (*fluctuatio animi*) which is the counterpart with respect to the emotions of doubt with respect to the imagination and which, Spinoza says, differs from doubt in nothing except magnitude (*Ethics* III, xvii, S).

So we rejoice when we imagine that objects of our love rejoice and we love what we imagine so affects them. We are disconcerted and pained when we imagine that they suffer pain, and hate whatever we imagine pains them. On the other hand, we love what we imagine causes pain to those we hate and rejoice when we think of them as suffering, and we hate what we believe gives them pleasure and regret their enjoyments. When those we hate are imagined to possess objects that we love we experience jealousy. When those we imagine to be like ourselves seem to us to experience pleasure or pain, we feel similarly in sympathy with them. When we imagine the objects of our love or hate to be future, our emotions become hopes and fears; when they are in the past, they become joy and sorrow, elation and disappointment. And all these emotions, according to circumstances, may be almost indefinitely complicated, in ways which Spinoza demonstrates with impressive logic and in considerable detail.

But we need not enter into all the details of his account of the affects.

It will be enough to take note of those features which have closest bearing upon, and most significance for morality.

When we imagine that others like us as well as those whom we love are affected by pain or sorrow, we too are sorrowful and when they rejoice so do we. This propensity is called commiseration.[8] The term applies also to the feelings of pleasure and pain which we experience when we imagine others to be affected by them who are like ourselves, but towards whom we have otherwise no particular feelings. When we sympathize with them in this way we strive to remove what we think gives them pain and to preserve what we imagine pleases them. This propensity is called benevolence.[9] So we endeavour to do what we believe others like ourselves will enjoy and approve while we strive to avoid what we believe they dislike and would disapprove.

We can and do ourselves become objects of our own love or hate. We love ourselves when we do what gives us pleasure and particularly when we do what we imagine pleases others, and this self-love and self-approval Spinoza calls *gloria*,[10] of which the best translation might be "priggishness" or "self-satisfaction." Spinoza uses a different term for "pride" (*superbia*) which he defines as overestimation of oneself beyond what is justified. The opposite feeling towards ourselves, when we imagine we have done what others disapprove, is shame (*pudor*). Self-satisfaction is also called *acquiescentia in se ipso*, complacency with oneself, and in certain circumstances it is regarded by Spinoza as both desirable and good, but in many, if not most, cases it can be highly offensive, in his words: "As it can happen that the pleasure, which somebody imagines he gives to others, is imaginary, and as everyone tries to imagine concerning himself what he thinks will give him pleasure, it can easily occur that a vain man (*gloriosus*) may be proud (*superbus*) and may imagine that he is pleasing to everybody when he is universally obnoxious." (*Ethics* III, xxx, S). Besides shame, he calls the contrary emotion repentance (*poenitentia*) when it depends more upon our opinion of ourselves than upon those of others about us (or what we imagine them to be).[11]

Akin to commiseration, or compassion, is our reaction to the way in which we imagine others feel towards what we love and hate. If we think they love what we love and hate what we hate, our own feelings become confirmed and more constant. On the other hand, if we think

---

[8] Cf. *Ethics*, III, xxii, xxvii, S; Definitions of the Affects xviii.
[9] Cf. *ibid.*, xxvii, C 3, S.
[10] *Ethics*, III, xxx S.
[11] *Ibid.*

they love what we hate or *vice versa* we suffer vacillation of mind.[12]

Though in general we try to make our fellows like what we like, if what pleases them can be enjoyed only to the exclusion of others (i.e. our selves), we seek to prevent their having it, and we become jealous if we imagine that anybody whom we love is loved by another and reciprocates that love. This is a conflict of love and hate towards the same object occasioned by conditions we have already mentioned, the tendency to feel sympathetically with those we imagine similar to ourselves and the conflicting tendency to resent the enjoyment by others of what we ourselves desire.[13]

Vacillation causing us to will what we do not wish and want what we do not will is fear, which when excessive becomes consternation. Anger is the desire to inflict hurt upon those whom we hate, and vengeance the desire to return evil for evil; and hatred begets hatred by which in turn it is increased. Nevertheless, if love is returned by one whom we hate our hatred may be overcome; for just as hatred begets hatred, so does love beget love. Thus love can overcome hatred, and when it does so is so much the greater because of the prior feeling of aversion over which it has prevailed. Love, therefore, is in the last resort more powerful than hatred, though the latter, in some circumstances, when we harbour it towards a person who returns good for evil, may simply conflict with the love normally aroused in response to love shown towards us. In such a case, if the hatred prevails it becomes cruelty. Usually, however, love imagined to be proffered without cause is requited, and lack of appreciation of benefits bestowed for interested reasons is resented.[14]

Just as we love or hate those who feel similarly to persons that we love or hate, so we tend to generalize our feelings towards others to include everybody like them, that is, those who belong to the same class or group.[15] But love and hate are diminished if the cause of our pleasure or pain is imagined to be multiple, and increased when we imagine the person who causes it to be a free (and thus an unaided) cause of our pleasures or our ills. And because the same things at different times affect the same man differently, and at the same time affect different persons differently, our affects towards the same objects are various and changeable. Nevertheless, we tend to judge others by ourselves and ourselves by comparison with others.[16]

[12] *Ethics,* III. xxxi.
[13] *Ethics,* III, xxxii, S, and xxxv.
[14] Cf. *Ethics* III, xxxix, xl, xli, xlii, xliii, xliv.
[15] *Ethics,* III, xlvi.
[16] *Ethics,* III, li, S.

4. Active Emotions

The account of the affects which we have considered so far makes it evident that they are for the most part the product of imagination and based, therefore, upon error or at best supposal. When the mind vacillates between conflicting emotions it is in the same sort of state, or indeed in the same state, as when it is in doubt. In all such cases it suffers rather than acts and is the plaything of circumstances and the shuttlecock of external causes. Such affects are associated with inadequate ideas; but there are other emotions which are the counterpart of true ideas and these are active emotions, or what H. F. Hallett calls "exertions." [17] Although it would be wrong to say that Spinoza is intellectualist in his account of human behaviour, in that (as I shall shortly show) he by no means attributes its motivation to the intellect alone, he does hold that of every state of mind the cognitive aspect is prior to the affective, so that every affect is primarily an "idea" whether imaginative (sensuous) or intellectual. In the *Short Treatise*, after listing the three kinds of knowledge, he writes:

"Thus we maintain that knowledge is the proximate cause of all the passions (*lijdingen*) in the soul. Because we hold it once and for all impossible, that, anybody who neither conceives nor knows (*begrijpt noch kent*) in the ways or on grounds above-mentioned, could be moved to love or desire or any other kind of volition." (*K.V.* II, Ch. II).

The objects of ideas are in all cases states of the body, and most of these are effects of external causes. The affects are ideas or awarenesses of these and, whether or not their objects are projected as "external," they are at once cognitive and affective. But as love and hate are defined respectively as pleasure and pain accompanied by the idea of a cause, without that idea no love or desire or any other kind of volition (seeing that these are the primary forms) would be possible.[18]

All desire, as we have seen is a manifestation of the *conatus*, and affects are the awareness of transitions to greater or less power of action (or "perfection"), pleasurable if to greater and painful if to lesser perfection. Consequently, the mind rejoices in the contemplation of itself and its own power of acting (*Ethics* III, liii); and as its power of acting is greater in proportion as it has adequate ideas, its pleasure and self-esteem increases with its knowledge. Desire, therefore, when we know

---

[17] Cf. *op. cit.*, Ch. VIII, 2.

[18] Cf. *Ethics*, II, Ax. 3: "The modes of thought, such as love, desire, or by whatever name the affects of the soul are designated, do not occur unless in the same individual there is an idea of the thing loved, desired, etc. But there can be an idea although no other mode of thought is given."

fully and properly, will issue in activity which is the counterpart of such knowledge.

Adequate ideas, moreover, are not the effects of external and fortuitous causes but are ideas of which the intellect itself is the adequate cause; and intellect strictly speaking and in its true essence is the intellect of God.[19] For adequate ideas are those which grasp their objects as they are determined by the appropriate attribute of substance, in their full system of relations with the universe as a whole. They are, therefore, in a sense, *causa sui*, or at least they are identical with ideas in God's intellect which is *causa sui*. Actions which are the expression of adequate thinking are, accordingly, free, in the only sense recognized by Spinoza as legitimate, that is, they are determined by themselves – or in them the mind is determined only by itself – and not subject to external compulsion. Free action is thus the goal and object of the urge to persevere in one's own being, for free action is the pure expression of one's own essence as that is an expression (or mode of existence) of the essence of God.

All the active emotions such as, in Spinoza's words, "follow from the affects which are related to the mind so far as it understands" he embraces under the term *fortitudo*. One might translate the word as "courage," but Spinoza clearly means something much broader and more significant than the common conception of that virtue. Perhaps "constancy of mind" would be nearer to his meaning, but "strength of mind" is the phrase usually reserved for *animositas,* one of the two forms of *fortitudo* that Spinoza distinguishes. The other is *generositas*. And he defines them as follows: "by strength of mind (*animositas*) I understand the desire by which each person tries to conserve his own being solely from the dictates of reason. By generosity, (*generositas*) however, I understand the desire by which each, solely from the dictates of reason, tries to help other persons and to join them to himself in friendship."

Such active emotions may well give rise to conduct which is superficially similar to that motivated by passive emotions of love, compassion, self-satisfaction and the like; but there is an essential difference in that active emotions are more constant and reliable, less likely to be changed by fortuitous events, less liable to conflict, and all related to pleasure and exhilaration, for all involve the maintenance if not the increase, of the power of acting. (*Ethics* III, lix and S.).

5. *"Human Nature"*

In his account of human emotions Spinoza shows throughout, deep

19 Man's mind is a "part" of the infinite mind of God; cf. *Ep.* XXXII.

understanding of common psychological facts, and demonstrates their natural connexions: how they tend to arise one from another by their very nature and the nature of the conditions which occasion them. Consider, for example, the following passage:

"This pain, accompanying the idea of our weakness is called 'humility'; but pleasure which arises from the contemplation of ourselves (is called) 'self-love' or 'self-complacency.' And since this is repeated as often as a man contemplates his own virtues or power of acting, so it happens that everyone revels in the relation of his own exploits and in displaying his powers whether of body or mind, and that men, on this account, are tiresome to one another. From which again it follows that men are by nature envious and rejoice because of the weakness of their equals and on the other hand are cast down on account of their virtue. For as often as each imagines his own actions he is affected with pleasure and the more so the more he imagines them to express perfections and to be more distinctive; that is, the more he is able to regard them as different from others and as singular things. For which reason each rejoices most in the contemplation of himself when he can see in himself what he denies of others. But if that which he affirms of himself he attributes to the universal idea of man and animal, he is not so pleased; and, on the contrary, he is chagrined if he imagines his own actions to be more feeble in comparison with those of others, a discomfort which he tries to remove by misrepresenting actions equal to his own or by embellishing his own as much as he can. It is therefore apparent that men are naturally prone to hatred and envy..." (*Ethics* III, lv, S).

Spinoza is under no illusions concerning the springs of human conduct, and rationalist though he is, and in spite of his firm belief that the essential nature of the human mind is the rational intellect, he is well aware that "those who persuade themselves that the multitude, or men perplexed by public business, can be induced to live by the prescription of reason alone, dream of the golden age of the poets or of a fairy-tale." [20] For it is impossible, on his showing, for men to be always rational. That is a rare and difficult achievement, the conditions for which we have yet to investigate, and, for the most part "men are led by blind desire rather than reason." [21]

It follows that what we frequently refer to as "human nature" has, for Spinoza, a double aspect. It is natural to man to be subject to emotions, to be appetitive and to be "led by blind desire"; but it is also of the nature of the intellect to frame true ideas. The nature of things involves the infinite series of finite modes that issue of necessity from the

[20] *T.P.*, I, 5.
[21] *Op. cit.*, Ch. II, v; *V.V.L.*, II, p. 6.

essence of substance; and among these are human bodies, and human minds which are the ideas of those bodies. They are but singularities among an infinity of singular modes, each subject to the influence of an infinite multitude of external causes. It is impossible, therefore, for the *conatus* of a mere finite mode to dominate completely the vast number of external determinants that govern its behaviour. It is impossible for man to be anything but a part of nature and the power with which he is able to preserve himself against the force of external causes is limited and infinitely surpassed by theirs.[22]

But the idea of the body involves the idea of that idea (the idea of the mind). It is consciousness, aware of itself and self-transcendent. It can and does, therefore, reflect upon itself and is aware of its own relation to other things, of its body (or *ideatum*) in its relation to other bodies and to the external causes that affect its behaviour. The mind is thus capable of framing adequate ideas as well as being subject to passions which result from the impingement upon the body of external influences. It not only feels and imagines but it is also cognizant of its own feelings and imaginings, and can thus become critical of its own ideas, aware of its own limitations, and of the external causes to which it is subject. To be aware of one's own limitations (as Hegel pointed out in his critique of Kant) one must already have transcended them. It is of the nature of the intellect to think in this more adequate fashion, for idea necessarily involves *idea ideae,* and thoughts and their concomitant actions issuing thus solely from the essence or nature of mind are adequate and free.

Human nature, therefore, has two sides to it. It is both finite and so subject to passions, and potentially infinite in so far as it is self-conscious and can think. Paradoxical though it may seem, it is as natural for men to be bewildered by the vagaries of imagination and to be "led by blind desire" as it is for them to think adequately and to act freely when they determine themselves by their own self-conscious "nature" alone. Consequently, it is no inconsistency for Spinoza to speak of actions as those of which man's nature is the sole or adequate cause, and also to say that man is by nature prone to hatred and envy, as well as to all the other passions; for it is man's nature to be finite, or a part only of the natural world, but it is equally his nature to be conscious and self-reflective. Conduct resulting from his nature as a merely finite being is, for that reason caused by other finite beings conjointly with his own, so that his own "nature" is only a partial or inadequate cause of it. But conduct resulting from his adequate thinking is caused by his own rational nature

<hr>

[22] Ch. *Ethics* IV, ii, iii and iv.

and (apart from God) by nothing else – or, in Spinozistic terms, God is the cause of the latter so far as he is considered as constituting the essence of man's mind (and body) alone, but of the former so far as he is conceived as constituting the essences of other things concurrently. Moreover, Spinoza is giving a true account of human nature as much when he dwells upon its impotence and "bondage" as when he speaks of its liberation and demonstrates the power of the intellect. Unless both aspects are included human nature is not truly represented and the description of it will be one-sided.

The power of the mind and its freedom will be the subject matter of what follows. Its weakness and vacillation has become apparent from the account so far given of the passions summed up by Spinoza in these words:

"And thus I think I have explained the principal emotions and fluctuations of the mind, which arise from the composition of three primary affects, namely, desire, pleasure and pain, and have demonstrated them through their first causes. From which it is clear that we are driven about by external causes in many ways, and that thence, like waves of the sea driven by contrary winds, we waver, ignorant of our fate and of its outcome." (*Ethics* III, lix, S).

6. Freedom

Strictly speaking there is only one free cause, and that is God, for God is *causa sui*. He is his own cause, subject to nothing external, because there is nothing external, no source of power other than his. Other causes, like the human intellect may be considered free only derivatively, because and in so far as they are expressions, activities, or "parts," of God's power. A free cause is what Spinoza calls an adequate cause of its effect, that is, a cause than which nothing else is required to explain the effect. It is what we should describe today as sufficient as well as necessary. If an activity is comprehensible solely through the nature of the agent (is caused solely by its own nature), it is free; on the other hand, if it is explicable adequately only by reference to causes external to the nature of the alleged agent, the activity is compelled and the subject of the activity suffers.

Compulsion, however, must not be confused with determination for what is free may very well be determined without being compelled. In Spinozistic language determination is negation and God is not determined by anything outside himself, though, as we saw, that is far from excluding determinations within him of his distinguishable attributes and modes, which are mutually determinant. God's power, issuing in free activity, however, expresses itself entirely in and as these attributes and modes; and as God's power is identical with his intellect, and his intellect is absolute and complete, there is nothing in any way conceivable which God could produce that he does not produce. For God's acts are systematic and rational and constitute the self-completed and total system of the universe in which everything is as it must be, is determined by everything else and by the structure of the whole, and could not therefore be other than it is. To imagine that God could have done otherwise is to imagine him and his work to be finite, so that there are other possibilities not included in his actual deeds. Thus to maintain that God's acts are determined and could not be other than they are, so far from implying, limitation upon his power, is to recognize its infinite and absolute self-sufficiency. God could not act otherwise than he does because there is no "otherwise" which is conceivably possible. For this reason, while his causality is free it is not arbitrary or capricious and he does not exercise "free will" in the sense that he could or could not, might or might not, act in a particular way, according as he feels disposed. To imagine God as exercising that sort of (allegedly) "free" will would be contradictory of his infinite and absolute power and is ludicrously inept. Everything that God does, therefore, is what it must be: there is nothing contingent, nothing indeterminate. Consequently, God's causation is at once both free and determinate and everything that he produces is determined, although he is in no way compelled. The same will apply to human action, in as much as it can be considered as God's action, so far as he constitutes the nature of man. When man acts from his own nature alone his action is free, because it is not compelled by external causes, but it is not in any degree indeterminate.

Once these distinctions between freedom and indeterminacy, compulsion and determination are properly understood the persistent misinterpretation of Spinoza's doctrine, which has prevailed ever since his own life-time, can be avoided. Lambert de Velthuysen, writing to Johannes Oosten in comment on Spinoza's *Theologico-Political Treatise,* in 1671, said:

"He declares that the form, appearance and order of the world are clearly necessary, equally with the nature of God and eternal truths which he holds to be constituted apart from God's choice (*arbitrium*); and thence also he expressly pronounces that all things occur by insuperable necessity and inevitable fate." (*Ep.* XLII).

In his reply to Oosten, Spinoza repudiates the misinterpretation emphatically:

"The basis of his argument is this, that he thinks I take away liberty from God and subject him to fate. That is plainly false. For I maintain that all things follow with inevitable necessity from God's nature, just as everybody asserts that it follows from God's nature that he understands himself: which clearly nobody denies does follow from the divine nature of necessity, and yet nobody conceives that God is compelled by some fate, but (rather) that he understands himself entirely freely, although necessarily." (*Ep.* XLIII).

And again he explains to Hugo Boxel, who had similarly misunderstood him:

"By what reasons you try to persuade me to believe that 'fortuitous' and 'necessary' are not contraries remains hidden from me. As soon as I see that the three angles of a triangle are necessarily equal to two right angles, I also deny that this happens to be so by chance. Similarly, as soon as I observe that heat is the necessary effect of fire, I also deny that it occurs accidentally. That 'necessary' and 'free' are two contraries seems no less absurd and opposed to reason: for nobody can deny that God knows himself and everything else freely, and yet all concede by common consent that God knows himself necessarily. Consequently, you seem to me to make no distinction between compulsion or force and necessity. That man wishes to live, to love, etc. is not a compulsory activity, but is nevertheless necessary, and much more so that God wishes to be, to know and to act." (*Ep.* LVI).

Thus necessity is opposed to chance but not to freedom and is not to be identified with compulsion. What is compelled (by external forces) is not free, but what is free from such compulsion, and free altogether (like God's action) can nevertheless be determined. Determinism is, therefore, not opposed to, or incompatible with, freedom, but it is opposed to and incompatible with chance or caprice.

There is not, however, only one kind of determination. Spinoza's favourite example is the mathematical determination of the three angles of a triangle by its figure, and here, in the letter quoted, he also mentions the necessary connexion between fire and heat. This is causal necessity, not mathematical. But both of these varieties are consequent upon systematic relations between the factors concerned (in the one case geometrical and in the other physico-chemical). Spinoza's conception of substance is of a single system of inter-related modes so interlocked that each is determined by the rest and by the ordered structure of the whole. It is in this sense that all events are determined. But from this it does not follow that the kind of determination is always geometrical or always physico-chemical. The determination of human behaviour by passions may be regarded as a determination of a different order, and Spinoza undoubtedly did contemplate a special kind of determination involved in the self-reflective character of consciousness, for reflection upon our own ideas can change their validity and convert them from partial and mutilated notions to adequate ones. Actions concomitant with such adequate ideas are (he said) free, but they are nevertheless rationally determined. It is hardly to be doubted that Spinoza conceived this kind of determination by self-conscious reason as the highest and most far-reaching kind to which other kinds were subordinate and of which they were, so to say, partial manifestations. For this is the sort of determination by which God freely produces his creatures and the sort of determination also by which man frees himself from the tyranny of desire and the turmoil and bewilderment of conflicting passions. As all determination is in the last resort that of the eternal laws of God's nature, and as the latter is necessarily self-conscious, we must surely conclude that the ultimate determination is that of infinite self-conscious thought.

The notion of determinism itself is thus constituted by a scale of degrees in which each kind of determination is a nearer approximation to the ultimate directive governance by the immanent causality of the whole of substance. Mathematical, mechanical, physio-chemical, psychological and rational determination are forms in a scale each progressively more adequately manifesting the comprehensive self-activity of God's power (or essence). That again is immanent in each form, or is the dynamic exerting itself in these various (yet continuously progressive) ways. It is *Natura Naturans* issuing in them as *Natura Naturata,* which is thus revealed as a dialectical scale of degrees of perfection to which each kind of determination is appropriate and which at each step is proportional to the degree of determinism displayed. The totality is immanent in each but is only fully expressed in the last, most highly developed (or concrete), most fully perfect (or completely real). As this final grade of the scale is the most comprehensive, it absorbs the whole of the scale into itself and is both the final grade and the totality in one. Every developmental or evolutionary process displays a dialectical series of this kind, and such dialectical progression is the essential character of what is properly called teleological. I shall go on to argue that Spinoza's doctrine, despite his constant and well-deserved attacks upon the contemporary notions of teleology, is itself essentially teleological in the only legitimate meaning (as I shall explain) of that term. In the last resort, the only consistent way of conceiving Spinoza's Substance is as a dialectical whole, and although he nowhere sets out his theory in precisely the way that I have presented it in this paragraph, there is good evidence in several different contexts in his writing that he himself conceived Substance as just such a scale of degrees of increasing perfection. With this in mind we may now address ourselves directly to the topic of teleology and to the problems of human will and responsibility.

7. Teleology

It is hardly possible to discuss teleology, or the presence in nature of final causes, without reference to notions of good and evil, or of human will and purposiveness. Nor does Spinoza separate these topics in his critique of "prejudices which might prevent (his) demonstrations from being grasped." Nevertheless there is much to be said about each of these three subjects, so without attempting to separate them rigidly, I shall give attention to each in turn. What is common to Spinoza's criticism of current opinions on all three matters, final causes, good and evil, and freedom of will, is that it is directed against inadequate and incoherent theories rather than against the concepts themselves as rightly understood. He constantly reiterates that what he censures are the products of imagination which men indulge instead of trying to understand by reason. "All those principles (*rationes*)," he says, "by which the common people are in the habit of explaining nature are only different forms of imagining, and do not point to the nature of any (real) thing, but only to the constitution of the imagination." (*Ethics* I, App.) What he says of such confused thinking, should not blind us to those aspects of his theory which show a more positive approach to the ideas under discussion. Equally we should not be misled into thinking that Spinoza contradicts himself because, for instance, in the Appendix to the first Part of the *Ethics,* he is satirical and scathing in his account of popular notions of good and evil, and yet in Part IV (and elsewhere) he himself entertains ideas of human welfare and perfection. No more is it an inconsistency in his thought that he repeatedly rejects the doctrine of free will, yet devotes pages to the explanation of human freedom. To show that his arguments are mutually compatible will be one of my objects in the following sections, as well as to reveal features of his doctrine which are commonly overlooked and neglected or misunderstood by commentators.

The kind of teleological explanation which Spinoza attacks is that which attributes purposes to natural phenomena similar to, or even identical with, the ends commonly pursued by men. First it makes the assumption that what appeals to man's appetites and is therefore imagined by him to be good is also the attraction, or causal influence, directing natural processes. Because man seeks what is profitable to himself and regards as means to this end whatever helps him to attain it, he tends to regard all things as means to ends and to explain occurrences as if they happened in order to produce such ends as their effects. Secondly, he finds numerous things useful to himself as means to the satisfaction of his desires, and so he imagines them designed for the purpose: "plants and animals for nourishment, the sun for giving light, the sea for feeding fish, and so forth." And as he has not created these things and cannot imagine them to have created themselves, he concludes that God must have created them for his benefit. Then imagining God on the analogy of an earthly ruler, man assumes that God has done all this to make man beholden to him and to induce him to give honour and praise to his maker. "This is the reason why each has devised, according to his own bent, a different form of worshipping God, so that God might love him above others and direct all nature to the service of his blind cupidity and insatiable greed." [23]

The first error, therefore, is the attribution to God and nature of ends and desires typical of and peculiar to man. This involves the further error of imagining that God acts for ulterior ends in order to bring about what initially he lacks; and that implies a deficiency in God which he must endeavour to supply and an imperfection that he strives to make good – an idea altogether incompatible with God's infinite nature.

This method of explanation, moreover, leads us back through a series of alleged purposive actions to an eventual desperate appeal to God's inscrutable purpose in order to cover our ignorance. A stone falls from a roof on to a man's head and kills him. This is explained by saying that the stone fell in order to kill the man (presumably as a punishment for sin). But you may say, the stone fell because the wind blew. Then why did the wind blow just at the time that the man was passing? Should we say because the weather was stormy and the man had been invited by a friend? But, again, why was the weather stormy just precisely then and why did all these chance events concur? . . . Finally, "you fly to the will of God, that is, the refuge of ignorance."

Further, because things disposed in certain ways are easier to imagine than when not so disposed men call such dispositions orderly, and finding many things in nature easily imaginable in this fashion they say that God has created an order in nature, ignoring all exceptions and counter-instances. In so doing they attribute imagination to God, or alternatively assume that God has so disposed things as to aid the imaginations of men.

[23] *Ethics* I, App.

Thus some philosophers have persuaded themselves that the celestial motions produce a harmony, forgetting that the pleasure we take in certain combinations of sound depends on the constitution of our bodies and the nature of our senses and is not a quality of things themselves, "all of which sufficiently shows that everyone judges of things according to the disposition of his brains, or rather accepts the affections of his imagination in place of things."

The ridicule Spinoza heaps on such notions is purely negative criticism and is richly merited. He leaves it to his reader to see for himself why such opinions are ludicrous in the light of what has been demonstrated of God and Nature in the foregoing proposition of the *Ethics*, and he leaves what he considers the true account of these matters to develop itself in those which follow. Consequently, many commentators, taking this polemic along with Spinoza's professed determinism, have concluded that he intended to deny any form of order to the universe and to exclude teleological processes altogether, however conceived; and that, as must be apparent from what has already been said in foregoing chapters, is certainly wide of the mark. The dynamic character of God's power, the process of causes and effects governed by the *facies totius universi* and the doctrine of the *conatus* are by themselves sufficient evidence against any such view.

The inadequate and largely ludicrous notion of teleology of which Spinoza is so contemptuous, would be almost universally rejected today by philosophers as well as scientists. To imagine that a present event can be "caused" (conceiving cause and effect as a linear sequence) by a future event is to reverse the natural and intelligible order of things. Efficient causation is always *a tergo* never *a fronte*. To explain matters of which we are frankly ignorant by alleging that they are brought about by the will of God for inscrutable purposes is mere obscurantist superstition. But simply to reject all this is to give no intelligible account either of human purposive action or of numerous other natural processes for the explanation of which efficient causation *a tergo* is inadequate. In this regard Spinoza succeeds far better than many modern critics of teleological explanation. For there is another and better conception of teleology which is not vulnerable to Spinoza's attack, and one which is implicit in all his own thinking. It is a conception of teleology which is not exclusive of efficient causation and which is compatible with, not contradictory of, mechanism. For typical mechanisms are human artifacts made for specific purposes and serving purposive functions, and all mechanisms are systematically designed structures of which the principle of organization governs the performance of their function and alone makes it possible. This determination of function in the part by the principle of organization of the whole is the key characteristic of teleological process.

It is generally admitted that human purposive action is teleological in character, even if nothing else is; for that is the meaning of the term – namely, what pursues an end or objective. But human action is far from being undetermined and is never independent of efficient causes. As Spinoza maintains it is only because men, while aware of their desires, are ignorant of their causes that they believe themselves to have free will. But this is not to deny that they do pursue ends towards which their desires are directed. And the ends that men pursue are not isolated objects or events as yet unrealized which exercise a mysterious causal influence upon them *a fronte.* They are in all cases the completion of a structure or whole already implicit in their minds; in instinctive activity the structure is one of organic and biological functions maintaining the systematic totality of the organism in health and completeness; in more deliberate action it is a plan or design that is being fulfilled. This is the nature of teleological activity properly understood: it is a process generating a totality, in which every phase and detail is constituted and directed by the principle of organization (or structure) universal to the system that is being generated and fully realized only in its completion. It is a pattern of form and action in which every nuance is determined by the requirements of the whole. When this is the case adequate explanation always proceeds from the whole to the part, from the universal principle of organization to its diverse manifestations in the course of its realization.[24]

Teleological process, therefore, from one point of view is action neither *a tergo* nor *a fronte,* for it requires an entirely new conception of causality, not as a linear determination of successive events each by its immediate predecessor, but as reticular mutual determination of events in systematic relation, each fixed and defined by, as well as defining, all the rest, in accordance with a governing principle of structure that integrates the whole. From another point of view, it is determination both *a tergo* and *a fronte,* for the causal influence is reciprocal among the parts because the governing principle of order is universal to the whole, so that when the system is generated in time what comes earlier is as intimately related to what is subsequently to emerge as it is to what has previously been realized. The end, as potential, is already present at the beginning,

---

[24] Cf. my "Teleology and Teleological Explanation," *Journal of Philosophy,* LVI, 1959, and *Foundations of Metaphysics in Science,* Ch. XIII.

and equally each phase of its realization is determined by the prior process. Throughout, and at each stage, the principle of organization of the whole structure is the immanent cause of the entire process.

Now this sort of conception and this sort of explanation is persistent in all Spinoza's thinking. Every particular thing and event is to be explained in the light of the whole system. Nothing can be or be conceived without God-or-Substance-or-Nature, which is the immanent cause of all particular finite events. These flow in an infinite series from the eternal nature of substance. In their sequence they are mutually determined and their relations are governed by the totality of the entire universe in which the ratio of motion and rest is maintained constant. Causal determination is ubiquitous, and nothing is "free" in the sense of uncaused, random, or accidental, but the ultimate cause of all is God's infinite nature and that is a free cause in the only legitimate sense. It is *causa sui*.

Thus Spinoza objects to the false notion of teleology saying:

"... this doctrine concerning an end altogether overturns nature. For that which is in truth the cause it considers as the effect and *vice versa*. Again that which is first in nature it puts last; and, finally, that which is supreme and most perfect it makes the most imperfect. For (passing by the first two assertions as self-evident) it is plain. ... that that effect is the most perfect which is immediately produced by God, and to the extent that a thing requires many intermediate causes for its production, it is the more imperfect." (*Ethics* I, App.).

That which is immediately produced by God (we have seen) is the infinite mode of the relevant attribute. In the case of Extension it is motion-and-rest, giving rise directly to the *facies totius universi*. This is the more perfect cause which determines all finite events in the physical world, in its self-maintenance as an individual totality with a constant ratio of motion and rest. The governing influence is the principle of the whole; thus all processes within it are teleologically directed, in the proper sense of that word, and all satisfactory and complete explanation will in the last resort be teleological, in terms of that governing principle. This is clearly the character of *scientia intuitiva,* defined as knowledge which proceeds from an adequate idea of the formal essence of certain attributes of God to the adequate knowledge of the essence of things – knowledge which comprehends things in the light of the ultimate totality to which they belong. Needless to say, what is true of Extension and physical processes is even more obviously true of thought and of the nature of mind. To contend, therefore, as some commentators do, that Spinoza held a mechanistic conception of human nature and action and denied its purposive and teleological character, is a complete misunderstanding and a gross misrepresentation.

Before turning to that, let us note two further examples of Spinoza's teleological thinking. Despite his denial of an order in nature such as would aid the imagination of man, he himself describes (often in the same context) an order of nature of another kind. For instance he repeats his denial of an *imagined* order in the world in the letter to Oldenburg (*Ep.* XXXII), in which he explains so fully and so beautifully how different bodies, by mutual adaptation of their activities and functions, may constitute a single individual, and extends this principle to the universe as a whole. In his reply (*Ep.* XXXIII), Oldenburg astutely remarks that Spinoza's proof of the interconnexion of things is itself an admission of the existence of an order in nature.[25] And indeed the whole structure of Spinoza's account of Substance, its attributes, its infinite modes and the infinite sequence of finite entities in which its eternal nature expresses itself – the whole gamut of *Natura Naturata* – is obviously and essentially the account of a rational determinate order of infinite scope and completeness, in which (to use F. H. Bradley's language) "the whole is in every part and informs each part with the nature of the whole." What Spinoza is rejecting, therefore, is only the kind of "order" facilely concocted by wishful thinking, which, ignoring the evidence, postulates a neat and convenient arrangement specially designed for the benefit of man. That kind of "teleological explanation" is stupid and unsupportable; but to see that it is does not warrant the abandonment of the legitimate form of teleological explanation in terms of systematic order, to which Spinoza consistently adheres. The force of his critique is to correct, not to abolish the conception of order as it applies to the real world. A similar piece of evidence of teleological thinking, in the very context of criticism of the popular confused form, occurs in the passage at the end of the Appendix to *Ethics* I, where he replies to the question: "If all things have followed necessarily from the most perfect nature of God, whence then so many imperfections in Nature? That is to say, the corruption of things till they are putrid, the deformity of things which produce nausea, confusion, evil, sin, etc." After repeating that evil and corruption are not to be judged according to their effects on the human senses, but *"ex sola earum natura et potentia,"* solely from their own nature and power, he concludes:

---

[25] In *Ep.* XII Spinoza actually uses the phrase in his own exposition.

"To those, therefore, who ask why God did not create all men so that they are governed only by reason, I reply simply that it is because he did not lack means for the creation of all things, from the highest to the lowest degree of perfection."

As we proceed we shall find ample reason to hold that, as this passage testifies, Spinoza viewed the world as a scale of degrees of perfection "from the highest to the lowest." And, moreover, that he envisaged a process within it tending persistently towards greater perfection – *a nisus* towards atonement with God, toward the full realization of the immanent infinity in each singular finite being.

The principle motivating this process is the *conatus* of each singular thing to persist in its own being. We have observed Spinoza's theory of the scale of complication among bodies, of the way in which simpler bodies become more complex by amalgamation with others, in which combination a constant proportion of motion and rest is maintained. The ideas or minds of such bodies vary with them in complexity and capacity, for the more complex a body becomes the more capable it is of doing and suffering many things, and, to the same extent, its mind is capable of perceiving many things. "Moreover, we cannot deny that ideas differ from one another as do the objects themselves, and one is more pre-eminent than another, and contains more reality, just as the object of the one is more pre-eminent than the object of another and contains more reality." (*Ethics* II, xiii, S). Hence the more complex a thing is in this way the more capable it is of acting and persisting in its own being. For "the more the actions of one body depend solely upon itself, and the less other bodies are involved (*concurrunt*) in its action, the more is its mind capable of understanding distinctly." (*ibid.*) The *conatus* will therefore be a striving towards the realization of such capacity, for whatever in-creases the power of understanding likewise increases the power of acting and the degree of reality (or "perfection") of a thing. Here we see like-wise the source of man's capacity to purify and improve his intellect, to free himself from confused ideas and from subjection to the passions. Clearly, therefore, there is, in Spinoza's system, a principle of develop-ment which so far from conflicting with his theory of total determinism, is actually involved by it – a fact which will become even more apparent when we consider his teaching concerning the will, responsibility and human freedom.

8. The Will and Human Responsibility

As his criticism of teleological explanation is not a denial of teleology properly understood, but is a rejection of false and confused notions of teleology, so Spinoza's attack on the doctrine of free will is not a denial of freedom to man but a repudiation of a false conception of freedom. What he deprecates is the identification of freedom with indeterminacy, the contention that the will acts without any prior cause. No finite principle of action, he maintains, is without a cause, and nothing is really indeterminate. What seems indeterminate to us is the purely contingent, what happens by mere chance, and it only seems so because of the deficiency of our knowledge. To regard the will as indeterminate, therefore, is to reduce deliberate action to the level of accident which is precisely the opposite of what the advocates of the doctrine intend.[26]

Our common unease at the denial of free will springs from our desire to regard our actions as our own and ourselves as responsible persons. If our will were not free, but were simply the effect of causes beyond our control, we should not be responsible for our actions and our very individuality would seem to be taken away. But it is to be noted at the outset that responsibility is not saved by making our actions unaccountable, as they would be if they resulted from no cause whatsoever. Acts which are purely arbitrary are merely capricious and the reverse of responsible, and what occurs as if by pure chance has no resemblance to deliberate choice. Spinoza was clearly aware that the desire and urge to believe ourselves masters of our own decisions could not really be satisfied or consistently justified by a belief in a will that is independent of any determination.

The aim of his attack is two-fold. First, as is clear from the Appendix to Part I of the *Ethics*, he wishes to ridicule and dispose of incoherent popular beliefs, often adopted and repeated by unreflecting theologians. Secondly, he is anxious to oppose a doctrine for which he has considerable respect but which he saw to be inconsistent, namely, that of Descartes. His opposition to Descartes, again, has two main sources. Descartes held that God acted by a will that is absolutely free and so is inscrutable to, and unaccountable by, men. That, Spinoza saw was subversive of Descartes' own theory of God's perfection, and of the credibility of human knowledge, which Descartes made dependent on God's veracity.[27] Further, he opposed Descartes's doctrine that man's susceptibility to error was due to his free will, which, being infinite in scope, could affirm propositions that, owing to the limitations of his intellect, he did not clearly and distinctly perceive. Spinoza, as we observed above,[28] saw that every

---

[26] Cf. *Ep.* LVI, quoted above, p. 124.
[27] Cf. Leon Roth, *Spinoza, Descartes, and Maimonides* (Oxford, 1924; New York, 1963), Chs. I and II.
[28] Ch. V, pp. 89-98.

perception (or cognition) is implicitly an affirmation or denial and that there is neither need of any further principle to effect assertion nor the possibility of affirming or denying what the intellect did not perceive (whether clearly or confusedly). "For what else is it to perceive a winged horse than to affirm of the horse that it has wings."

At the end of the second Part of the *Ethics*,[29] he discusses at length and with care the Cartesian arguments and shows them to be untenable. (i) It is maintained by the Cartesians that men do not require any larger faculty of assent than they already have in order to affirm an infinite number of things which they do not perceive, whereas they would need a greater intellectual capacity to understand them. This Spinoza denies because, he says, he sees no reason to believe that the will, or power of affirming, extends any further than that of perceiving, or feeling (*sentiendi*), for there is no limit to what we can perceive in successive perceptions, and we can by no means affirm anything that we cannot cognize at all.

(ii) The Cartesians point out that we can suspend judgment upon matters of which we are uncertain and thus we can choose freely whether or not to affirm them. But such suspense of judgment, Spinoza retorts, is simply our awareness that we do not perceive or understand the matter adequately. He has already explained that we doubt about something only if we have some other idea that conflicts with it and no means of deciding between the two. Doubt or suspension of judgment is vacillation of the mind, not the exercise of free will.

(iii) The Cartesian argument asserts that to affirm what is true involves no greater capacity of assent than to affirm what is false, but a greater capacity of intellect is needed to distinguish the more real from the less. Spinoza rejoins that this is not so, because what is false is simply a privation in idea, or a mutilation of the truth. To affirm as true what is true, therefore, does require a greater capacity than to affirm what is false, as much of "will" as of intellect. The main error here, moreover, is that "will" is being used as a general term, or as the name of a general faculty, and this is a mere *ens rationis*. There is no such thing as will in general but only particular volitions, which the general term is used to cover indiscriminately. It therefore appears as if we refer to the same capacity indifferently whatever is being asserted. But this is not the case for each assertion differs with content judged.

(iv) It is argued that if a man had no free will he would be immobilized

---

[29] *Ethics* II, xlix, S.

and unable to act at all whenever equal and opposite attractions (or motives) acted upon him at the same time, like Buridan's ass placed equidistant between two equal bundles of hay. Spinoza retorts that a man so placed in equilibrium would be unable to decide and to act. "If you ask me," he continues, "whether such a man should not be considered an ass rather than a man, I say I do not know, as also I do not know how he should be considered who hangs himself, or how children, fools and madmen should be judged." The implication is that a man so placed should be capable of forming an adequate idea of the situation and of acting rationally, as an ass cannot.

In brief, there is no such thing as a "faculty" of willing. There are only particular acts of will and these are indistinguishable from the things willed, or in other words, the ideas affirmed. For willing is identical with asserting or denying. "In the mind there is no volition, or affirmation and negation, except that which the idea involves so far as it is an idea" (*Ethics* II, xlix), and "will and intellect are one and the same" (*ibid.* Corol.).

In rejecting the untenable view of free will, however, Spinoza is not denying the possibility either of human responsibility or of human freedom. He does indeed reject the common opinion that men are to be held responsible for their passions and to be blamed for the behaviour that they cause. He protests vigorously against those who express disapproval of human passions, weep over them, or ridicule and condemn them, as if they were independent of natural causes and not subject to (and products of) the laws of nature, like everything else.[30] Because they are natural they are not to be despised as defects, for nothing in nature is defective or other than it must be. We regard the passions and the behaviour to which they move men as vicious only in relation to our own wishes and the ends we set before ourselves in the pursuit of our desires.[31] Men who give way to passion and are swept by them this way and that "like the waves of the sea," who are moved by anger, envy, jealousy and fear and so become embroiled in enmity and strife with their neighbours, are rather to be pitied than to be reviled. Men's conduct, he holds, is always determined but that does not mean that it is always on the same level. You do not blame a horse for being a horse, but that does not make it the same as a man,[32] and even though wickedness is not committed by free will and is

---

[30] Cf. *Ethics* III, Preface.
[31] Cf. *ibid* and *Epp*. XXI and XXIII.
[32] *Ep*. LXXVIII. Observe, once again, how Spinoza implicitly ranges things in a scale of degrees of perfection or reality.

the result of necessary causes, that does not make it desirable or less pernicious,[33] nor does it equate it with righteousness.

A man who acts from passion behaves under the influence of external causes, for such action is merely the practical expression of imagination and confused thinking, which is the mental aspect of the effects upon the body of outside causes. Such behaviour, therefore, is neither free nor responsible. But men are conscious of themselves and of their passions and through reflection can form true and adequate ideas of things, and so act from the necessity of their own nature alone. Such action is free, though not undetermined. It is determined by reason, yet it is free because autonomous. Equally, rational action, which is determined by the intellect alone, is for that reason eminently responsible, as it is what the agent does of himself. And as intellect and will are one and the same, in such action the will is free, in the same sense as God (with whose intellect our ideas coincide when they are adequate) is a free cause, and acts as freely and as necessarily as he thinks.

On this foundation Spinoza develops a system of ethics that is both consistent and morally satisfying. It is consistent in that it advocates love and compassion while it does not, like so many other moral creeds, revile the dissolute and the wayward. Wickedness, Spinoza holds, is in itself and in its consequences evil and repulsive. It requires no further punishment so that the wicked are not to be castigated so much as pitied. In the Short Treatise where he treats of Devils he says that, if there were such an epitomy of evil, they would be infinitely pathetic objects only to be pitied, and the proper attitude to them should be only to desire their conversion. But, in fact, as evil is nothing positive but is (like error) only privation of "reality" (see p. 152 ff below), no such beings as devils can exist.[34] The morality he envisages is one of benignity and toleration. Before entering upon its details we may do well to outline the summary which Spinoza himself gives at the end of the second part of the Ethics of what he calls the advantages (or usefulness) for living conferred by his doctrine:

(i) It teaches us that we do everything by the will of God and that our actions become more perfect the more we understand God. This gives the greatest repose to the mind and teaches us that our highest happiness consists in the knowledge of God alone, by which we are persuaded to do only what love and piety dictate. Beyond this we seek no reward, "as if virtue itself and the service of God were not happiness itself and the highest liberty."

---

[33] Ep. LVIII.
[34] Cf. K.V. II, Ch. XXV.

(ii) It teaches us to accept and bear with equanimity the accidents of fortune and what is not within our control.

(iii) It conduces to social harmony, for it teaches us not to hate, envy, despise, mock, or rile against anybody. Also it teaches us to be contented with our lot and to be helpful to others, not from sentimental pity, partiality or superstition, but as reason, time and circumstance demand.

(iv) Finally it gives guidance to the community in so far as it shows how society should be governed in order that citizens should not be subservient but should do freely what is for the best.

In succeeding chapters we shall try to show how Spinoza develops his ethical and political doctrines so as to reach these admirable results.

PART IV

HUMAN WELFARE

CHAPTER VII

GOOD AND EVIL

In different works, and in different contexts of the same work, Spinoza has made differing statements about the nature of good and evil, creating an appearance at times of inconsistency and at least of confusion. But once again this is only appearance, for the differing accounts are not incompatible and each statement can be given its appropriate place in his system so that they can be seen to cohere. I shall begin by listing and explaining these apparently diverse accounts and shall then show how they fit together in a comprehensive grasp of Spinoza's total system.

1. Aids to the Imagination

(i) He repeatedly denies the applicability of the adjectives "good" and "bad" to Nature as a whole, or, for that matter to any of its parts.[1] Everything in Nature is as it is, and Nature as a whole is "perfect." But the term "perfect" is to be understood simply as meaning completely real (*Ethics* II, Def. vi). This is clearly the case with respect to God or Nature; and every mode of substance, in so far as each is a necessary part necessarily occupying its determinate place in the entire system, is a necessary factor in that perfection.

(ii) As we commonly use the words "good" and "evil," however, they are merely relative terms and relations we are told, are simply *entia rationis* and do not exist or refer to anything that does exist. All that exists in reality are things (*zaaken, res*) and actions (*werkingen, actiones*).[2] They are relative in two senses: first relative to human desires, for what we desire and find pleasant we call good, and what we find unpleasant we call evil, and this may vary as between different people;[3] and, secondly, relative to circumstances, for what seems better in one set of circumstances

---

[1] Cf. *K.V.*, I, vi; *Epp.* XIX, XXI, XXIII; and *Ethics* IV, *Praef.*
[2] Cf. *K.V.* I, x, and *Ethics* IV, *Praef.*
[3] Cf. *K.V. loc. cit.; Ethics* I, App., and *loc. cit.*

seems worse in another. "For example, music is good to the melancholy, bad to those who mourn and neither good nor bad to the deaf." [4]

Here, however, we must issue a *caveat*. Spinoza's remark that relations are only *entia rationis* and do not exist in nature is made in what is probably his earliest work, and should not be taken as evidence that he excluded all distinctions from reality. We have already seen good reason to hold that he conceived substance as essentially self-differentiating and self-diversified. But comparisons *as we make them* between different appearances are largely and most frequently the product of *imaginatio*; and we ourselves say of many ideas, when we mean to dismiss them as illusory, or at best as just aids to thinking, that they are "merely relative." Such, for instance, are ideas of largeness and smallness, weight (as opposed to mass), strength and weakness, and so forth. So when Spinoza speaks of relations as unreal he is referring to *imaginatio* and the false distinctions that it constantly makes, not to the true essences of things as understood by *scientia intuitiva* in the light of the attribute of Substance to which they belong.

(iii) It would seem to follow that if good and evil are merely relative terms, they are nothing real, and indeed that is what Spinoza maintains.[5] He asserts very clearly that evil (at least) is nothing positive. For what we call evil is held to be so by comparison with something regarded as good, either because that is more complete according to our idea of what it should be (e.g. a blind man lacks what we conceive should belong to the complete or "perfect" man), or because it gives us more pleasure (*laetitia*) than what we are judging to be bad. In either case the badness of the thing is the result merely of what it lacks, is a mere privation. Obviously this is so in the first case, and, in the second, what gives us pain does so because it is concomitant of imaginative or inadequate ideas, which are fragmentary (and so false), that is, they are inadequate, false and painful because of deficiency or privation.[6]

(iv) The term "perfection" as opposed to "imperfection" originally refers to human intentions. If a craftsman intends to make some artifact, or if a man intends to carry out some plan, when the work is completed (either the work of art or craft or the plan as conceived) we say that it is perfected (*perfectum* or fully made). We then say that something is im-

---

[4] *Ethics* IV, *Praef.*, Cf. *TdIE.*, I, 1 & 9, *V.V.L.* I pp. 3-5.

[5] *Ethics* IV, Praef.: "*Bonum et malum, quod attinet, nihil etiam positivum in rebus, in se scilicet consideratis, indicant, nec aliud sunt praeter cogitandi modos, . . .*" "So far as good and evil are concerned, they too indicate nothing positive in things, considered that is to say in themselves, nor are they anything other than ways of thinking . . ."

[6] Cf. above pp. 92, 96-98, and *Epp.* XIX, XXI and XXIII to Blyenbergh.

perfect so far as it falls short of completion. Next we transfer the term to natural objects because we form general ideas of them according to the properties they have in common and which strike our imaginations most strongly. What conforms to such a general idea (for example of horse or man) we say is perfect and what lacks any of the distinctive properties which we combine in that idea (e.g. a lame horse or a deaf man) we call imperfect. But in actual reality there is nothing positive that corresponds to these terms, which are only terms of comparison. General ideas are abstractions and at best only aids to the imagination; and human intentions are variable and human artifacts have "value" only via relation to human desires.[7]

(v) Not unconnected with the accounts of good and evil so far listed, is the equation of these terms with what is and what is not profitable to man. In the Appendix to *Ethics* I, Spinoza writes: "Here it will be sufficient if I take as fundamental what ought to be conceded by everybody . . . that all men have an appetite, of which they are conscious, to seek what is useful to them (*suum utile*)." And "after men have persuaded themselves that all things which have come into existence have been produced for them, it follows that they judge that to be most important in each thing which is most useful to themselves, and assess as most valuable all those things by which they are most beneficially affected. Whence, of necessity, they form those notions by which they explain the nature of things, such as *good, evil, order, confusion, . . .* etc."

Once again it is the way in which men imagine things in conjunction with the affects these imaginings produce in their minds that leads them to judge the imagined causes of their affects good and bad. So that, for the most part the ascription of these predicates is inept, variable and inaccurate.

In all these ways the terms "good" and "evil" may be explained as standing for confused ideas typical of the imagination, which uses them as aids in its comparison of one thing with another according to its attractiveness or repugnance. But Spinoza gives other accounts of ways in which we may use "good" and "evil" and "perfection" which are less subject to the strictures and limitations of the above uses. Let us next consider them.

2. True Good and Supreme Good

It is a universal propensity in all things, including man, that they strive to persevere in their own being; and, in conscious beings like ourselves,

---

[7] Cf. *Ethics* IV *Praef.*

we have already learnt, this *conatus* is felt, and we are conscious of it as an urge to increase our capacity for acting. What enables us to do this is "useful," or "profitable" to us in a proper sense of those words and we may consequently regard it as good. On the other hand, what reduces our active capacity gives rise to painful affection and is said to be evil. We are thus led to two further ways in which the terms "good" and "evil" may be used, which Spinoza sanctions as legitimate, and this is how he defines the terms in the fourth Part of the *Ethics*: "I. By good I understand that which we know for certain to be useful to us. II. By evil, however, that which we know for certain hinders us from the possession of any good."

In the unfinished *Treatise concerning the Improvement of the Understanding,* having maintained (as he does elsewhere) that good and evil, perfect and imperfect are merely relative terms, and that rightly understood all things are produced according to an eternal order and certain necessary laws, Spinoza proceeds to say that human weakness is unable to follow that order, and so men conceive an ideal of human nature much more steadfast and capable than their own, and see nothing that stands in the way of their acquiring it. So they are moved to seek the means which will lead to this perfection of themselves, and they call whatever serves as such means truly good. Actual success in acquiring and enjoying this perfected nature, man then regards as the supreme good, each seeking it for himself along with as many others of his fellow men as is possible. And that supreme good, Spinoza says he will show in its proper place, is the knowledge of the union of the mind with the whole of nature.[8]

In the Preface to the Fourth Part of the *Ethics,* he virtually repeats these statements. Having explained at length the relative and variable uses of the terms ("good" and "evil"), he says that he will continue to use the terms, because he wishes to frame an idea of human nature that may be regarded as an ideal (*exemplar*). Thus whatever we know for certain is a means to the progressive approach to the ideal, he will call "good," and he will call "bad" whatever hinders or prevents that progress.

3. Perfection

Further, when a man is said to pass from a less to a greater perfection, or *vice versa,* this is to be understood to mean that he approaches nearer to or recedes further from, the conceived model of human nature, not that he changes his essence – for "a horse would be destroyed as much if

[8] *TdIE.,* II, 13.

it were changed into a man as if it were changed into an insect" – rather we must understand it as meaning that his power of acting, as far as that is understood through his own nature, is increased or decreased.

In general, however, perfection must be understood as meaning the same as reality, that is to say, the essence of each thing itself so far as it exists and acts in a certain manner, without reference to its duration. For nothing is considered more perfect simply because it has lasted for a long time. (*Ethics* IV, *Praef. loc. cit.*)

4. One coherent doctrine

Now in all these various, and perhaps seemingly conflicting, statements about good, evil, perfection and imperfection, there is nothing really incoherent; nor shall we think them so if we keep in mind Spinoza's distinction between *imaginatio,* on the one side, with its inadequate ideas, and, on the other, the adequate thinking of *ratio* and *scientia intuitiva.*

The world, Nature, God, Substance, is absolutely complete, in the fullest sense real and, therefore, in the most proper sense perfect, both as a whole and in every detail. But within this whole there are grades or degrees of "perfection" differing according as the essences of the things concerned are more or less comprehensive – nearer to or further from the wholeness which constitutes Substance. Infinite modes are more real (or perfect) than finite, and finite modes, as we have seen, may be less or more complex, less or more apt to do and suffer many things together, less or more capable of action, both physical and mental; and their degree of perfection will depend on the extent to which they are autonomous, or self-sufficient in their activity and effectiveness. In man, the measure of his self-dependence is the degree to which he thinks adequately, and of his impotence the degree to which he thinks inadequately.

Accordingly, the true good for man is what enables him to perfect his intellect, whatever helps him to frame adequate ideas and so increase his power of acting – his dependence for action solely upon his own essence. And we can know what that is for certain, if and only if we do think adequately. Thus we can form an adequate idea of the perfection of man, which, the more clearly we understand it, the more fully we realize, is knowledge and love of God and consequent atonement with him. Of this, as Spinoza says in *TdIE.,* we shall speak in its proper place. Meanwhile, this is what we are to understand as the model or exemplar of human nature and may legitimately refer to as man's perfection, and in relation to this ideal and their contribution to it, or their failure to contribute to its realization, we may call things good or bad for man.

But this is far from being the way good and evil are thought of by the general run of men, who for the most part think imaginatively and are "led by blind desire," subject to passion and driven this way and that by their lusts, like waves of the sea swept by contrary winds. To them good and bad are whatever happens to please or displease. The ends they pursue are the objects of their casual and fortuitous desires; what seems good to one seems evil to another and to a third is wholly indifferent; and the same thing at different times may appeal differently to the same man, or leave him quite unaffected. In these circumstances, the terms "good" and "bad" are purely relative, and designate no real or stable property in anything.

In confused imaginative thinking we form general ideas of things and we then call them perfect or imperfect according as they happen to conform or not to conform to the ideas we have formed of them. But as these general ideas are themselves only ways of thinking, mere aids to the imagination, the terms "perfect" and "imperfect," thus applied, are no better; and they indicate nothing real in the nature of things, which considered in themselves are neither "good" nor "bad," "perfect" nor "imperfect," as these terms are used and applied in imaginative thinking. In short, our confused ideas of good and evil at this level of thinking are simply false, and, when they are attributed to God, simply ludicrous. "And in this manner (men) ignorantly attribute imagination to God himself," says Spinoza. "But while they seek to show that Nature does nothing in vain (that is, what is not useful to man) they seem to have shown nothing other than that Nature and gods are just as insane as men." [9]

Nevertheless, even in imaginative thinking men are impelled by the urge to persist in their own being, or essence, and so to increase their own power of acting. Consequently, what actually does increase that power really is useful to them, although at the level of *imaginatio* they think so confusedly that they fail to see what that is. The more they come to think adequately (and by what means they come to do so we shall see presently), the more will they understand what really is of advantage to them, while at the same time they will actually be acquiring it. Then they will be brought to comprehend their true good, and will be able to form an adequate idea of perfection. Then they will see how it properly applies to God or Nature, and so derivatively to themselves as an ideal worthy of pursuit.

The moral ideal is thus directly and logically derivative from the nature of man, from the nature of his feeling and knowing, as that is

[9] *Ethics* I, App.

derivative from the nature of substance. Whatever may be the opinions of later thinkers concerning the relation of fact to value, of Hume and Kant along with their present-day successors for instance, Spinoza's doctrine is a demonstration *in extenso* of the possibility of deducing the ought from the is – the morally binding from the factually necessary. The key to this derivation is, of course, the teleological character of Spinoza's thinking, rooted in his identification of the true and the good ultimately with the infinite completeness of the whole (i.e. with God), and his conception of essence, whether of substance or of finite modes, as dynamic: in the one case a power of being and of creating, in the other, a *conatus* to self-preservation and the augmentation of the power of action.

Failure to appreciate this characteristic of Spinoza's thought is the source of many errors of interpretation among his commentators who seize upon the factual and descriptive aspect of his exposition and accuse him of obscuring, or abolishing, the axiological aspect. They then find elements in his doctrine which imply recognition of the latter and accuse him further of inconsistency.

5. Spinoza and Plato on the Good and the Expedient

We find in Spinoza, much as we do in Plato,[10] an explanation and a reconciliation of the ideas of advantage or profit, and of moral goodness. What men by and large pursue and what they see as their advantage, is what they happen to desire and that for the most part is the result of passion and confused thinking (what Plato would have called *eikasia* or, at best, *doxa*).[11] But in desiring and pursuing such ends, which are largely delusive and ultimately frustrating,[12] they are nevertheless motivated by an innate urge towards what, if they could see it clearly and distinctly, would be their true advantage or ultimate good. For Plato, this urge is Eros, and the true knowledge of the Good is *epistēmē*. But in pursuing the objects of casual desire, under the influence of the passions, men are pursuing illusory ends. What they take to be their advantage is really quite the contrary, for it makes them even more subject to passion, even more the plaything of fortune and chance. Moreover, it generates within them conflicts, which distract and frustrate them as individuals,[13] while it drives them into mutual hostility which undermines those conditions of social living upon which their welfare depends.[14]

[10] Cf. *Gorgias* and *Republic,* I-IV.
[11] Guesswork or mere opinion.
[12] Cf. the opening passages of *TdIE.*
[13] Cf. *Phaedo,* 66b.
[14] Cf. *Republic* VIII and IX.

What men commonly see as their advantage, therefore, and what they regard as expedient, is just the opposite, and, from the point of view of adequate thinking, and by comparison with what, if properly conceived, really is their advantage, is evil. Thus, as Plato tells us, the philosopher who knows the true nature of justice and virtue, sees that, and understands why, the tyrant is the weakest and most miserable of men. He knows that justice, so far from being the "advantage" of the stronger (or the ruler), is the true advantage of the whole community served by each of its members according to his capacity. He knows, further, that ultimate happiness and satisfaction is to be found only in the highest knowledge.[15]

Spinoza propounds a similar doctrine. The passionate man, a slave to his desires sees as his advantage what is really only a figment of his imagination. What pleasure he may gain from it is both precarious and illusory. For, not only will it involve conflicts of desire and vacillation of mind, but as it is the effect of causes mostly outside his own control it is very uncertain of achievement, and as liable as not to lead to a decrease in his power of action which is actually the opposite of the pleasure he seeks. Such putative advantage (or expediency), therefore, is really the exact contrary of the true good for man. It is what hinders, not what assists, his progress towards greater capacity for action.

The pursuit of desires, therefore, and subjection to the passions, the libidinous, the jealous, the irascible, the vengeful, the cunning, the avaricious and, in general, all such conduct as the wise man, who thinks rationally, would see to be "wicked," is sheer misery. It is not so much to be censured, in Spinoza's view, though it is never to be approved, as to be pitied. The proper attitude towards vice is not indignation and wroth, which would themselves be simply other examples of wickedness. Rather it is pity and compassion coupled with the effort to convert the depraved and assist the wayward to find the right path. The devil, we are told (K.V., II, xxv.), if there were, or could be, such a being, would be a most miserable creature, deserving only compassion.

The notion, therefore, that God could be angry with the sinful and devise special pains for them as punishments, is arrant nonsense, once again setting God on the level of the man of imagination and passion. Sin is its own punishment, and God (not being subject to passion) has no resentment or any other sentiment towards man for his conduct. Equally, we shall find, virtue is its own reward. But punishment of law-breaking

---

[15] Cf. *Republic* I, IV, VI, IX.

in society is quite another matter, and we shall examine the principles which should regulate that at a later stage of our discussion.

Just as for Plato all desire is for the good (if only we could know what it really and truly is), so for Spinoza the *conatus*, consciousness of which is desire in us, is always for a greater power of acting – or, if you prefer, of being your real self, of maintaining your own essential being. Accordingly, man's real or true good, what, if he could but know it, he always wants, is what truly increases his power of action. And that is strictly nothing other than adequate thinking. So man's real perfection is to be achieved, in the last resort, only in the contemplative life, which will lead him ultimately to the true knowledge and love of God. Moreover this, as we shall see, does not conflict with, but requires and involves, the love and service of his fellow men. It is not an exhortation to forsake the practical life and neglect one's social duties. Political principles and the means of social order flow from it just as well and just as necessarily as do moral principles. For this ultimate ideal of human nature provides the key to human happiness and final satisfaction as well as to the proper ordering of human relationships.

6. Moral Weakness

Just as there is a parallel between Spinoza's theory of goodness and advantage and that of Plato, so his view would seem to share with Plato's the difficulty of accounting for moral weakness and the actuality of moral evil in the deliberate choice by man of what he clearly knows to be wrong. Plato maintains that nobody can do evil voluntarily, for once he really and truly knows that it is evil he can no longer prefer it to the alternative, which he knows to be good, and thus he cannot choose voluntarily to do what he knows to be wrong.[16] But Plato's critics, like Aristotle, assert that this view is contrary to the facts and that men frequently do choose to act in ways that they clearly know to be evil and wrong.[17] Moral turpitude *par excellence,* say the critics, is the deliberate choice of what we know to be evil. Even though we may rationalize our choice and produce what seem to be excellent arguments in support of it, such arguments are really only given in what Sartre calls "bad faith." They are how we deceive ourselves and others that our moral failure is really not culpable. Such action is responsible action and for that reason is essentially evil; and it really happens.

Spinoza's position once more seems not unlike Plato's. Behaviour

---

[16] Cf. *Gorgias,* 467c-468b; *Meno,* 77c-78a.
[17] Cf. Aristotle, *Nicomachean Ethics,* Book VII.

which he identifies as vicious is that in which we are overcome (at least in some measure) by passion. Its causes, therefore, include external things and it is not solely due to our own nature or *conatus*. Thus we are not fully, if at all, responsible for such action. We may be said in some sense to do it voluntarily, for will, so far as Spinoza recognizes it, is the same as desire, and, in vicious behaviour, we do follow our desires. But such behaviour is externally determined and is not properly our own doing. It is really only in virtuous, or rational, action that we are fully responsible and the act is fully our own. It would seem, therefore, that we can never deliberately choose, with full and clear knowledge of the nature of the action, to do what is vicious, for to act with clear knowledge is to be free of passion, which is the result of only partial knowledge, or imaginative thinking.

But this is not the whole story and is not an adequate representation or understanding of Spinoza's position. True it is that man's action when fully responsible and autonomous is rational and virtuous; but no such action is devoid of emotional tone or can be effected without conation. It must be motivated by some "exertion." Nevertheless, when a man knows clearly what is right it does not follow automatically that he will act accordingly, for the accompanying "exertion" may be insufficient. No idea *per se* is the cause of any bodily motion, for each is a mode in a different attribute; and, further, "nothing positive in a false idea is removed by the presence of a true idea, in so far as it is true" (*Ethics* IV, i). Thus the appearances of the sun as only 200 feet away is not immediately removed by the knowledge of its true distance, and, when it is reflected in water, though we know the contrary, it still appears to be in the water (ibid. S.). For the same reason, a false idea may still have a strong emotional appeal, even after it is seen to be false. Again, no passion can be overcome except by a stronger passion (*Ethics* IV, vii); and finally the power of man, as a finite being, is always surpassed by the effects of external causes (*Ethics* IV, iii).

It is very easily possible, therefore, for a man to know what is good and to be overcome nevertheless by desires which are not good; and so far as he is conscious of his appetites he knows what he is doing and chooses voluntarily to do it. Spinoza can, accordingly, accommodate in his theory a perfectly consistent account of moral weakness, which, though not altogether the same as Aristotle's, is not very different. We shall have occasion to return to it in the next chapter, but before we proceed let us remind ourselves that the voluntary choice which Spinoza identifies with desire is not the exercise of free will. That he emphatically denies. Choice is never uncaused, and, in the case of moral weakness, when passive desires overcome active emotions, it is not rational or self-caused. Its unfreedom is in itself part of the fact that it is evil, but that remains a relative term. For evil is evil only in that it falls short of what is better. Absolute evil would be sheer negation, pure nothingness, complete absence of all reality, or positive action of any kind; and that would not be moral conduct at all. Even the man who deliberately does what he knows by certain standards to be wrong, does it because it appeals to him as in some way good – or he could not desire it – that is what accounts for his rationalizations and self-persuasion, bad faith though they well may be. After all, to say that he "rationalizes" his action only means that he tries to make it seem right, both to himself and to others – that he recognizes the rational criterion as ultimately valid and, if only tacitly and implicitly, submits to it. His action cannot, therefore, be wholly and utterly evil, but always has in it some seeds and potentiality of good; and that precisely, is what is positive in the act – it is that through which the agent strives to persevere in his own being – whereas what is evil is the negative aspect.

Another objection frequently raised to the position common to both Plato and Spinoza is that it makes all moral action, even the best, merely selfish, for it is always the pursuit of one's own (best) advantage. It would seem impossible, accordingly, if not actually immoral, on such a view, to forego one's own advantage for the sake of that of another. Selfishness and unselfishness, however, as generally understood, refer only to the imaginative conception of advantage (or to what Plato would have called "opinion"). The advantage that a selfish man pursues at others' expense, turns out, if understood rightly, to be no advantage at all. It consists in his enjoying certain pleasures while depriving others of them, or acquiring wealth at others' expense, or achieving honour or position or social predominance by repressing the legitimate claims of other men. We shall find as we investigate the matter further and have already seen to some extent, that action of this kind merely gratifies the passions, generates conflicts and anxieties, disillusion and remorse, and is in fact no true good for the selfish individual; nor incidentally is it truly evil for those apparently deprived. What is truly good for anybody proves to be equally good for all, and is strictly only enjoyable in concert and community.

Unselfishness, therefore, if it is the pursuit of the real advantage of others will turn out to be equally the real good of the unselfish person. If performed through mere sentiment, or a desire for approval (whether one's own or that of one's associates) it is not genuine unselfishness, the motive for which must be solely the others' true good. It is not enough to indulge his appetites or grosser desires, for that is not really in his interests. What really is in the last resort for his benefit is that he should himself become a morally good person – or in Spinoza's terms, a free man. But that, as we shall see, is equally in the interest of the person bestowing the benefit, for the true good is common to all.

Moreover, it is psychologically impossible to act deliberately for an approved end without judging it to be in some sense good. Both Plato and Spinoza are entirely right on this point. Even when I do out of weakness what I know to be wrong I do it because it appeals to me at the time as in some sense desirable and attractive. And when I act in the interests of others, it is either because their good means more to me than the conveniences or pleasures I forego; or else it is because, as we say, I could not live with myself, if I neglected them, let them down, or callously ignored their needs. For any action to be deliberate, responsible and properly speaking voluntary, it must have some self-regarding aspect, otherwise it is not something which I consciously choose to do. And it is only responsible acts which are subject to moral judgement.

7. The Reality of Evil

Theories like those of Plato and Spinoza seem to many to involve yet another serious and rather complex difficulty, not unrelated to the last two. Plato believed that ultimately everything is what it is "because it is best for it to be so," [18] and from that it should follow that nothing can ever be what it ought not to be and that evil does not exist. Likewise, in morality, both Spinoza and he held that whatever we deliberately choose to do, we do because we believe it to be good, and it is only when we are ignorant and misconceive the good that we go wrong. So, in a sense, all moral evil is nothing but ignorance and error which would be dispelled if only our knowledge were complete and perfect. And even our blunderings are not part of reality because they take place in and are the products of, the sensible world of changing appearances which is not in truth the real world, either for Spinoza (so far as it is the product of *imaginatio*) or for Plato (so far as it is not wholly intelligible).

Everything, Spinoza asserts, follows necessarily from the infinite and eternal essence of Substance. It could not be other than it is, and to say that it "ought to be" different is to use words without meaning. "Ought" and "ought not" apply only to the way we wish things to be. Good and

---

[18] Cf. *Phaedo* 98b.

evil are relative only to our desires, or, at best, to standards we have ourselves devised, they are largely the product of imagination and are based
upon illusion. Both what we commonly take things to be and our satisfaction or dissatisfaction with the way they are result from distorted and
truncated thinking, so that our ideas of good and evil are, for the most
part, false and unreal. The final outcome seems to be that ultimately evil
is not real, that what we take to be evil is mere illusion and in the world
itself evil does not exist.

The critics object that even if it were true that our ideas of evil are
illusions, the very fact that we make such errors and are the victims of
illusion is itself an evil, to be free from which would be a good, irrespective
of our desires. But, surely, it is *not* true, for all the suffering endured,
often needlessly, by mankind and animals is palpably evil. It is not itself
illusory nor is its disvalue, and no amount of knowledge or correct thinking could dispose of either. Nor can they be written off as mere privation.
We might be more hesitant about the good [19] because the best of our
experiences leave something still to be desired; and there is less agreement, more doubt and more dispute about what ultimately is good. But
everybody agrees that intense and needless suffering is evil and admits
that it occurs. Is this not an insuperable obstacle to the adoption of a
theory like Spinoza's?

The question of the reality of evil is a large one the full discussion of
which would take us beyond the bounds of our subject. I shall consider
here only how Spinoza does or could consistently reply to it, leaving aside
whatever might be said in addition to his theory.[20] Spinoza's answer,
however, is one of the most penetrating and is more satisfying than many
another, so in confining ourselves to his view we may not be neglecting
much of great importance.

First we must insist that the summary of Spinoza's position given
above, though not inaccurate, is incomplete and it has frequently been
sadly misinterpreted. What we have already said should have made it
clear that it is a misrepresentation of his position to declare unreservedly
that nothing in reality is either good or evil, and that the terms are only
applicable to and in the illusions, themselves inconstant, of the finite
mind. Nevertheless, the misinterpretation is common and persistent.
God, he is often alleged to hold, neither is nor contains good or evil and

[19] Despite Plato's confident identification of the Good with ultimate reality. But
our object here is to discuss Spinoza's position, not Plato's, and Spinoza seems *prima
facie* to deny the reality of both good and evil.
[20] The topic is discussed in my *Revelation through Reason* (Yale University Press,
New Haven, 1958, Allen & Unwin, London, 1959) Ch. VI.

is indifferent to both, and his view of the world is represented as a fixed and rigid system which just is what it is, and to which value judgements are inapplicable and irrelevant. As for man, so the misinterpretation continues, having no free will of his own, even if there were any such thing as goodness in the world or in his nature, he could not freely or deliberately try to realize it, and so should strictly speaking be incapable of moral action. Whether he acts well or ill by any criterion, his acts are equally caused and determined by God, who is indifferent to both evaluations.

So van Blyenbergh objects to Spinoza: "Therefore, it seems clearly to follow from your position that God wills villainies in one and the same way as he wills those acts which you call by the name of virtue." And further: "You say, as I see, that the upright worship God; but from your writings I cannot grasp anything other than that to serve God is only to do such acts as God has willed that we should do; and you ascribe the same to the wicked and licentious. What difference is there then, in relation to God, between the service of the upright and of the wicked? You say also that the upright serve God, and by service continually become more perfect. But I do not understand what you mean by 'become more perfect' nor what 'continually become more perfect' signifies. For both the impious and the pious receive their essence and the conservation, or continuous creation of their being from God, as God and not as judge, and both in the same way fulfil his will, according to God's decree." [21]

To this Spinoza replies, as we have noted before (p. 97 above), that God cannot be the cause of evil, error or villainy, because what makes these evil is mere negation and does not consist in anything that expresses essence. He objects further that not all things are on the same level of perfection: "Finally," he proceeds, "I should like it to be noted that although the actions of the upright (that is, of those who have a clear idea of God in accordance with which all their actions, as also their thoughts, are determined) and of the wicked (that is of those who scarcely possess an idea of God, but only ideas of earthly things, according to which their actions and thoughts are determined) and lastly, of all who exist, flow necessarily from the eternal laws and decrees of God and continually depend on God; nevertheless they differ from one another, not only in degree, but also in essence. For allow that a mouse is equally dependent upon God with an angel, and pain (*tristitia*) equally with pleasure

[21] *Ep.* XXII.

(*laetitia*), yet it is not possible for a mouse to be an angel nor pain to be a kind of pleasure." (*Ep.* XXIII).

We can see what in Spinoza's doctrine might prompt such misconceptions, but also we should now be able to realize how far they are distortions of his true intentions. There is, for him, a sense in which what men commonly take to be good and evil are mere illusions and the product of imagination. But it does not follow that because men can often be mistaken, good and evil have no legitimate meanings. Man thinks inadequately, when he does, because he is a finite mode of substance, but finite modes themselves are not the products of illusory thinking. They do actually exist, even if temporal and spatial appearances are, in some measure at least, dependent on our imagination and so, *ipso facto,* are incomplete and fragmentary. Moreover, as they actually are in themselves, finite things differ in the degree of their perfection. Yet the very nature of reality is such that finite partial modes strive to maintain themselves in their own true essence. That essence is a necessary element in the whole, is made what it is by the whole, and can be conceived adequately only in and through the whole. Therefore, the whole is immanent in it; and that immanence is its *conatus,* its own essence or power, which is at the same time the power and essence of God manifesting itself and working through the finite mode. This *conatus* is a striving towards greater completeness or perfection and epitomizes the teleological aspect of Spinoza's system as I have explained it above.[22]

For all these reasons: man's propensity to imagination (fragmented thinking) and passion, as well as his capacity for adequate conception; his consequent *conatus* or urge to realize his own true essence as an intellectual being, whose nature it is to frame true ideas; the power of God immanent in his nature, which impels him constantly to know, understand and thus (as we shall see) to love God – for all these reasons, there is a legitimate and very significant sense in which a distinction may be drawn between good and evil, and a sense in which man can act and be morally responsible, and can strive to realize a perfection in which alone he finds ultimate satisfaction.

It is also true that God or Substance, reality as a whole, is precisely what it is, for it lacks nothing. It is perfect in the sense of being absolutely complete, and what in it appears to us as evil is only relative to our uncomprehending desires and the deficiency of our imaginative knowledge. If, and so far as, we see such "evils" in proper perspective, in their full circle of relations, both physical and moral, and realize that there is still much

[22] Pp. 129-132.

that we cannot comprehend, we see that what to us seems evil in these things is merely privation, and affects us adversely only because of the mutilated view of the whole which we entertain. Nevertheless, that substance is as a whole fully complete and perfect does not entail that the whole of this reality is present and realized everywhere and at all times. And because God "does not lack the means for creating all things from the highest to the lowest degree of perfection," there are in his infinite nature all possible gradations. Thus there is also a legitimate sense in which we may say that even in God there are less and more perfect phases of his being, in the infinite series of causes and effects that flow necessarily from his eternal essence, and in the process of continual augmentation, or evolution, of bodies and the concomitant purification or "improvement" of the understanding. Evil, therefore, is real, but only as the incident of a low grade of perfection, and it is sublated and overcome at higher grades. Hence it remains relative: absolute evil would be absolute non-entity, and in the completeness of the whole of substance all evil is shed away.

If this completes the answer to objections such as Blyenbergh's, can it also dispose of the further objection, that there is unmistakable evil in excessive needless suffering which actually occurs in plenty in the world, however man may view it? Men and animals suffer, often through no fault of their own and in ways that cannot be compensated by any consequent or countervailing good. Is not such suffering inexpungeably real and such as cannot satisfactorily be explained away either as illusion or as privation, nor overcome in any perfection of the whole?

We can only infer from what Spinoza says of related matters what his answer would have been to this question. First, we must remember that pain is defined as the idea (or awareness) of the transition from greater to lesser perfection. In neither limiting term is there anything positive which corresponds to evil, which derives its meaning only from comparison of the latter with the former, indicating a merely relative property. But the transition is painfully felt and Spinoza concedes that in itself pain is never good (*Ethics*, IV, xli) because it is in itself a lessening of the subject's power of action. Nevertheless, the subject is, and in such cases must always be, a finite mode of substance, and the transition felt as pain is a minute part of the infinite process of changes and transitions which are perpetually occurring in the common order of nature. Seen as the subjection of the finite mode to the overwhelming influences of external causes it is painful. But seen in this way it is the object of *imaginatio*. Seen *sub specie aeternitatis*, it is one of the innumerable processes which are regulated to maintain the constant physical configuration of the whole universe (*facies totius universi*) and in this context, if we could but understand it (which generally we cannot), it would not be seen or (presumably) felt as a transition to lesser perfection. For the whole is complete and perfect.

Even so, pain is an ambiguous term and in Spinoza's word "*tristitia*" the sense is a feeling of dejection and frustration as much as (or more than) physical sensation. The feeling of dejection and frustration might be covered by the foregoing argument, but what of the physical sensation? In relation to that our argument seems less plausible. Possibly we ought not to identify physical pain completely with evil any more than physical pleasure is to be unreservedly identified with good. But Spinoza does say that *tristitia* in itself is always bad, even if, in certain circumstances, the goodness of *laetitia* may be called in question. If then pain is always bad, intense and needless pain, undeserved and uncompensated, must surely be unmitigated evil. Cases of deep sorrow or grief may be disposable in Spinoza's theory as the result of imaginative thinking, which, however understandable, is always remediable (as we shall see further below) by adequate thinking which sees their objects *sub specie aeternitatis* and so dispels the negative passion. But can we dismiss intense physical pain in this way?

For Spinoza such pain would be an intense awareness of transition (presumably steep and sudden) from a greater power of action in the body to a lesser. As it is physical pain we are concerned with, the transition must be conceived to have a predominantly physiological character. It will also be the result of external causes. Now Spinoza proves (*Ethics* II, xxiv, xxv, xxvii, xxviii) that our sensations do not involve adequate ideas of our own bodies, of the physiological processes that go on in them, or of the external bodies that cause the physiological changes that we feel. Therefore intense physical pain undoubtedly would be a confused and inadequate idea and would involve inadequate ideas of all of these. Adequate ideas of them, if they could be attained, would not (as we have shown above) automatically remove the sensation or its painfulness. But adequate ideas are never wholly devoid of affective value and are accompanied by active emotions. If these were strong enough they could (at least in principle) overwhelm the passive affect. Completely true knowledge of the physiological processes and their causes (a) might presumably enable us to remove the latter and so change the former as to reverse the transition from greater to less perfection, and (b) would involve a knowledge of God and his infinite modes such as altogether to transform our conception and consciousness of the body.[23]

The extent of the power of the mind over its consciousness of the body and the degree of conscious (or unconscious) control we can achieve over physiological processes is still only very partially known. Evidence from the fire-walking of fakirs in India and Roman Catholic peasants in Spain, as well as the extraordinary phenomena of hypnotic control demonstrated in psycho-somatic therapy, witness to possibilities far beyond what is commonly believed. Spinoza could hardly have had knowledge of such phenomena but he had remarkable insight into the relation of the mind to the body and undoubtedly believed in man's ability so to expand and purify his awareness of his world as completely to transmute his emotional reactions to it. In the *Short Treatise* [24] he claims that the mind, in the fourth kind of knowledge (what in *Ethics* becomes *scientia intuitiva*), becomes united with God in the same way as in *imaginatio* it is united to the finite body. In that case all pain would be banished from consciousness in a transforming sense of the totality which is complete and perfect. How this union of the mind with the whole of nature is to be understood, and whether it is consistent with Spinoza's contention that body and mind are identical in substance, are matters to which we shall give further attention in a later chapter. The outcome, in any case, is that Spinoza considered it possible for the finite entity to achieve a degree of development, both physical and mental, in which consciousness, becoming purified of error and evil, transcends pain in an all-encompassing tranquillity, an experience that Spinoza calls "blessedness."

A persistent critic may nevertheless object that at finite and imperfect levels pain is experienced and is intense, and that this cannot be obliterated or compensated by some other experience elsewhere or at another time, however sublime and joyful. In reply, we must insist that both the mind of man and still more emphatically the totality of substance are wholes or unities in which parts and phases are not separable in reality, and are imagined as self-contained, or mutually independent, only by inadequate thinking. In such a whole the states (*affectiones*) of the subordinate moments are not autonomous. In a developed and complex organism, for instance, the fate of single cells which are constantly destroyed and replaced as a condition of the health and welfare of the whole, is not significant, is in fact subsumed into and obliterated by the perfection of that whole. So the perfection (so far as attained) of the finite

---

[23] Cf. p. 240f, below.
[24] *K.V.* II, xxii, xxiii.

mind does absorb and nullify the suffering of its own finite phases, and the infinite perfection of God overrules, overcomes and transmogrifies the relative imperfection of finite phases of nature.[25]

If I have interpreted Spinoza correctly his solution of the problem of evil would include physical pain, however apparently needless and intense, in the same way as other forms of evil. That too would be incident upon a low grade of perfection. It would be possible only for finite modes incapable of adequate awareness at their particular level of finiteness but potentially capable of acquiring adequate knowledge through which their degree of perfection would become progressively increased so as to resolve and nullify the conflict causing pain. That there should be in the infinity of substance all possible gradations of perfection is, moreover, necessary; for unless God did contain such infinite variety he would be merely finite and so not God; *"quia ei non defuit materia ad omnia, ex summo nimirum ad infimum perfectionis gradum creanda."* [26] A purely "perfect" entity (in some sense of "perfect" not synonymous with wholeness or self-completion), one that excluded all finiteness or any imperfect and subordinate phase, is itself a mere product of imaginative and abstract thinking. Any such alleged "perfection" would be the blank, featureless and abstract unity of which the idealist critics of Spinoza (e.g. Joachim and Caird) complain. But, I have argued that to understand Spinoza's substance as excluding all diversity and self-differentiation is a misinterpretation; one which, I believe, Spinoza would himself have repudiated. There can be no absolute perfection that does not involve within itself all possible degrees of imperfection, which, nevertheless, it absorbs, sublates and abolishes in the final consummation of its own completeness. Only in his transcendent wholeness is it true of God that he is "of purer eyes than to behold evil?" [27]

---

[25] A truth pictorially expressed in the final speech of Demogorgon in Shelley's *Prometheus Unbound:*

> "Love, from its awful throne of patient power
> In the wise heart, from the last giddy hour
> Of dread endurance, from the slippery, steep,
> And narrow verge of crag-like agony, springs
> And folds over the world its healing wings."

[26] See p. 132 above.

[27] Habbakuk I, 13.

CHAPTER VIII

THE MASTERY OF FATE

1. Of Human Bondage

Spinoza's account of morality begins in Part IV of the *Ethics,* in his usual fashion with definition of terms. He then proceeds to explain and demonstrate man's inevitable subjection to passion and the kind of behaviour it occasions, indicating the extent to which it may be regarded as good or bad in accordance with the definition of these terms that he has given. By way of comparison and contrast, he gives an account of action according to reason and an outline of the good life, but he reserves the explanation how it is possible for man to overcome the passions and to act according to reason for the first half of Part V. For while Spinoza sees the passions as natural, and passionate behaviour as something to be treated and explained by the same geometrical (or scientific) method which he uses for everything else, and though he proves man's liability to passion to be unavoidable, he believes nevertheless that this very scientific understanding of the natural causes of passion is a step towards overcoming and controlling them. In very considerable measure man can subordinate passion to reason and can act accordingly, and his power to do this can also be demonstrated *geometrico ordine.* It is moreover only by cultivating his rational capacity that he can attain happiness, and it is for the sake of happiness, or peace of mind, that the intellect is to be cultivated, not in order to repress passion. On the contrary, it is because and so far as reason is followed that passion and suffering are overcome.

We are subject to passion because we are parts of nature, nor can we bring it about that we should not be parts of nature and should not follow the common order of nature in our every-day living (*Ethics* IV, iv, C, and App. vii). For man's body is at best a finite mode of Extension and his mind is the awareness of that body. Presently we shall see that this description requires important qualification, nevertheless it is true and inescapable that man is a finite being, and that as such his *conatus in suo esse perseverandi* is limited. It is, moreover, infinitely surpassed by the *conatus* of other finite modes by the causal influence of which he is constantly and unavoidably affected. It is, therefore, impossible that man should ever be entirely free from passion and to imagine that he could be is pure fantasy. Indeed it would not even be desirable that he should be altogether devoid of affects, for all conduct requires some motive force, and no untoward affective drive can be overcome except by some other superior in power. In short, it is only by good affects that bad ones can be subdued. Spinoza's rationalism is very far from the sort (if any such exists) which regards man as even potentially capable of acting solely from pure reason, of suppressing and disregarding emotion entirely, and of thinking and behaving in some super-refined region of pure logic. Nothing could be further from his teaching and no view of human nature more readily moved him to ridicule and contempt.[1]

The good, as we have seen, is what men desire, and what aids them in its attainment is the useful. What obstructs that attainment is bad. Further, man's desire is his consciousness of the *conatus* to persist in his own being, hence whatever assists that effort and help to preserve his existence is good and useful to him and whatever hinders him in that endeavour is evil. The good excites in him pleasure (*laetitia*) and the evil pain (*tristitia*) and his ideas of these constitute his knowledge of good and evil. Each idea is related to its appropriate affect, Spinoza tells us, as the mind is to the body (*Ethics* IV, viii). The affect, however, so far as it is a passion of the mind, is itself an idea; it is, in fact, the idea of the transition in both body and mind either from lesser to greater power of action or from greater to lesser. Thus the knowledge of good or evil is idea of an idea, and, as we learnt from Prop. xxi and its Scholium in Part II, such a reflex idea is related to that of which it is the self-aware-ness as the mind is related to the body. It is this self-reflexiveness of our knowledge of the affects that we shall shortly find of fundamental im-portance for the mastery of the passions and the ascendancy of reason in practical life. Meanwhile, we must note that power of action is what Spinoza identifies as virtue. We may summarize then by saying that what assists the *conatus* to self-preservation is good, useful and pleasant, and so far as it ministers to and increases our power of action it enhances our virtue.

We shall be misled if we accept too readily the *prima facie* appearance of hedonism in this position, for Spinoza does not identify pleasure wholly with the good nor with virtue. It is more accurate to say that the pleasant

[1] Cf. *Ethics* III, *Praef.*; *T. P.* Ch. I.

is what we commonly call good, but what may, in fact, be and often is, bad. For what presents it to us as good is for the most part imagination, which is deceptive. On the other hand, what is truly good [2] is always in some sense or degree pleasant, because by nature and definition it is, or involves, transition to a higher degree of perfection.

Virtue, moreover, is the power of acting from the essence of one's own nature alone – that is, one's own essence must be the adequate cause of the action (*Ethics* IV, Def. viii). This could never be painful in itself; but could we be perfectly virtuous and act wholly from our own essential nature (which Spinoza shows to be impossible for finite entities like men), we should be unaware of any transition from a lesser state of perfection and thus should not be conscious of good and evil, nor should we be affected by pleasure (Cf. *Ethics* IV, lxviii). The supreme good for man, therefore, if fully realized would not be identifiable with pleasure at all. It could, however, not be painful, and Spinoza calls the state of mind appropriate to it beatitude. But that is hardly an affect and certainly not a passion. It is at least analogous to God's state of mind and he can suffer no passions and experiences no affects such as pleasure or pain. "If pleasure (*laetitia*) consists in the transition to greater perfection," says Spinoza, "beatitude should certainly consist in this, that the mind is endowed with perfection itself." (*Ethics* V, xxxiii, S.)

Wolfson, accordingly, is far from correct when he writes: "There is no difference therefore between virtue and emotion, or, to be more exact, between what is called virtue and vice and the emotions of pleasure and pain (Prop. VIII)." [3] Proposition viii states that the knowledge of good and evil is nothing but the consciousness of pleasure and pain, and that conforms to Spinoza's definitions of these terms and to his teaching about good and evil as I have explained it above (Chap. VII). But virtue is the power to act from our own essential nature alone, and vice is impotence so to act caused by the supremacy of external influences, or, in other words, submission to passion. There is, therefore, considerable difference between virtue and emotion. First, emotion may or may not be active. It is more frequently passive. But virtue is action *par excellence*. Secondly, pleasure and pain are not always the same as virtue and vice. Sometimes vice may be pleasant, for it may involve transition to a greater degree of perfection which is not yet fully adequate to virtue, or the pleasure may be in various ways delusive and transitory. Consequently, though virtue is always in some sense pleasant and always more *desirable*

---

[2] Cf. p. 144 above.
[3] *The Philosophy of Spinoza*, Vol. II, p. 225.

than vicious pleasures, it cannot be identified unreservedly with the emotion of pleasure.

For example, pride is a pleasurable form of self-complacency, or self-love, according to Spinoza; that is to say, it is the affect of pleasure with oneself as the imagined cause, occasioned by the idea of oneself as doing what is approved by others.[4] But one's ideas of oneself and of one's actions as well as one's ideas of the approval of others may all be products of imagination and therefore false. As imaginative thinking they are the effects of external causes as much as or more than of one's own nature. Accordingly, although the proud man derives pleasure and encouragement from his false ideas of himself, and although this may in some way and degree enhance his power of action, it is far outweighed by the restriction of that power involved in the associated passions to which he is subject through imagination. His pleasure, such as it is, is liable to be short-lived, for his pride, as Spinoza says, is really obnoxious to everybody. His pleasure is the awareness of a transition to greater power only within limits. It is based on a misconception of the attitude of others towards him, possibly a response to the sycophantic flattery of a coterie of associates who have interested motives of their own for humouring him. Within these limits he may feel his power of action enhanced, but in so doing he is in large measure deceived and his pleasure is partial and spurious affecting only a limited aspect of his life and accompanying only a restricted and mutilated consciousness of his world. He will, therefore, at some stage become sorely disillusioned by the behaviour of others towards him, and will suffer even more and more painfully than in his former self-deception. Such pride, therefore, though in a degree pleasant, is by no means a virtue. Similarly ambition [5] which is the endeavour to do what will please others, will, so far as it succeeds, be pleasant, if only because we take pleasure in the pleasure felt by others like ourselves. But Spinoza defines ambition, as distinct from "humanity," as an effort to please the common herd so strong that, carrying it out, we injure ourselves and others. Clearly under this condition the pleasure involved cannot be virtuous and must be very circumscribed.

The relevant distinction seems to be between pleasure affecting only part of the body and mind, and pleasure affecting the whole. The former Spinoza calls titillation (*titillatio*), and the latter cheerfulness or exhilaration (*hilaritas*).[6] Titillation admits of excess and may be evil (*Ethics* IV,

---

[4] Cf. *Ethics* III, xxx and S.
[5] Cf. *Ethics* III, xxix, S.
[6] Cf. *Ethics* III, xi, S.

xliii), whereas of exhilaration we cannot have too much and it is always good (*ibid.*, xlii). Moreover, many if not all vicious pleasures are closely related to kindred virtues, into which they can be converted with a significant change in their conditions, which we shall presently examine. Thus ambition, when the desire to please others is disinterested, becomes humanity; and pride, when one's conceit of oneself as pleasing others is not self-deceptive or excessive, is self-esteem (*Acquiescentia in se ipso*), self-respect, or self-contentment.

Once again, the obscurity of the relation between pleasure and virtue can be cleared away by realizing that Spinoza thought of these matters in terms of degrees, or gradations, of reality and perfection. Pleasure and pain are incident upon transitions up or down the scale, but virtue and vice, good and evil depend upon the position on the scale and are relative, both to each other and to an ultimate ideal of human nature in which the third and most adequate kind of knowledge dominates the personality. There is some degree of good (or virtue) in every act. As we have seen, no state of body or mind is ever wholly passive; and evil, we have been told, is only negation or privation, and nothing positive in any state of affairs, or in any behaviour, is so far evil. Everything and every deed, in that it depends on God and fulfils a particular necessary function in the system of the universe has, according to its place in that system, a certain necessary perfection. Nevertheless, the degrees of such perfection in different things and in different kinds of conduct depend upon the comprehensiveness of their essences (or that of the agent in the case of conduct). A mouse is as much dependent upon God as an angel, but that does not turn a mouse into a sort of angel.

Human virtue, however, is strictly action, and that means autonomous or self-determined thought and behaviour. Pleasure on the other hand is the feeling of transition to greater perfection, which always accompanies virtuous action but is neither confined to it nor identical with it. Pleasure is common enough, but virtue is something more rare and difficult to come by. Most people, and all of us for much of the time, are in bondage to passive affects many of which are pleasant, yet our conduct is more liable to be sinful than righteous.

At the level of *imaginatio* we are subject to passions and things which please us appeal according as we imagine them to be present or imminent; those which repel us likewise do so more or less strongly in proportion to their proximity in space and time. Accordingly, the greater good, if more remote in space and time, will appear less attractive than one which is less advantageous but more accessible. Similarly evils which are anticipated in the distant future deter us less than those nearer at hand, and we are liable to embrace present pleasures though we are aware that they bring evils in their train, because the evils are not present and will occur only later. For similar reasons, pleasures and pains which are thought to be contingent affect us less strongly than others thought to be necessary, and the more probable have greater effect than the less.

True knowledge of good and evil, on the other hand is not subject to this variability with the proximity or remoteness of the object, for adequate knowledge views things *sub specie aeternitatis*. Nevertheless, true knowledge by itself cannot restrain passions, but only if and so far as it is accompanied by stronger affects than those it opposes, and as true knowledge is the mental aspect of bodily action of which the sole and adequate cause is our own essential nature, the affects it arouses are liable to be considerably exceeded by the causal influences upon the body and mind of external things. Combine this fact with the influence upon the mind of goods imagined as present, as compared with that of goods known to be future or thought to be uncertain, and it is easy to understand why we frequently know what is good and nevertheless do what is evil. "The good that I would I do not; but the evil that I would not that I do." [7]

Finite man, therefore, is always in some measure subject to passion and can never free himself entirely from evil impulses. He can never by his own efforts become completely virtuous and such virtue as he can attain is always liable to be overwhelmed by the strength of his emotions. Nevertheless, the more his body is capable of doing and suffering many things at once, the more apt is his mind for adequate thinking, and the greater, in consequence, is his power of action (or virtue); and even finite man has in his nature that capacity which, if developed and exercised, can liberate him to a significant extent from the influence of passion, and enable him to live a life of contentment, relatively free from vacillation and distraction. More than this, the power of the intellect, which in the last resort is the true essence of man, is such that it can, through the third kind of knowledge (*scientia intuitiva*), bring him to the knowledge and love of God — "the love towards an eternal and infinite being (which) feeds the mind with joy alone and is free from all pain; that is intensely to be desired and to be sought with all one's might." [8]

---

[7] *Romans,* VII, 19, Cf. Ovid, *Metam* VII 20: "Video meliora proboque deteriora sequor," quoted by Spinoza in *Ethics* IV xvii, S.

[8] *TdIE,* I, 10. I have here translated *laetitia* as "joy" as a term more appropriate to the infinite object of devotion.

2. The Mastery Over the Passions

How this supremacy over the passions may be achieved we may now consider, as Spinoza explains in the first half of Part V of the *Ethics*. I shall then return to his account of the life of Reason as described in Part IV, reserving his teaching concerning blessedness and human immortality for a later chapter.

The Stoics believed that reason had absolute power over the emotions, but, much as he was influenced by Stoic philosophy, Spinoza considered that in this they were mistaken (for reasons we have already outlined). He also disagrees with Descartes who believed that pure thought could act directly upon the body through the pineal gland and so counteract the effects of passion. This theory, Spinoza maintains, is physiologically unfounded and metaphysically unsound. It is also associated with the doctrine of an uncaused free will which Spinoza considers himself to have conclusively refuted. Not only is the anatomical evidence for Descartes's theory lacking, the nerve paths in the brain and their relation to the gland being other than Descartes supposed, but pure thinking being the direct awareness of bodily motions, is not and cannot be their cause. So these views of the way in which the mind can control and regulate the passions are dismissed by Spinoza in his preface to Part V.

He begins his own account of the matter by reminding us that the order and connexion of ideas is the same as that of the states or affections (*affectiones*) of the body. Thus our bodily states are as much a reflection of the way in which our ideas are ordered (or disordered) as *vice versa*. Accordingly, modification of our mental attitudes towards things will be concomitant with similar modifications in our physiological and emotional reactions to them. The relation between mind and body is fundamental to the correct understanding of Spinoza's ethical theory, and a brief recapitulation of the doctrine and its implications, which will serve to anticipate possible misunderstanding, will repay us at this point in the discussion.

The sole source of all passive affects as well as of confused and erroneous ideas is *imaginatio*, and that is the "feeling" or awareness of changes in our own bodies produced by external causes. The affects themselves, however, are feelings of our *conatus* or striving to persist in our own being, and the augmentation or diminution of its power by the effects upon our bodies of their commerce with external bodies. Love and hate, therefore, are the affects (respectively) of pleasure and pain associated with the objects imagined to be their causes. Consequently, any modification of the ideas affecting the imagined causal relation between the imagined external objects and the emotions felt will involve a modification of the emotions (or affects) themselves.

The causal relation, however, is (a) between an imagined object and a felt emotion, both of which are ideas, and (b) between processes in the body and its contacts with external bodies, of which the ideas are the feelings, or awarenesses. The bodily movements are not and cannot be causes of the ideas for each is in a diferent attribute; nor can the ideas be causes of bodily changes. Accordingly, it is impossible for "mere thinking" to *produce* physical or physiological changes, and similarly impossible for "mere thinking" to have any effect upon the passions, which are the awareness of the *conatus* of the body. To counteract a passion nothing is effective except another affect of equal or greater intensity. Spinoza declares, therefore, that the true knowledge of good and evil, so far merely as it is true, cannot restrain any affect, but only so far as it is considered as an affect itself (*Ethics*, IV, xiv).

For Spinoza there is no such thing as "mere thinking." All ideas are ideas of bodily states and all ideas are in varying degrees (as are all bodily states) active or passive, so that they all have emotional tone, either pleasant or painful. Any change in the content or character of an idea, therefore, is liable to carry with it a change in affective value, and at the same time it will be either the registration in idea of a bodily change or actively expressed in bodily movement. To raise the level of thinking from *imaginatio* to *ratio* is, therefore, to modify concomitantly the affect attendant upon the imaginative idea. Hubbeling misses this point when he writes: "This impotence of true knowledge is a weak point in Spinoza and does not fit well into his high estimation of this way of knowledge in the fifth book of his *Ethics*" (*Spinoza's Methodology*, p. 75.) For what Spinoza maintains is that true knowledge of good and evil is inefficacious only so far as it is merely true, but not in so far as it is affective, which it always is. And, oddly enough, Hubbeling states this position correctly in the sentence immediately prior to the one I have quoted.

In Chapter II, above, I drew attention to Spinoza's argument in *TdIE.* that, by reflection upon our ideas and especially by relating them to our idea of God, we are able to correct the errors and dispel the confusion of *imaginatio*. By such reflection, as he shows in the *Ethics*, we become aware of the characteristics common to our own bodies and to all other bodies, and are thus able to form adequate ideas of these common characters. So it becomes possible, we may conclude, to distinguish by reason between what in our imaginal ideas is due to the nature of our own body and what to the nature of external bodies. We shall thus form adequate ideas of the causes of our affects and thereby, as has just been shown, modify them. But imagination, as it is the sole source of error, so it is the sole source of passion (the passive affects); and the transition from imagination, with its inadequate ideas, to reason, of which the ideas are adequate, is a transition from passion to action. The accompanying affective tone of the rational idea is an active emotion (an "exertion") in place of the passive emotion accompanying the former imaginal idea.

Accordingly, reflection on the passions and the formation of adequate ideas of the way in which they are caused through the inadequate apprehension of the influence of other bodies upon our own, produces clear and distinct knowledge which is wholly active and not (like imagination) mainly passive. This is a transition to greater power and autonomy and so is truly good, and conduct expressive of the adequate knowledge so generated will be virtuous.

By failing to observe the self-reflective character of ideas and so (a fortiori) of reason, Wolfson completely misrepresents Spinoza's position with respect to the power of the intellect. Impersonating Spinoza he states (in the first person) what he takes to be the position thus:

". . . the only way in which an action can be changed is by another action which is stronger than the first on account of its being caused by external causes which are stronger than those which caused the first action. Now, among the external forces which determine action as well as emotions is the power of reason, or that kind of knowledge which I call the second. It is a power within us, or, if you prefer, I will call it virtue, for the original meaning of the term 'virtue' is power, and that power or virtue, when once fully developed within us, acts as do our physiological reflexes, without any intervention of what you call free will." [9]

Apparent on its face is the contradiction in this passage between the statement that the power of reason is among the *external* forces which determine action and the subsequent description of it as a power *within* us. Spinoza says quite explicitly that it is precisely because reason is not an external force that it is a power of action, as opposed to a passion,[10] or rather an imagination which is largely passive. And so far from acting "as do our physiological reflexes," reason consists of adequate ideas and is a mode of Thought, whereas our physiological reflexes are motions in the body which is a mode of Extension. The awareness, if any, of our

[9] *The Philosophy of Spinoza,* II, pp. 225-6.
[10] Cf. *Ethics* IV, xxix, dem., and V, iii, dem.

physiological reflexes would be sensation, confused ideas by no means identical with or in any way similar to the reflexive, adequate ideas of reason. No more gross an error could be made than to confuse the two. While Spinoza undoubtedly would have denied any "intervention of what *you call* free will." He did not, as we have seen, altogether deny free will as properly understood; and he identified it with reason.[11]

So Wolfson, ignoring the reflective character of reason, sees the active emotions accompanying it, which are able to counteract the passive emotions, simply as mechanical forces. That again is a failure to appreciate the distinction which Spinoza maintains between the attributes as well as the relation of substantive identity between them. Physiological reflexes may be mechanical forces (though even that description might have to be modified if all the implications of Spinoza's theory of bodies were fully developed and pressed); but ideas and emotions (which are *qua* conscious nothing other than ideas) are not and cannot be mechanical forces. Accordingly, when Wolfson argues that since reason is a part of nature for Spinoza (which is undoubtedly correct) it is "the blind tool of nature," [12] he is simply failing to understand Spinoza's conception of the nature of reason. It is indeed a part of God's intellect, but a part shared in the adequacy of its ideas by man. It is therefore clear and distinct perception of its objects, the very antithesis of blindness, a term which Spinoza applies only to the passions and to them only metaphorically.[13] For even the passions, though confused, are ideas, and a profound mistake is made by those who "look upon ideas as if they were dumb pictures on a tablet, and, being obsessed with this prejudice, do not see that an idea, so far as it is an idea, involves affirmation or negation." (*Ethics* II, xlix, S.).

Let us now return from this critical digression to Spinoza's account of the way in which reason may overcome the passions. Love and hate are affects towards objects imagined as the causes respectively of pleasure and pain; if then we can dissociate these feelings from the external objects we imagine as their causes we shall destroy the love and hatred towards the objects and the fluctuations of mind occasioned by them. Now the better we come to understand the passions and their causes by reason, the more easily we can do this. In fact an affect ceases to be a passion as soon as we form a clear and distinct idea of it, for a clear and distinct idea is by its very nature an action of the mind. Thus the better we

[11] Cf. Above p. 136, and *Ethics,* II, xlix. C.
[12] *Op. cit.,* II p. 232.
[13] *T.P.,* II, 5: "*Sed homines magis coeca cupiditate quam Ratione ducuntur.*" Note that it is desire not reason that is blind.

understand a passion the more is it in our power to control; and we can always form some adequate idea of every affect, for they all have common properties that can be grasped by *ratio*. Everybody, therefore, has some (if not an absolute) power of understanding his passions clearly and distinctly and so can bring it about that he is less subject to them.[14]

It follows that every passion, and the behaviour consequent upon it, can become an action and the same desire arising from an inadequate idea can arise from an adequate one, so that conduct which is vicious (i.e. done from bad motives) can become virtuous. To convert our passions in this way, by divorcing the emotions from their imagined causes through an adequate understanding of their real causes, should be our chief aim and concern, for we cannot devise a better remedy for the mental disturbance and distraction which the passions occasion than a clear understanding of them and their true causes.[15]

Spinoza exemplifies the possibility of converting vicious into virtuous action from the account he has already given of ambition and pride and corresponding virtuous actions which he calls piety. But we can easily find our own examples from common experience. A man who shows ill-temper and speaks brusquely to his wife when he returns home from work is mollified as soon as he realizes that his irritation is more the result of his own fatigue and hunger than of any provocative shortcomings of hers. In more extreme and abnormal cases, psycho-analysts are constantly demonstrating that as soon as a neurotic patient can be made to see and understand the source of his neurosis his behaviour becomes normal. Again, a man thinking only of his own immediate advantage, who supports a political cause (say racial equality) as a means to obtaining office and position, could equally well seek those same objectives, not as ends, but, if he thought in terms of more universal ideals, as means to fostering racial justice. In one case the motive of self-seeking ambition prompts similar behaviour to what, in the other case, is motivated by benevolent concern for the oppressed. Spinoza's contention, however, is that the virtuous action (so far as it is virtuous) always springs from adequate understanding. Mere sentimental benevolence as well as pity and remorse may well be vicious. "He who is easily touched by the affect of commiseration, and is moved by the misery or tears of another, often does something of which he afterwards repents, as much because we do nothing from emotion [or sentiment] which we certainly know to be good, as because we are easily deceived by false tears." (*Ethics* IV, l. S.).

[14] Cf. *Ethics* V, ii, iii, iv and S.
[15] *Ibid.*

But the knowledge of good and evil, which arises from adequate ideas – not that which is simply imaginative consciousness of pleasure and pain, but the reflective awareness of that experience, which is rational, – is certain knowledge; and it brings with it consequences for the affects which are of far-reaching importance. In the first place, rational knowledge sees things *sub specie aeternitatis* and recognizes events and actions as necessarily caused. It cannot therefore attribute an action to an agent as a free cause that it views as the product of innumerable causes. But it has been shown by Spinoza that an affect is more intense if its object is regarded as the sole cause of the pleasure or pain it occasions than if it is regarded as but one of many, thus it is more intense if the cause is viewed as free rather than necessary.[16] If all events are seen as necessary the affects towards them are reduced accordingly in strength and become more controllable. Thus when we are deprived of something we love we are less affected by sorrow if we reflect that the loss could by no means have been prevented.

Secondly, as reason views things *sub specie aeternitatis,* future goods are to it equal with present goods if they are intrinsically equal, and present evils seem no worse than similar ones which are more remote. The disparities of time and space which so distort the assessment of imagination can therefore be counteracted by clear and distinct understanding.

Thirdly, images related to many objects are more vivid and constant than those related to only one or a few; and what we clearly and distinctly understand are the common properties of things, which are the same in their parts as in their wholes, and so are most constantly and ubiquitously presented to us. Thus we can more easily connect images to things we clearly and distinctly understand than to such as are vague and confused, and the affects associated with those images will then become more constant and insuperable (*Ethics* V, xi, xii, xiii). Examples might be culled from psychology to support this contention. We more easily remember what has in it a systematic pattern or rational order than what is disorderly and random. Words and sentences are more easily retained than nonsense syllables; and once we have understood a proof in mathematics we can remember it more easily than if we do not see the mutual connexions of the steps and simply try to learn them by rote.

Further, to the extent that we are less subject to mental conflict and passions which distract the mind from thinking clearly, the easier it is to

[16] Cf. *Ethics,* V, v, vi, viii, ix; and III, xlix.

order and arrange the affections, or states of the body, according to the order of the intellect (V, x). This is because passions which run contrary to our nature – that is, evil passions – cloud the intellect and reduce its power of action. The less we are affected by them therefore, the more reasonably we can think and act. Accordingly, rational behaviour has a cumulative effect. The more rationally we behave, the less we are afflicted by contrary passions; and the less we are so afflicted, the more easily we can order our feelings so as to act rationally.

Therefore, says Spinoza, we should commit to memory and constantly practice general rules, or maxims, of conduct which will keep us free from damaging emotions, and so strengthen our capacity for rational thought and behaviour. What such rules might be I shall presently detail. They are at once the product of rational reflection and, when put into practice, the means of supporting and perpetuating the habits of rational reflection.

These, then are the ways in which reason can overcome the passions: not simply by demonstrating theoretically their detrimental character or by offering an alternative to imagination that is theoretically proved to be preferable; but by transforming the objects of the imagination, ordering and connecting them in a logical manner and presenting them in new contexts and in a new light, so that the emotions they arouse are of a different kind, are more active and exclusive of passive affections.

3. The Dictates of Reason

Reason requires nothing that is contrary to nature, for it is itself nothing but activity which springs solely from our own nature and is the expression of our nature *par excellence*. Our essence expresses itself in and as the endeavour to persevere in our own being, or in our nature's effort to conserve itself. But, as the whole trend of Spinoza's argument persistently establishes, the true being and nature of man is his intellect: that activity of his mental (and physical) power which is least subject to interference from, and the contribution of, external causes. The augmentation of this power is man's true good, and to seek it is what is most useful to him. The primary dictate of reason, therefore, is that we should seek what is useful to us and whatever will preserve our true essence or being. The *conatus* is thus the foundation of all virtue, which is neither more nor less than to follow the law of one's own nature.[17]

From this it follows that no man can desire to destroy himself who is led by reason, and any who do so desire must be forced to extremities by

[17] Cf. *Ethics* IV, xviii S.

external causes and consequently by passion. For none can desire to do well and be happy unless at the same time he desires to live and to act. "A free man," says Spinoza, "thinks of nothing less than of death; and his wisdom is not reflection upon death, but upon life." (*Ethics* IV, lxvii).

The more a man strives to conserve his own being the more strength (*virtus*) or virtue he acquires, for what is contrary to our nature is evil and we are averse to it, but we naturally desire what we judge to be good. To succeed, therefore, what is desirable above all is to purify that judgement – in short, as we saw at the beginning, to purify the intellect of confusion so that it will, according to its own proper nature, frame adequate (or true) ideas. "What we strive to do by reason is nothing other than to understand; nor does the mind, so far as it uses reason judge anything to be useful to it unless it conduces to understanding." (*Ethics* IV, xxvi). Consequently we know for certain what is good or evil only by knowing what leads to or hinders understanding (*Ibid.*, xxvii). Here we find the aim of all virtue and the true object of all desire. This is the Spinozistic version of the Platonic doctrine that virtue is knowledge. But whereas for Plato the highest object of that knowledge was the Idea of the Good, for Spinoza the ultimate goal of the intellect is the knowledge of God, which is the highest good for man and the consummation of virtue.

This highest good is common to all men, so the rational man will desire nothing for himself that he does not equally desire for all other men, and as nothing is more useful to man than what is akin to his own nature, nothing is more advantageous to him than the mutual cooperation of men who are led by reason.[18] No man can live in complete solitude, for none is sufficient to himself, and in order to live well, to get what they need both physically and mentally, and to protect themselves from external dangers, men must, of necessity, help one another. They do this best, most efficiently and in greatest harmony when they act according to reason. That, however, is the exception rather than the rule, and the paramount need for mutual aid demands some method for regulating men's passions and desires through law and the imposition of sanctions. The discussion of such regulation and its rationale is the subject-matter of political philosophy which we shall defer to the following chapter. Here we shall simply note the contrast between rational and irrational conduct, the superiority of the former and the ways in which the latter may be overcome and transformed.

So far as men are subject to passion they do not agree in nature, for

---

[18] Cf. *Ethics* IV, xxxv and C 1 and 2, xxxvi, xxxvii.

passions are the effect of diverse external causes and they are for that reason the negation of our own power. But, Spinoza maintains, things can be said to agree in nature only with respect to their positive powers, not in respect of what they are not. To say that things (e.g. a man and a stone) agree only in being finite, impotent, overwhelmed by alien forces, etc. is just another way of saying that they have nothing positive in common.[19] Thus passionate men come into conflict, and one who through passive affects strives to make others live as he wishes becomes hateful to them. Similarly, one who seeks to possess what can be his only if others are deprived of it is at variance with them and is apt to defeat his own ends.[20]

On the other hand, a man who tries to lead others by reason to act rationally, does not use force or vituperation, and his conduct is humane and benign. "Minds are not conquered by arms but by love and generosity" (*Ethics* IV, App. xi). So the reasonable man returns good for evil and his enemies do not yield to him through fear and weakness, but are won over by gratitude willingly to virtue. For virtue is sought for its own sake and for no subsequent reward, because there is nothing better than virtue and when it is properly understood, nothing can be preferred to it, or can be an improvement upon, or embellishment of it.[21] It is for its own sake, then, that the reasonable man seeks virtue whether for himself or on the part of others, and he succeeds (when he does) in persuading others to be virtuous, by reasoning as well as by example and benevolent action, which prevails more effectively than force in convincing other men that virtue is indeed a good in itself.

In this way Spinoza deduces from the universal impulse in men, as in all things, to persist in one's own essence and to preserve one's own being, that it is good and right to pursue one's own true advantage, and that this is nothing other than to perfect the understanding so as to come to know truly and adequately what the good for man is. From this again he concludes that action in accordance with adequate knowledge will be benevolent and altruistic so far as it reasonably seeks for others the same good as it seeks for the self and does so only by means of rational action.

4. Selfishness and Self-sacrifice

Is this doctrine merely one of enlightened selfishness? Can the principle of self-preservation really (or even plausibly) be made the foun-

---

[19] Cf. *Ethics* IV, xxxii and S.
[20] Cf. *Ethics* IV, xxxvii, S 1.
[21] *Ethics* IV, xviii, S.

dation and sole source of all morality? Could it at all convincingly account for the self-sacrifice of the Christian martyrs, or the conscientiousness of Socrates in his submission to the death penalty, or the heroism of such men as Leonidas, Regulus, or Captain Oates of the Antarctic? Is it at all compatible with the belief that "greater love hath no man than this, that a man lay down his life for his friends."

In the case of Socrates or of the Christian martyrs it might be argued that their belief in the immortality of the soul and its continued existence in a better world beyond death made the sacrifice of their lives no less an endeavour to preserve themselves (their souls) and to persist in their own true being, especially as that sacrifice was seen as a condition contributory, if not indispensable, to the attainment of immortality and salvation. Spinoza himself has a version of this doctrine that we shall examine later and which, if accepted, would reconcile such examples to his philosophy. But what of the sacrifice of men who may have no such confident conviction of disembodied survival or eternal bliss?

In the first place, no deliberate act, as I have argued above, is ever completely devoid of self-regard, even though the agent may entirely identify himself and his own well-being (in the ultimate sense of the term) with that of another for whose sake he makes the sacrifice. For Spinoza such complete mutual identification is the dictate of reason, because the good at which the reasonable man aims is identical for all men and is unattainable in full measure by any one unless attained concurrently by everybody. For men agitated by passion are contrary in nature to one another and nothing contrary to our nature is good, whereas when led by reason men agree in nature and their good is common to all, the more so in that they are by nature interdependent and cannot live solitary lives.[22]

In the second place, to rank as a genuinely moral act sacrifice must be rationally justifiable. If it is made from blind impulse, or wild passion, or superstition, it is not virtuous; yet it is still an expression of the urge of the living being to express its vitality, as prompted by imagination and as excited in extremity. But if the self-sacrifice is rational, it must be the case that the circumstances render it impossible for the agent to continue to live rationally – that is, according to principle – if the sacrifice is not made. Thus, for Socrates it was impossible to escape the death penalty imposed by the Athenians unless he committed what he knew to be injustice, and his continued life would then have been marred by what to his own conscience was wrongdoing, or irrational conduct. Thus the only

---

[22] Cf. *Ethics* IV, xxxii to xxxvi.

way to preserve his own essence, in Spinoza's sense, that is, the integrity of his own intellect, was to drink the poison. To do otherwise, as the argument of the *Crito* demonstrates, would have been to live a contradiction.

Self-sacrifice for any other reason, or for none at all, or as a mere surrender to passion, Spinoza would have considered stupid, vicious, or even insane. But he made no defence of cowardice, nor did he condone the fear of death, and he had no admiration for wrong-doing prompted by such fear. The free man, who acts according to reason, he says, can scarcely fear death,[23] and its prospect could not deter him (so long as he retained his freedom, and rationality) from acting rightly. For there is nothing better than living virtuously or worse than a life of wickedness; so that if the latter were the only condition of survival it would be better to die, and if the only virtuous course involved death, it is still to be preferred:

> "For they who know that they are blameless (*honestos*) do not fear death as criminals, nor do they deplore the punishment; indeed, their minds are not tormented by remorse for evil deeds, but, on the contrary, they consider it an honour rather than a penalty to die for a good cause, and glorious to die for the sake of liberty" (*T.Th.P.*, xx).

What is to be preserved is one's power of action, and that consists in adequate thinking (the true essence of the mind) and right conduct. The death of the body is the inevitable demise of a finite mode, which must eventually occur whatever happens. In Hamlet's words:

> "If it be now, 'tis not to come; if it be not to come, it will be now; if it be not now, yet it will come: the readiness is all ..."

A man thrust into a situation such that to avoid death is equally to sacrifice his freedom to act rightly and to think honestly – a situation like that in which the Athenian judges placed Socrates – finds, so long as he thinks adequately, that the *conatus in suo esse perseverandi* is best satisfied by submitting to physical death.

5. *Vice and Virtue*

All actions are good, passions are some good but mostly bad. Pleasure is not in itself evil whereas pain is; the evils resulting from pleasure are derivative and indirect, but pain, so far as it is the feeling of diminution of power to act, is in itself evil. However, titillation, the pleasure of some part only of the body, can be detrimental to the whole and therefore may

---

[23] Cf. *Ethics* V, xxxviii, S. and xxxix, S.

be excessive; while cheerfulness or exhilaration, the pleasure of total well-being can never be too much. On the other hand, obsessions with certain sources of satisfaction, like a miserly love of money, produced because (as Spinoza says) money is imagined to bring us everything, or sexual love, or ambition, these may become so excessive as to be pathological, like disease, and are varieties of insanity. Thus love, though often good, may at times be excessive and bad, but hatred is never good and its attendant passions are always to be deplored.

In the *TdIE.* and the *Short Treatise* we are shown how love for finite and transitory objects is a constant source of anxiety and disappointment. In the *Short Treatise* Spinoza tells us that love involves union of the self with the object of its love; accordingly if that objects is perishable, or still worse imaginary and really non-existent, like honour, wealth or pleasures (*Wellusten*), or if its possession is fortuitous and beyond our control, we are rendered constantly miserable and wretched and we may even be destroyed by our pursuit of such objects.[24] Hatred, of course, is even worse, for it follows from imagination, and so misconception of the object, which, if inanimate, may well be good for us at some time even if it seems bad for us at others, and, if it is a person, we inevitably regard with malevolence.[25] In the *Short Treatise* Spinoza exhorts his reader to free himself from hatreds lest they deprive him of true goods and because he should always strive to improve, not to injure further, what is already in some degree evil.[26]

In themselves hope and fear are signs of weakness and so, consequently, are over-confidence, desperation, joy (*gaudium*), remorse and the like; for the more a man is led by reason the less he is subject to hopes and fears, but he directs his actions by firm, well-thought out policies (*certo Rationis consilio*).[27] Overestimation of oneself easily leads to pride, and excessive sympathy or commiseration is not good in itself. The desire to help others in trouble can as well spring from reason alone. The rational man, therefore, finds nothing contemptible, hateful or derisory, and equally nothing worthy of pity, for he knows that everything is necessary and occurs according to the nature of things. But not to be moved at all by nature (whether by passion or by reason) to sympathy and the desire to help others would be inhuman in the proper sense of that word. (*Ethics*, IV, l. S.).

Humility and repentance are not themselves virtues, but they are

---

[24] Cf. *K.V.* II, v, and *TdIE.*, I, 8-9.
[25] See p. 117, above.
[26] Cf. *K.V.*, II, vi.
[27] *Ethics* IV, xlvii, S.

beneficial more often than not because they restrain men from worse evils. For the most part, pride and self-subjection are the products of ignorance, but, again, the latter is less harmful and most easily remedied because pleasure prevails more easily over pain than the reverse. But both of these vices involve envy of others and a tendency to depreciate their virtues; the proud do so in order to aggrandize themselves, and the abject to find consolation in other people's faults.

Vainglory is simply a desire for the approbation of others, especially of the mob, which being fickle is apt to cause anxiety and despondency. On the other hand, reasonable self-approbation is not a vice, and shame, which is not really a virtue, has the saving grace that it involves a desire to behave well and to avoid misconduct.

But while many passions may have beneficial effects, no good deed which results from passion could not be performed better as prompted by reason (in which case it would truly be action and virtue), and no desire arising from reason can be excessive. Reason gives equal weight (*ceteris paribus*) to present and future goods, though our awareness of time, being largely imaginative, is never adequate. This is why it so easily happens that with the best will in the world we may neglect future good in favour of present pleasure. Nevertheless, reason *per se* seeks the greater future good and accepts the lesser present evil for its sake.

A reasonable man does not act from fear and so is not restrained from vice by superstitious beliefs in divine punishment. In fact he seeks virtue for its own sake and thus avoids evil incidentally. He is like the healthy man who eats wholesome food, not the invalid who is persuaded by fear of greater evil to take nasty medicine. And as the reasonable man is not subject to fear and surperstition, so he does not shun innocent pleasures. He embraces a life of moderate and beneficial enjoyments: indulges in moderation in the pleasures of eating and drinking, refreshes himself with sweet odours of flowers and the beauty of green plants, takes pleasure in beautiful adornments, in music, the theatre and the arts, and whatever he finds revivifying without attendant harm.[28] As Spinoza wrote to Blyenbergh, "I endeavour to pass my life not in dolefulness and groaning, but in tranquility, delight and cheerfulness." (*Ep.* XXI).

A free man, moreover, is as virtuous in avoiding danger as in facing it, when the need for either arises. Courage, after all, is more the knowledge of what ought to be feared than indiscriminate fearlessness.[29] Further, a free man living among ignorant people avoids, so far as possible, ac-

[28] *Ethics* IV, xlv, C 2, S.
[29] Cf. Plato, *Republic*, IV, 429d-430b.

cepting favours from them, but he will decline their proffered gifts with tact and circumspection so as not to give offence. He does this because ignorant men look for gratitude for favours, not so much as a sign of appreciation but in order to gratify their own self-esteem. The wise, on the contrary, bestow benefits without expectation of return, although it is only between free men that genuine gratitude is exchanged.

Further, the reasonable man is not cold and altogether unfeeling. We have seen that adequate ideas have an affective status of their own and that there are active as well as passive emotions. Though rational action is not prompted by sentimental pity or shallow sympathy, still less by the amorousness of erotic attraction, all altruistic action based on reason is generous and loving. He who follows reason (as has been said) tries always to return good for evil and gratitude for benefits. He desires to assist others, whether by advice or practice, in order that together they may enjoy the highest good and therefore he seeks their love, not their adulation, and strives to move men through joy to the love of virtue and the rule of reason (Cf. *Ethics* IV, App. xxv).

Action according to reason is always honourable and honest. To behave dishonestly would be to act self-contradictorily. For if it were virtuous to deceive it would be right and good for all men, but then it would follow that it would be more advantageous for men to believe lies than the truth, which is absurd. The argument, therefore, that a man may break faith, or lie, to avoid present danger or death, does not hold; for if it did, it would always be right for all men whenever their immediate interest dictated. But then no undertakings between men would ever be reliable, no agreements dependable and no promises trustworthy. Ordered life in society would then become impossible.[30] In this argument it is not unlikely that Spinoza had in mind what Thomas Hobbes identified as the third Law of Nature: "That men perform their Covenants made: without which Covenants are in vain." [31] It is also interesting to note that Spinoza here anticipates the argument of Kant, that what cannot be universalized without self-contradiction must be morally wrong.

Finally, a reasonable man lives more freely in society with other men, and the more so the more reasonable his fellow citizens are, it will therefore be his chief aim to educate them so far as he is able and induce them to see reason. For, as we have found, nothing is more beneficial to man than other rational beings. No man is sufficient for himself, nor could any survive in isolation. We need one another's help and cooperation and

[30] Cf. *Ethics* IV, lxxii and S.
[31] *Leviathan*, Ch. XV.

can achieve little or nothing without it, and our highest good is common to all and ultimately attainable only in common. Thus, our account of the good life, the life of reason and virtue characteristic of free men, brings us naturally to consider the nature of society, and its proper organization. This will be undertaken in the next chapter. We may end this one by stressing Spinoza's point that for man nothing exceeds moral virtue in value, and the life of reason cannot be improved by any additional rewards or extraneous consequences.

If a man follows reason he does what he knows to be most important in life, he is not misled by ignorance and imagination and so acts responsibly. He is the adequate cause of his own actions and so is free. The value of such action and the virtuous life is paramount for man even apart from what we later find to be its supreme consequence, the blessedness and immortality realized in the love and knowledge of God, to which the life of reason naturally and logically leads. Even the humanist, therefore, will find the life of reason the best and will see virtue as the highest good.

CHAPTER IX

THE STATE AND POLITICS

1. Ethics, Politics and History

Political Theory has been a shuttlecock between the historians and the philosophers for centuries, from the time of Thucydides and Plato. To-day the social scientists claim it as part of their domain while philosophers have largely abandoned the attempt to enunciate political principles. The reason for this has been a preoccupation by philosophers with logical and epistemological analysis to which political philosophy seemed alien and which led its practitioners to view the elaboration of political creeds as mere ideology – a view which incidentally brought them into agreement with the sociologists.[1] Such estrangement between philosophy and political theory is, however, abnormal and perverse, for the inescapable connexion between morality and social order ensures that ethics, inseparably bound on the one side with the philosophy of mind (and thus with metaphysics and epistemology), is equally enmeshed with the rationale of social and political institutions, on the other. This is not, of course, to say that history and social science have no part to play or that philosophers turning their attention to the principles of political order should neglect what the historian and the social scientist can reveal.

Spinoza does neither, though the condition and character of these sciences were very different in the seventeenth century from what they are in our time. Just as Spinoza was a learned and close student of ancient and mediaeval philosophy and theology, both Jewish and Christian, and as he was probably the foremost scholar of his time in the Cartesian system of philosophy (with much of which he came to differ), so also he was well versed in the writings of the time on political theory, including the works of Macchiavelli, Hobbes and Hugo de Groot (Grotius), and

---

[1] Cf. Henry Aiken, "The Revolt Against Ideology" in *Commentary*, 1964, and "Morality and Ideology" in *Ethics and Society* (Ed. R. DeGeorge) ; Daniel Bell, *The End of Ideology*, and Raymond Aron, *The Opium of the Intellectuals*.

he took keen and active interest in the politics of the Netherlands, counting among his friends many prominent political figures. On one occasion, he went, with the consent of the de Witt faction at the Hague, as a secret emissary to the headquarters of the Prince of Condé (then invading the Netherlands) in the hope of persuading him to an honourable peace settlement between Holland and France. His political treatises are thus no mere speculative philosophizing; yet, like everything else to which he turned his attention, the ideas he develops in them have grown from roots embedded in his metaphysics and the logical coherence of his thinking remains rigorous and intact.

2. Philosophical Roots

In the *Ethics* the basic principles of human association and the rational ordering of human relations have already been demonstrated, on the foundation of the dual nature of man as subject to passion yet capable of reason. The natural and essential interdependence of men for survival has been noted, as well as their inevitable tendency under the influence of the passions to come into mutual conflict. Nevertheless, because of the *conatus* and man's persistent pursuit of what is ultimately good for him, love is shown to be stronger and more efficacious than hate even on the level of passion.[2] Moreover, it follows from the interdependence of men that their most helpful and valuable aid in the effort to survive and to assure their own welfare is the cooperation of other men, the more so the more they are led by reason. For the dictate of reason is to embrace all means to increasing the power of action and its aim is a good necessarily common to all.

When we turn to politics, however, the primary fact with which we have to reckon is that the majority of people are led by blind desire and only a few by reason, so the mutual cooperation which is so indispensable has to be assured by the subjection of vicious tendencies to control in the interest of the whole group. The psychological principles of such control have already been demonstrated, and the theory of social order is built upon them.

There can, therefore, be no question that, although Spinoza adopts concepts and adapts for his purposes, doctrines current in his day, using language common to writers like Althusius, Grotius and Hobbes, his own political theory is of a piece with the rest of his philosophy. There is no need to maintain, with Hubbeling, that in his politics he uses a different

---

[2] Cf. *Ethics* III, xliii, xliv, and p. 117 above.

methodology,[3] although, as I have argued, he does not always use the geometrical order for the development of doctrines that are mutually germane. His political principles flow logically from those we have already examined, and he reinterprets the current notions of Natural Law, the State of Nature and Social Contract (where he admits them) in the light of his own metaphysical, psychological and ethical teachings.

3. Natural Law, Natural Rights and the State of Nature

The doctrine of Natural Law as it had been developed in the Middle Ages was at once the law of reason and the law of God. So it is presented by Grotius who regards it as the precepts that reason prescribes, of fair dealing, respect for property and good faith, without which no society could maintain itself. While identifying it as God's law, he distinguishes laws so fundamental that God himself cannot change them without self-contradiction, from those which are imposed by God's will and are changeable by his decree. It is only the former to which he applies the term, Law of Nature.

According to Hobbes "a law of nature is a precept, or general rule, found out by reason." [4] He says nothing of divine origin, but like Grotius he thinks of natural law as a body of moral rules binding upon men in certain respects, but not laws of necessity from which divergence is physically impossible. The Mediaeval view of natural law as well as that of other sixteenth and seventeenth century thinkers was similar. Strictly it was a law of morality and not a law of physical nature as we should understand that phrase. Nevertheless, it was thought to prevail prior to and independently of all civil law and society and in some way to be the source and foundation of both.

As the law of nature was prior to the civil law, so there was thought to be a state of nature prior to the civil state. In the natural state man was subject only to natural law by which he possessed certain natural rights, and to remove men from the state of nature and establish a civil society, a special act of mutual agreement, or contract, was required.

Versions of these doctrines varied from one writer to another. For some the state of nature was already a quasi-social condition in which men naturally obeyed the law of nature and recognized each other's natural rights. For others, like Hobbes, the state of nature was a state of war of every man against every man, so intolerable that reason dictates a covenant between men "to confer all their power and strength upon one

---

[3] Cf. *Spinoza*, p. 109f and *Spinoza's Methodology*, pp. 7, 40, 68f, 78.
[4] *Leviathan*, Ch. XIV.

man, or upon one assembly of men, that may reduce all their wills, by plurality of voices, into one will . . .", and so to create a commonwealth.[5] Other writers, who took a more benign view of human nature and the natural state, found other reasons for requiring an original social contract as the origin of the civil state, whether they believed in it as an actual historical event or merely as a legal fiction to give rational justification to political authority.

For all these ideas Spinoza finds some use, though latterly, at least, he departed from the notion of contract; but in his system each of them is given a somewhat different and more tenable interpretation. As he identifies nature with God, the law of nature and the law of God are, as a matter of course, the same. And as the law of nature governs all things so too it determines the nature of man; so the law of nature is, at the same time, the law of human nature. Human nature, however, is, as we saw, dual. Man is by nature subject to passion and a creature of desire, and this follows from the supreme law of his (and all other) nature that he strives to persist in his own being. But from this law it follows with equal necessity that he strives to increase his power of action, and that depends on the degree of adequacy of his thinking. The law of his nature demands, therefore, that to achieve his highest good he should think and act according to reason. In the last resort, then, it transpires that the law of nature is also the law of reason. In all this there is no break, as there is with other philosophers, between the law of nature as the law of the physical world, the law of nature as that of man's physiological and psychological make-up, and the law of nature as the moral law and the foundation of the civil state.

Nevertheless, "the law of human reason" may be read ambiguously. It may mean the law of nature which determines how human reason operates, or it may mean the dictate of human reason with respect to human action, and that is subject to the limitation of human knowledge. Both because of this limitation and (what is really a consequence of it) because man's nature is two-fold, the law of nature does not wholly coincide with the law of reason. "Nor is this surprising; for nature is not bounded by the laws of human reason, which aim only at the true interest and preservation of men, but by other infinite laws relating to the whole eternal order of nature, of which man is but a minute part." (*T.Th.P.*, XVI).

As it is the law of man's nature to desire to seek his own advantage, whatever he is able to do to that end he has a *natural right* to do. In this

[5] Cf. *Leviathan*, Chs. XIII and XVII.

regard Spinoza follows Hobbes, who identifies natural rights with natural powers, maintaining that in the condition of nature every man has a right to everything he can get. (*Leviathan*, Ch. XIV); for whatever he can make use of may be a help to him in preserving his life, to strive to do which is his primary right. But Spinoza does not envisage a state of nature preceding society and he uses the phrase rather to indicate natural propensities in men and the results which they would produce if given free rein. He maintains, therefore, that it is quite wrong to regard man in nature "as a state within a state," [6] that is, as autonomous and obedient to the law of reason independently of society and its order. Because men by nature mostly follow "blind desire" they are not autonomous, but they are, nevertheless, always striving to maintain and preserve their own being, so that whatever they can do to satisfy their desires they do by nature and by natural right.

Having thus identified natural right with natural power, Spinoza proceeds almost at once to show that such power, apart from reason and the order of society is virtually nil. It would follow that, practically speaking, there are no natural rights. In the state of nature, as each man follows his own advantage as he thinks best and is bound to obey nobody but himself, there is no common consent as to what is good or evil, thus there is no sin. Likewise as there is nothing (apart from the opposition of others) to prevent anybody from taking whatever he wishes for his own use, there is no such thing as property and so no injustice.[7] In short, apart from society there is no morality.

On the contrary, the natural pursuit by each of his own desires leads men into mutual conflict, and, because they are more cunning and resourceful than other animals they are by nature enemies. "In so far as men are tormented by anger, envy or any passion of hatred they are driven apart and are at odds with one another, and are the more to be feared the more capable, crafty and cunning they are than other animals. And because men are naturally very greatly subject to these passions, they are by nature enemies." (*T.P.*, II, 14). Accordingly, the state of nature gives no security and no prospect of success in the pursuit of one's desires and the power of the individual in such circumstances would be nugatory.

It has already been shown that men subject to the passions are virtually incapable of action and are devoid of freedom. The power of action comes only with adequate thinking and by following reason. But that

---

[6] *Ethics*, III, *Praef.*, and *T.P.*, II, 6.
[7] Cf. *Ethics* IV, xxxvii, S 2.

also is the aim of the *conatus* and the end of desire, for "among the affects which relate to the mind so far as it acts there are none but those which are related to pleasure and desire." (*Ethics* III, lix.). Accordingly, men have power or freedom in any degree only when they follow reason to some extent, and the dictate of reason is that the true good is common to all (*Ethics* IV, xxxvi). The condition, then, of the realization of rights is the recognition of a common good.

> "Hence it follows that as long as human natural right is determined by the power of each individual and belongs to each [separately], it is nothing (*nullum*), but exists more in opinion than in fact, since there is no assurance of its being possessed. And it is certain that every man is so much less capable, and consequently has so much less right, the more cause he has for fear. Add to this that it is hardly possible for men to sustain life and cultivate the mind without mutual help. We may conclude, therefore, that the right of nature which belongs to the human race can scarcely be conceived unless where men have laws in common, men who can at one and the same time appropriate to themselves the lands which they inhabit and are able to cultivate, protect themselves and repel all force, and live by the common consent of all." [8]

Thus natural right and civil right coincide, a consequence not in conflict with human nature; for, as Spinoza puts it in *Ethics* IV, xxxvii, S 2, "If men lived by the direction of reason, each would possess this right without any injury to another." And, as he says earlier in Chapter II of the *Tractatus Politicus,* "Moreover, since everything strives as far as in it lies to preserve its own being, we cannot have the least doubt that, if it were equally in our power to live from the prescript of reason as to be led by blind desire, all men would be led by reason and would order their lives wisely; which by no means happens." (Ib. 6). Thus ordered living is implicit in the pursuit of desire and the civil condition in the natural.

The identification of natural right with natural power and the consequent "admission of the possibility of a right in the individual apart from life in society," T. H. Green stigmatizes as "the cardinal error of Spinoza's 'Politik.' " [9] It should now be clear, however, that it was no error at all, if we accept Green's own view of rights, and was little more than a concession, on Spinoza's part, to the theoretical conventions of his time. For he quite explicitly says that natural right apart from society is "*nullum,*" and so it is not a possibility that he admits. Moreover, what Green requires is that rights should exist only where there is "recognition by members of a society of a correlative claim upon and duty to each

[8] *T.P.,* II, 15.
[9] *Lectures on the Principles of Political Obligation* (London, 1924), B, p. 56.

other, as all interested in one and the same common good" (*ibid.*); and that is just what Spinoza goes on to assert.[10] Green traces the alleged error to Spinoza's rejection of final causes, which, I have argued, is a misinterpretation of his doctrine; but even apart from that, Spinoza does not deny, but rather insists on, the purposive activity of human beings in their recognition of a supreme good for man and the true value of everything that conduces to it. Green finally concedes almost as much when he writes, "The conclusion, then, is that Spinoza did really, though not explicitly, believe in a final cause determining human life" (*ibid.*, p. 59). In fact, Spinoza does so explicitly. His identification of *jus naturale* with *potentia* is in part an aspect of his derivation of the normative (the "ought" and the "right") from the positive (the "is," or the natural), and in part it is an identification of right (*jus*) with that which constitutes for him the supreme good, the perfection of the intellect in rational thought and action, in which alone, he held, power to act (*potentia*) really consisted.

In the *Tractatus Theologico-Politicus*, which Spinoza wrote between 1665 and 1670 (the date of its anonymous publication),[11] his account of the natural condition and its disadvantages is closer to Hobbes' position. There we even find traces of the contract theory, for he says that men brought it about that the right of each to everything should be held collectively and should be determined by the power and will of all together instead of each individually. Each man, to bring this about, must (he says) firmly have promised, or contracted, to be directed by the dictate of reason; and as no contract has force except by reason of its utility, and as good faith among men is uncertain because of the difficulty and rarity of obedience to reason alone, they must be compelled to keep their pact by the power which they have transferred to the commonalty and which, therefore exceeds by far, that of any individual. So we are led to the right of sovereignty next to be examined.[12]

The elaborate argument presented here to show that there is nothing in nature to compel men to keep promises except the expectation of greater advantage by so doing, is sufficient to make it clear that the con-

---

[10] Cf. also *T. Th. P.*, IV: "*Lex quae a necessitate naturae dependet, illa est, quae ex ipsa rei natura sive definitione necessario sequitur; ab hominum placito autem, et quae magis proprie Jus appellatur, est ea, quam homines ad tutius et commodius vivendum, vel ob alias causas, sibi et aliis praescribunt.*"

"A law which depends on natural necessity, is that which follows necessarily from the nature or definition of the thing itself; but one arising from *the agreement of men,* which is more properly called *right,* is that which men prescribe for themselves or others for the sake of safer or more convenient living, or for other reasons" (my italics).

[11] Cf. *Ep.* XXX.

[12] Cf. *T.Th.P.*, XVI.

tract is otiose. For Spinoza has just asserted that "nobody can doubt how much more advantageous it is for men to live according to law and the dictate of reason, which aims at nothing but the true good of men." This obvious advantage must then be a sufficiently powerful motive to induce men to live in the civil state and the contract falls away. No reference is made to any such instrument in the later *Tractatus Politicus,* which was written shortly before Spinoza died and was never completed.

4. Sovereignty and Law

The outcome of the argument is that men effectively possess natural rights only when they hold them in common "and are guided as if by one mind" (*T.P.,* II, 16). And the more men there are who unite in this way, the more power (and so the more right) they collectively possess, but, by the same token, the power or right that the individual can claim against the community is proportionately lessened the greater and the more united the community is. It stands to reason, however, that the more united the community is, the less will any of its members wish to claim rights against it, because it is in its unity that his own rights are realized and in that same unity that its strength, to which his own contributes, consists. To make claims against the community is dissension, which weakens the union, and to the causes and effects of which we shall presently return.

"This [corporate] right," Spinoza continues, "which is defined as the power of the multitude, is usually called sovereignty." (*T.P.,* II, 17).

The paramount advantage of the life according to reason, though rationally incontestable, does not alter the fact that men, as finite parts of nature, are more liable to passion. Even on that level, however, it must be obvious to them that cooperation is indispensable. Not merely is it obvious, but it is a practical condition of survival and so cannot be avoided. Cooperation, however, necessarily demands limitations upon individual licence and requires the mutual accommodation of conduct; but the liability to passion prevalent among the majority of men tending to generate envy, hatred and mutual conflict runs counter to this demand, and some effective means of restraint upon the passions is, accordingly, essential. Such restraint is not forthcoming from pure reason alone, merely in so far as it propounds the truth or demonstrates the greater benefits of peace and concord, because immediate advantages bulk larger in the imagination, exerting stronger influence than the more remote, and affects can be counteracted only by more powerful affects. Social order can only be maintained, therefore, if men's anti-social impulses are opposed and overcome by other impulses excited by sanctions and the fear of punishment for the transgression of an imposed law.

It is only with the imposition of law by a sovereign authority that right and wrong, justice, injustice, righteousness and sin, properly come into being, for in an assumed state of nature nothing is forbidden "except what nobody desires and what nobody can do" (*T.Th.P.*, XVI). Without the law, as St. Paul teaches, there is no sin (*Rom.*, IV, 15). A state of natural innocence (as we call it) is one prior to the consciousness of laws and prohibitions, in which whatever the agent does is done, certainly, according to the law of nature; but that is a law that cannot be transgressed. Thus animals, predatory though they may be, act only according to their natural instincts and commit no wrong-doing. But men are capable of reflecting upon their own impulses and natural desires and of judging the superior advantages of living in society under a law which they impose upon themselves, or upon one another. So they live, in Kant's phrase, according to the idea of law, and only thus are they moral agents liable to transgress as well as to observe the laws which their social inter-relations involve.

To say that vice and wrong-doing are actions contrary to reason, therefore, comes to the same thing as saying that they can occur only under the law of a civil society, for it is only in the civil condition that a life according to reason becomes possible, even though the law of the state is by no means always what reason would approve. If, however, the law of the state is made to conform to the dictates of reason, the welfare of all its members will be best provided.[13] But of that, more is to be said below.

The prime condition of civilized life is the maintenance of a social order, and the minimum condition of social order is obedience to law. But, we have seen, the majority of men are led by blind desire and not by reason. Therefore the law must be enforced by sanctions and those who do not obey willingly in recognition of the common welfare must be made to do so through fear of the penalty. The common welfare requires at least external conformity, whatever may be its motive. So the law must be obeyed if only through fear. Yet this, if a necessary minimal condition of social order, is far from sufficient; for men kept in subjection by fear alone will be unwilling and unreliable subjects, and a state the tranquillity of which rests solely on the servility of its subjects is no true state but rather "a desert" (*T.P.*, V, 4). For the aim of human association is a genuinely human way of life, "the true virtue and life of the mind," not just the persistence of men's vital functions like that of other animals

[13] Cf. *T.P.*, II, 20-21.

(ibid. 5). Other motives than fear must therefore be enlisted for obedience to the law if the state is to attain its proper end; and other motives are available. Rulers may appeal to the hope of rewards as well as fear of punishments, and besides these they can appeal to love of country and to the pursuit of advantages such as wealth, safety or peace. Equally, obedience may be prompted by love, respect or admiration for the persons of the rulers themselves (*T.Th.P.* XVII). But of course the best and most desirable motive, which is the most efficacious for good, is strength of mind (*fortitudo*), the love of wisdom and the intelligent recognition that the best life can be lived only in a well ordered state (*T.P.*, V, 4).

The real object of the law and the ultimate purpose of the social order is not apparent to the majority of people, but, at best, only to a few. That is why sanctions have to be attached to the law. But those who do understand it will obey the law because it is right and reasonable to do so, and will thus obey it with constancy of mind. These are the truly just (*T.Th.P.*, IV). They will obey because they realize that political order is the condition of peace and concord and the means to the common welfare; so that even when the government enacts what is not wholly in accordance with reason, it may be more reasonable to obey and suffer some inconvenience than to support or foster social disruption, the lesser evil being preferable to the greater (*T.P.*, III, 6; *Ethics* IV, App. xiv).

As for Spinoza power and right are the same thing, the combined power of all the members of a community is obviously supreme in both. This is the sovereign power, and the body of persons so combined is the civil state or commonwealth of which the members enjoying the benefits of civil right are the citizens. If the sovereign right is vested in particular people, one or more, it must be so by common consent (*T.P.* II, 17) for power held as the result of conquest is domination and its subjects are more slaves than citizens. They seek merely to avoid death, whereas free citizens seek to live (*ibid.*, V, 6). It is clear, therefore, that Spinoza conceives the sovereign power as vested in the people, who combine their forces by common consent in pursuit of common ends. Such a community he calls a free people (*multitudo libera*), and it is by their joint act that sovereign power is vested in the persons, whosoever they may be, who exercise political power in practice. It may be a monarch who holds supreme power, or a council, or the whole assembly of the people, but in principle the sovereign power resides in the people and Spinoza's preference is for democracy. Moreover, although he adopts the theory of sovereignty (usually called "juristic") as in some sense absolute, he is far from equating that with absolute monarchy (which is the predilection of Hob-

bes). The monarchy which he describes in Chapters VI and VII of the
Tractatus Politicus is very much a limited and constitutional monarchy;
for, he says, "those who believe that one man alone can hold the supreme
right of the state are greatly mistaken. For right is determined solely by
power . . . but the power of one man is far from sufficient to bear so great
a burden" (*ibid.*, VI, 5).

5. *The Rights and Powers of the Sovereign*

The extent to which sovereignty is absolute is just that to which its
power is unassailable. As the power of the whole community it cannot be
successfully challenged by the individual as such. There is no internal
force that can prevent the state, *qua* united power of the whole people,
from doing whatever it wills. So long as it has the power it has the right
which depends on that power; for law, to be effective, must be enforced,
consequently the only effective law is what the supreme power of the state
enforces, and its right to do whatever it will is therefore legal right. This
must not be confused with moral right, though the two may, under
certain conditions, coincide.[14] Thus the right of the state over the individual citizen is absolute just so far as the power of the state exceeds that
of the citizen virtually immeasurably (*T.P.*, III, 2). There are, however,
as we shall find, some respects in which the state has no power at all over
the citizen, and in these it has no right, for the citizen retains full natural
right over such activities (e.g. thought and opinion) as the power of the
government cannot reach (*T.Th.P.*, XX), and what cannot be enforced
is not within the right of the state (*T.P.* III, 8).

As the sovereign has the power to enforce law, so the sovereign alone is
the source of the law it enforces and has the sole right to interpret it.
Equally the sovereign authority alone has the right to punish transgression of the law, as well as to raise armies for defence of the commonwealth, appoint officials and settle disputes. It cannot do the impossible
and so is subject to the laws of nature, and there is a sense in which it is
also subject to the law of reason which we shall shortly examine, but so
far as there is no power that can prevent a government from acting
unreasonably (which often happens) it falls within its right to do so. For
the sovereign right is what results from the exercise of the united power
of the community acting as if with one mind, and so far as it expresses
that united power it is sovereign whether its acts be reasonable or not.
We must bear in mind, moreover, that there is always a modicum of
reason in government action, in as much as it is the action of a concerted

[14] See below p. 196.

body politic with a common interest in association and mutual cooperation, an interest prompted by reason in that the social condition is always preferable to chaotic anarchy and pervasive violence.

Even if we say that the state is subject to divine moral law, what that
law might be and how it should be interpreted could not be dictated to
the sovereign by any private individual. Private conceptions and interpretations of such law, so far as they are mutually at variance, are ineffectual,
and none can claim precedence over any other. The right to interpret
divine moral law, therefore, so far as it is recognized by the whole community, can only be vested in the sovereign power as that which has been
instituted by common consent. If it is to be effective, only the sovereign
can decide what the alleged divine law is and how it should be understood; for the one and only authority that can do this effectively is that
which has the power to make its decision good in practice ($T.Th.P.,$
XVI).

It stands to reason that the supreme political authority, which is the
source of the law, can neither break nor be subject to the law which it
makes itself and may with equal right repeal or change; for its acts *are*
the law and are *ipso facto* legal ($T.P.,$ IV, 5). This position is what has
been called the juristic theory of sovereignty expounded by such writers
as Hobbes, Jeremy Bentham, Blackstone and, at a later date, by John
Austin. Its truth lies in the fact that the state, so far as it does command
the force at the disposal of the entire community, is irresistible by any
private party and can do whatsoever it wills. But the condition is inde-
feasible – and none is more aware of this than Spinoza – that to be
supreme and sovereign the ruler must have at his disposal the whole
power of the people, and this can certainly be forfeited in varying degrees
unless he acts within certain definable limits.

What these limits are we shall presently consider. First let us note some
of the consequences which flow from the sovereign character of the state
for its relations with other states. Like Hobbes, Spinoza maintains that
states are to one another in the state of nature. That means there is no
superior law governing their relations except the law of nature. But, unlike Grotius, he does not conceive the law of nature as a code prescribing
rules of conduct analogous to the civil code. Rules of conduct there may
be, but they are those which result from the common tendencies of
human nature, not what are dictated by pursuit of a common good.
States pursue their own separate interests and so, like men, are by nature
enemies. They are able to defend their interests and territory, however,
more successfully than individual men.

The state will make alliances when and as it suits its interest, but they can have no greater, or longer, binding force than that interest requires. It may abrogate any treaty whenever it is more advantageous to do so than to keep it, and it would be failing in its function of preserving the welfare of its subjects if it kept a treaty to their disadvantage. The sole external consideration bearing upon any such decision (and one not unrelated to internal considerations) is the risk of provoking hostility of other parties to the agreement who may be stronger or more numerous. But if and whenever it is necessary to its safety or interests it may make war by its own sovereign right, and that presumably will occur when disputes between itself and its allies cannot be settled in accordance with the agreed terms of the treaty, or otherwise by mutual consent.

With reference to inter-state relations, as in all other political matters, Spinoza is a realist. In all dealings of the state with other states he saw the national interest as the paramount consideration, for he fully understood that where no common interest is recognized no law can be imposed, and over sovereign states there is no power other than conquest that can enforce legal rules. In international affairs the rights of the state are limited only by its power; and the same is true of the internal rights of sovereignty.

6. Limitations on the Power and Action of the State

By and large, we may say that only so far as the ruling power acts in the common interest as that is generally understood and recognized by its members, will it retain its power sufficiently to act as it wills. If it acts so as to bring its own laws into disrepute or disrespect it undermines its own power. The aim of government is peace, security and a commodious way of life, and if it attempts to impose upon a people by sheer force laws which they disapprove, resent and resist, they will not cooperate to provide it with the power it needs to enforce those laws and so far it will lose its right. The result of tyranny is sedition and rebellion which detracts through one and the same cause from the power and the right of the sovereign. Such rebellion and sedition, disrespect for law and the breakdown of social order are, Spinoza tells us, to be imputed to the corruption of government rather than to the wickedness of the subjects (*T.P.*, V, 2; *T.Th.P.* XVII) and similarly, the virtues of citizens are to be credited to good government. To maintain its power, therefore, a regime must act so as to retain the loyalty of its subjects and from this it follows that government itself is subject to limitations, which are set by what the people for the most part will accept as right, just, and in the common interest.

This probably accounts for Spinoza's preference for democracy as the best and most stable form of state. He says in the *Theologico-Political Treatise* (Ch. XVI), that it is rare for sovereign governments to issue utterly foolish commands for, if they are to retain their power, they must consult the common good and direct affairs in a reasonable manner. Tyrannical governments, he quotes Seneca as saying, never last long. Moreover, there is less likelihood of foolish government in a democracy than in other types of state, first because it is harder to obtain general agreement in support of absurd measures from a large assembly, and secondly because the primary aim of democracy is mutual restraint and a life of peace and harmony. Finally, he says, democracy seems to be the most natural form of state and to come nearest to preserving natural freedom, "for in it nobody transfers his natural right to another so completely that he is never again consulted, but each transfers it to the greater part of the whole society of which he makes one." The implication is that the stability of the sovereign power depends upon constant consultation with its subjects and action with their continuing consent.[15]

In still another way the power and right of the sovereign is limited. It has no right over what it cannot enforce, and it can enforce at most only overt actions. The state cannot enforce private judgements, opinions, or feelings, and so has no right to prescribe what they should be. The right to freedom of thought cannot be given up by the individual because the free activity of thinking cannot be prevented by the imposition of penalties. A government may in various ways influence opinions but it cannot successfully command men to think otherwise than their own private judgement dictates. (*T.Th.P.* XVII, XX).

Spinoza concludes that since thought must necessarily be free its expression ought not to be curtailed as long as it does not involve illegal or seditious action. Any attempt to restrict the freedom of expression, in view of the impossibility of preventing freedom of judgement, is likely

---

[15] Jan den Tex, in his paper, "Spinoza over de Tolerantie" (*Mededelingen van-wege het Spinozahuis*, XXIII, 1967), as well as in his book, *Locke en Spinoza over de Tolerantie*, alleges, despite the textual evidence, which he quotes, that Spinoza's inclination was really towards aristocracy. This opinion, however, is largely consequent upon den Tex's failure sufficiently to appreciate the connexion and continuity in Spinoza's thought between nature and reason. He seems also to overlook the fact that, whereas Spinoza completed his discussion of aristocracy in the *Tractatus Politicus*, what he had to say about democracy remained unfinished, and all we have, apart from his remarks in the *Tractatus Theologico-Politicus*, is the merest fragment.

to fail and would be excessively oppressive. For the original purpose of civil association is to free men from fear, not to enslave them by means of it. The restraints it imposes are upon passions and unruly conflicts, not upon rational activities. "The end of the state, I say, is not to make beasts or automata out of rational men; but on the contrary to enable them to exercise their mental and physical capacities in safety and to use their reason freely . . . The end of the state is, therefore, really freedom" (*T.Th.P.*, XX).

Accordingly, so long as men keep the peace and obey the law as it is promulgated, they should be allowed to express their opinions freely as they cannot be prevented from holding them. To speak freely is not to infringe any right of the sovereign, and is a benefaction and a duty if it is a rational criticism of the law or action of the government. Any such criticism it is conceded, must be submitted to the sovereign's judgement and may not be acted upon independently or seditiously. On the other hand, if the state attempts to repress expression of opinion it will at best generate widespread hypocrisy and deceit. Spinoza, in saying this, may have had in mind the experience of his own ancestors in Portugal and Spain, where, from fear of the Inquisition, many Jews outwardly professed to be Catholics without genuine belief or conversion. But, in fact, he continues, it is more probable that suppression will be resented and resisted, for men find few things so frustrating as having doctrines that they believe to be true branded as criminal, or their religious beliefs condemned as wicked. By such repression, the state will turn its most intelligent and best educated citizens, those most capable of independent judgement, into potential (or actual) rebels, for they will denounce the repressive laws and count it a virtue to stir up opposition against them. Thus proscription of beliefs affects mostly honourable men, not real criminals, and is moreover useless because honest and sincere believers cannot obey laws which forbid their beliefs. Punishment only makes martyrs of them and holds them up to admiration by the masses and exposes the government to ridicule.

Intolerance of religious doctrine, therefore, and the suppression of free speech is shown to be a danger to the state and a source of insecurity to the government. For it incites good men to opposition and rebellion while it encourages hypocrites and sycophants. Moreover, those whose beliefs are sanctioned become overweening in their arrogance, regard themselves as divinely inspired and proceed to dictate opinions and policies to the civil authorities. Spinoza concludes the *Tractatus Theologico-Politicus* with the claim to have shown what he set out as its

original purpose: that freedom of philosophical and theological speculation not only may be granted in accord with public peace and piety,
but cannot be denied without destroying both.

7. Political Freedom

We can now understand the sense in which the sovereign is subject to
the law of reason, for it is only to the degree that it acts reasonably that
it is likely to fulfil the condition that its subjects should loyally accept its
decrees as just.

"For it comes first to be considered that just as in the state of nature that
man is strongest and most his own master (*sui juris*) who is guided by
reason, so also that state will be most powerful and most fully *sui juris*
which is founded upon and directed by reason. For the right of a state is
determined by the power of a people (*multitudo*) which is led as if by one
mind. And this union of minds could by no means be conceived, unless
the state does all it can to aim at what sound reason shows to be good for
all men." [16]

Spinoza's theory of sovereignty is to be aligned as much with Rousseau's
as with Hobbes'; for, like Rousseau, he teaches, in effect, that because
and so far as the sovereign power is absolute it can belong only to the
whole people "led as if by one mind." And he teaches also that the
sovereign right of the state is most fully realized when it acts most nearly
in the best interests of the whole nation. What Rousseau identified as
sovereign was the General Will, and that was not the collective (actual)
will of all the individual citizens, but that ideal for which each man
would vote if he considered what was in the best interests of the whole
state, not simply what was in his own immediate interest.[17] This is
virtually the same as what Spinoza means by being guided by sound
reason, and is the "one mind" in which all reasonable men would agree.

Further, just as for the individual, freedom of action consists in acting
according to reason, just as in rational action he is autonomous (*sui juris*),
so the free commonwealth is the one which is wisely governed, which
maintains unity, peace and concord and expresses the free and reasonable
wish of all its members to live together harmoniously, happily and well.
Liberty, therefore, is not licence or the absence of government interference with the subject's unrestricted choice; it is not release from
regulation or exemption from restraint; but it is the ordered and self-

[16] *T.P.*, III, 7. Cf. also II, 21, and *T.Th.P.*, XVI.
[17] Cf. Rousseau, *Contrat Social*, Bk. IV, Ch. I.

regulated conduct of reasonable men acting in concert to achieve a common good. Thus the state is most free whose citizens obey the law willingly, from a sense of loyalty and with understanding that by doing so they act in their own best interests, as well as in those of the whole community (Cf. *T.Th.P.*, IV and XVI).

8. *Practical Considerations*

In the conviction that every political arrangement that is practically possible has at some time or other already been tried out, Spinoza declines to devise a perfect form of state. He does not believe (he says) that philosophers have produced anything but fantasies and useless impractical schemes by concocting Utopias, and he holds that mere speculation cannot lead to anything practically viable. He does, however, discuss at some length ways in which the three main forms of government, Monarchy, Aristocracy and Democracy, might arrange their governmental institutions and conduct their affairs so as to minimize conflicts of interests and maintain the most probable conditions of peace and prosperity. The unfinished *Tractatus Politicus* breaks off shortly after the beginning of his discussion of Democracy, depriving us of his wisdom on that form of constitution which he obviously preferred above all others. But what he has to say of it in the earlier *Theologico-Political Treatise* gives us a good idea of his views on the subject. These have been summarized above and there seems little need to detail his suggestions with respect to the other two forms of state for they are less relevant to modern politics and less philosophically interesting than the general principles we have been reviewing.

These practical suggestions of Spinoza's were made with an eye to the political forms and practices of the Netherlands of his day, in particular; as well as of other European countries of the time. They are of great historical interest but of not so great philosophical moment. I propose, therefore, to omit further reference to them in detail and may do so with less compunction because others have given excellent accounts of them, as well as of the influence on them of the historical circumstances in which they were written.[18]

A. G. Wernham makes the interesting point that Spinoza intended these constitutional suggestions as a demonstration of the practical possi-

---

[18] E.g., A. G. Wernham *Benedict de Spinoza, The Political Works* (Oxford, 1958), pp. 36-41; H. G. Hubbeling, *Spinoza's Methodology*, Appendix II; Theun de Vries, *Baruch de Spinoza* (Hamburg, 1970); L. S. Feuer, *Spinoza and the Rise of Liberalism* (Boston, 1964), Chs. 3-5.

bility of bridging the gap between the natural and the civil condition, which T. H. Green described as "an impassable gulf." The explanation Wernham offers is illuminating and ingenious, and is not a misrepresentation of Spinoza. But I have argued above that for Spinoza there really is no gulf between the state of nature and the civil state, and Green's view is based on a misinterpretation. Spinoza needed no bridge other than the *conatus* – man's universal desire (which, oddly enough, Green also postulates) to improve his own condition. But Wernham is quite right to point out that Spinoza was realist enough to know that neither subjects nor rulers habitually act according to reason, and that they can be brought to do what is in their own best interests more easily by fear of the consequences of acting otherwise, or by attractive rewards, if such can be devised. Spinoza devises means, therefore, in whatever way he can in his model constitutions, to balance interests and to give both citizens and magistrates incentives to do what will maintain peace and concord and the most favourable conditions for the exercise of moral and intellectual virtues.

The question may well arise, however, whether Spinoza's political theory has any significant message for modern man. Are not contemporary conditions so greatly different from anything he could have imagined as to make his ideas quite incompatible with modern political practices and objectives? In particular, is it possible to accept his account of the limitations upon state action, as arising from the need to retain the consent and loyalty of the governed, in an age when the instruments of coercion at the disposal of governments have grown immeasurably in power. With organizations of law enforcement such as are today available to those who wield power, and with mass media of propaganda exercising incalculable influence upon men's minds, how true is it that governments need fear resistance from their subjects or that opinions cannot be moulded or compelled?

It is indeed true that Spinoza could hardly have anticipated modern developments, but he understood very well the fundamental basis of political power, which has not changed; namely, that political organization has no other justification than the maintenance of tolerable conditions of life. He understood also that the power to enforce laws of any kind is never at the command of one or a few men, unless by the common consent, tacit or expressed, of a large number of those over whom they rule. Only with the cooperation of large numbers can police forces, armies, intelligence services, propaganda campaigns, newspapers, radio and television networks, and all such machinery of modern social manipulation be maintained. The large numbers, therefore, must in some way, to some extent and at least through acquiescence, give their consent to the exercise of power by these means. And if that exercise makes life intolerable for them, which it would become if their security were sufficiently undermined, their cooperation is liable to be withdrawn and resistance is liable to grow.

Not the most sophisticated methods of coercion and brain-washing have wholly succeeded, even in the most stable of modern dictatorships, in completely suppressing dissent and disaffection; and in the most notable of them Spinoza's warnings have been borne out, that they have turned their most intelligent and potentially valuable citizens into rebels. Even so, no state has ever been so tryrannical that it could ignore the common needs and the prevalent desires of the bulk of its subjects without in due course forfeiting its power; and no modern state whether dictatorship of the right or of the left, or dominated by the wealthy, or ruled by an élite, has been able to retain its power without the consent of at least a large number of its subjects. Even the domination of white minorities over large black majorities in Southern Africa can be maintained only with the approval of the bulk of the white community, and it ensures the acquiescence of the majority of the black by maintaining among them their traditional tribal ways of life approved by and familiar to the bulk of the indigenous population.

The lesson is still to be learned by modern governments (not least that of the United States) that disruption and defiance of authority is more the result of bad and unjust laws than of bad character among its citizens. Concurrently, however, it must be borne in mind that individual character and social order are mutually interdependent. As Spinoza says, the virtue of the citizens is equally to be attributed to the wisdom of the government.

Spinoza's insights into the nature of international relations and his understanding of inter-state practice are entirely sound. They are more perspicacious than those of Grotius and are still applicable today. It is still the case, in spite of the United Nations and all the high flown sentiments about world peace which politicians mouth, that national interests take precedence over common interests in world affairs, that sovereign nations form alliances – and break them – in accordance with strategic advantage, and that treaties are honoured only so long as it suits the interest of the contracting parties. Nations still make war whenever they feel strong enough, and keep the peace only so long as the power of potential enemies deters them from using force to gain their ends. And all this is because sovereign powers are not and cannot be subject to higher authority which can impose upon them a superior law.[19]

Spinoza's principles are, therefore, still exemplified today – if only his insistence that men are for the most part led by blind desire rather than by reason. It is, moreover, no less true that the remedy for social evils is neither despotism nor violent rebellion, but mutual consensus and rational order. For Spinoza does not pretend that the mass of men can be brought to see reason easily, and certainly not by extreme or violent measures (unless they learn by the disastrous results). Yet he does insist that if peace, concord and happiness are to be enjoyed, it will be only if and so far as reason prevails. That this seldom happens he is the first to admit; "but all excellent things are as difficult as they are rare" (*Ethics* V, xlii, S.).

[19] See *The Survival of Political Man* (Johannesburg, 1950) and *Annihilation and Utopia* (London, 1966) by the present author.

CHAPTER X

RELIGION

1. Philosophy and Religion

The opening passages of the *Treatise on the Improvement of the Intellect* made it plain that Spinoza was not embarking upon an enterprise of speculation purely for its own sake. He was not seeking any mere theoretical discovery or pursuing philosophical insight simply as an academic accomplishment. Philosophy was to be for him, as it was for the ancients, a total way of life and one to be preferred to the alternatives of commerce (for the acquisition of wealth) or politics (for the sake of social advancement). He adopted the philosophical way of life as the best and the most desirable, as affording true good or advantage and as constituting real freedom. What this way of life is we have found set out in the fourth and fifth Parts of the *Ethics*. It is the life of reason with all that follows from and is involved in it. But the crown and goal of reason is the knowledge and love of God – the eternal object that fills the mind with joy and excludes all pain, for love, as we are told in the *Short Treatise*, is the union of the mind with its object, and when that object is infinite and eternal the mind will partake of the same sublimity as the object possesses. The twenty-eighth proposition of the Fourth Part of the *Ethics* states that "the highest good of the mind is the knowledge of God, and the highest virtue of the mind is to know God." Thus all philosophy, for Spinoza, is ethics, and ethics, in the final outcome, is religion. "Whatever we desire and do, of which we are the cause so far as we have an idea of God, or so far as we know God, I refer to *Religion*," he writes (*Ethics* IV, xxxvii, S. 1).

In short, the distinctions between the highest and best kind of knowledge, morality and religion are no distinctions; the three are one and the same. The rectification of the intellect is at the same time the liberation of the mind from passion and the purification of the moral character; and all this, as we learned from the first, in *The Treatise on the*

Improvement of the Intellect, follows from relating our ideas to the idea of God. So they become adequate and the desires and actions which express them are (Spinoza says) to be referred to religion. Moreover, he asserts that the true and universal religion – universal in the sense that any and all who practice it have thereby attained salvation – is nothing other than the knowledge and love of God and the consequent practice of charity and justice towards men [1] – "Thou shalt love the Lord thy God with all thy heart and with all thy mind and with all thy might, and thy neighbour as thyself." This is the essence and epitome of all true religion, and whoever abides by it and carries it out in his life has in himself the spirit of him who in these words first gave it expression.

The idea of God is strictly the object of the divine intellect, an infinite mode of the attribute of Thought, and in the *Short Treatise* Spinoza calls the infinite modes "sons of God." [2] In the Scholium to Proposition lxviii of *Ethics,* Part IV, he says that the idea of God is "the spirit of Christ," and he speaks of it again in the *Theologico-Political Treatise* as the holy spirit. This idea of God is immanent in all minds and works in and through all activities as the *conatus in suo esse perseverandi,* which (as we saw) is at once the essence of the thing striving to preserve itself and the essence of God in so far as it is expressed in, or constitutes, that thing. But it is properly and adequately expressed only as the final goal of the *conatus,* the ultimate realization of the being that feels it as desire. That goal is to understand its own essence as part of and existing in the infinite and eternal essence of God. It is attained in the third kind of knowledge, which is, on its affective side, the intellectual love of God.

2. *The Intellectual Love of God*

This third level of knowledge, we shall remember, is a grasp, in a single apprehension, of the principle of wholeness that governs the detailed character of each and every finite mode of Substance, and so understands the finite in, and by means of, its understanding of this holistic (or teleological) principle.[3] Accordingly, knowledge of this kind necessarily involves ideas of God and his attributes, and these, as the forty-fifth, forty-sixth and forty-seventh propositions of the second part of the *Ethics* demonstrate, are adequate ideas. Adequate ideas, moreover, are actions (not passions) of the mind and transition to them from less adequate thinking is felt as pleasure. The cause of this pleasure clearly is, and in

---

[1] See below, p. 223.
[2] *Korte Verhandeling,* I, ix.
[3] Cf. p. 130 above.

scientia intuitiva must clearly be seen to be, God; and pleasure associated with the idea of the object which causes it is love. Thus he who understands things adequately by the third kind of knowledge (*scientia intuitiva*) loves God with an intellectual or rational love, the active affect which is a necessary aspect of true knowledge. When the finite modes understood in this way are our own emotions and impulses, the passive, painful and illusory character, which they have on the level of imagination, is abolished and transformed into the joyous active awareness of adequate ideas seen in relation to God, so that the conquest of the passions by reason issues in the intellectual love of God,[4] the most perfect and developed form of religion.

This love of God occupies the mind more fully than any other idea or affect (*Ethics* V, xvi), it cannot be changed into hatred, for nobody can possibly hate God, in as much as hatred is a passion and the idea of God is necessarily adequate and active. Even the knowledge that the causes of pain are part of Substance, so that in some sense one might say that God is the cause of pain – even such knowledge does not contaminate the love of God with sorrow or resentment, for, as we have seen, evil is strictly nothing positive, and once the causes of pain are adequately understood the passion (or suffering) is transmuted. "Therefore, to the extent that we understand God to be the cause of pain to that extent, we rejoice" (*Ethics* V, xviii, S.).

Further, the love of God cannot be adulterated with jealousy or envy but increases the more we imagine others to be bound to God by the same ties, for the good we seek and find in the love of God is the good common to all persons and we desire it as much for others as for ourselves (*ibid.* xx). It is the sort of love that seeks no return or reciprocation. God strictly does not love (much less hate) anybody, for he cannot be affected with pleasure or pain – in him there is no transition from one level of perfection to another. Thus nobody who understands adequately can wish that God, whom he loves with the intellectual love here described, should be other than he is, or should be such as could be affected by pleasure or pain. It is therefore love that seeks no requital, that is wholly unselfish; and this must apply to men as well as to God; for, just as one who loves God cannot be jealous of others who also and similarly love God, and cannot wish that God should return love to anybody, he will not expect a reciprocal love of the imaginative variety from men (love of the sort which is susceptible of jealousy), because what he desires of others is only that they should be rational and act reasonably, not that they be

[4] Cf. *Ethics* V, xiv, xv.

moved by passion. The criticism that Spinoza's ethic is nothing better than enlightened selfishness is finally confuted by this doctrine of intellectual love, which is utterly selfless and wholly absorbed in the obsessive awareness of the infinite object.

It follows that no passion or emotion can possibly be contrary to, or prevail over, the intellectual love of God, for it is that which overcomes and subdues all passions. It is therefore the most constant of all mental states and indeed fills the mind with joy excluding all pain. Consequently it is the consummation of virtue, which is to understand things by the third kind of knowledge, and its achievement is the aim of the most intense effort of the mind (*summus mentis conatus – Ethics* V, xxv).

Spinoza argues at the same time that the intellectual love of God is identical with the love by which God loves himself, for God enjoys infinite perfection and has knowledge (or idea) of himself as infinitely perfect, that is, as cause of himself and his own perfection. Though pleasure as a transition to greater perfection is incompatible with absolute completeness, the actual enjoyment of perfection itself Spinoza calls blessedness. This God necessarily enjoys and it is accompanied by the idea of himself as its cause. He therefore loves himself with the same intellectual love that man feels towards God. And so far as God's essence is expressed through that of the human mind (though not so far as he is infinite) this love is equally a love of God for man. In short, Spinoza concludes, the intellectual love of God is one and the same whether it be God's love for man or man's for God. It is nothing other than the enjoyment of the knowledge of God's perfection – or blessedness.

Nothing can counteract or destroy this love of God, which (as we shall see further anon) is eternal. In this, Spinoza tells us (*Ethics* V, xxxvi, S.), our salvation consists, which he identifies with our liberty or blessedness, and which he says is appropriately called "glory" in the Scriptures, for it gives the highest satisfaction to the mind (Cf. Def. of Affects, xxv and xxx). This salvation, then, is the final fruit and highest attainment of religious devotion, for "whatever we desire and do, of which we are the cause so far as we have an idea of God, or so far as we know God, I refer to religion." It is the holy spirit come to fruition in the mind of man, for the essence of the intellect is to know by the third kind of knowledge,[5] and the mind falls into error only so far as, being the consciousness (or idea) of a finite mode of Extension, it registers in imagination the effects of other bodies upon its own. So far as we can, as it were, strain out the impurities of imagination from our ideas, by the means already

---

[5] Cf. *Ethics* V, xxxvi, S.

explained, they become adequate and true and are the same as exist eternally in the mind of God; for it is of the essence of the intellect, so purified, to frame adequate ideas,[6] which it does so far as it sees all things in God; and it is impelled to do so by its *conatus* which is the power of God working in it – the holy spirit.

3. *The Tractatus Theologico-Politicus*

The enjoyment of blessedness through the purification of the intellect and the attainment of *scientia intuitiva,* with the intellectual love of God in which it issues, is a rare achievement and it is possible only for a small minority of human beings. For the majority of people we should have to despair of salvation if the sole means to it were the attainment of philosophic wisdom.[7] Accordingly, Spinoza recognizes another path to redemption besides that of following "the natural light." This alternative is the way of revelation and faith. It is not that revelation does not come through reason and the natural light. Indeed that is its chief source, and Spinoza is severe in his castigation of "those who absolutely despise reason, who reject and turn away from the intellect as being corrupt by nature, [and] these, forthwith (what is most outrageous) are believed to possess the divine light." [8] But revelation is also given in prophecy as recorded in the Scriptures. How these are to be interpreted, what the nature of prophecy is and how it is related to reason, what is the function of theology and how it is to be distinguished from philosophy, as well as the setting out of reasons why the state should allow freedom of religious belief, are the matters treated in the *Theologico-Political Treatise,* a work of great genius and compelling interest, too often neglected by students of Spinoza's thought.

The book was published in Spinoza's life-time and was written while he was still working on the *Ethics.* Part of his purpose in writing it was to vindicate himself from the charge of atheism which, as he says in *Ep.* XXX (to Oldenburg), the common people persisted in making against him. Possibly, therefore, it contains material which he had written earlier to rebut the accusations that had caused his expulsion from the Synagogue. Nevertheless, with his usual caution, he had it published anonymously, even the name of the publisher being disguised. Nor was it well or sympathetically received but was bitterly attacked as a pernicious and atheistic tract,[9] so that when he heard that somebody had translated the

[6] *TdIE,* IX, 73.
[7] Cf. *T.Th.P.,* XV *ad fin.*
[8] *T.Th.P.,* Praef.
[9] Cf. *Ep.* XLII from Lambert de Velthuysen to Oosten.

Treatise into Dutch and proposed to publish it, Spinoza expressed alarm and begged his friend, Jarig Jelles, to prevent its being printed (*Ep.* XLIV). So anxious was he not to give offence or occasion for dispute and censure that he anticipates in his preface (lest the reader should lack the leisure or inclination to persist to the end) what he protests in the conclusion, that he has written nothing that he would not willingly submit to the highest political authorities for approval, and that he would retract whatever might be regarded as contrary to the law of the land or harmful to the public weal. Despite the care which he has taken to write only what was compatible with piety, law and good conduct, he confesses that he is only human and is aware of his own liability to error.

Such anxiety to please the authorities and to withhold his own writings have been thought by some to be evidence of timidity or even of hypocrisy; but these are not characteristics which reveal themselves in what is reliably known of Spinoza as a person. If "the highest political authority" referred to above were Johan de Witt, Grand Pensionary of Holland, the statement could well be a plain report of actual fact.

It has been suggested that in the *Tractatus* Spinoza wrote with double meaning to give an appearance of orthodoxy, which he did not really embrace, to heterodox views obliquely expressed.[10] Dr. Hubbeling quite rightly rejects this interpretation as wholly out of keeping with the character of the man as revealed in his letters and in his reaction to the disapproval and condemnation of the Amsterdam Synagogue. Moreover, there is little difficulty, despite the strictures of some commentators, in reconciling the doctrines of the *Tractatus* with those of the *Ethics* (many of which are repeated in it). As Dr. Hubbeling remarks, Spinoza is quite explicit about the occasions on which he uses terms, making concessions to popular belief, in senses other than those he holds to be strictly correct; and he explains his meaning in his letters too plainly for the allegation of any deliberate *double entendre* to be countenanced.

Spinoza's reluctance to publish or even to allow his opinions to be imparted to those of whose intellectual sincerity and honest literary intentions he was not assured, was due to his complete lack of desire for fame, his abhorrence of controversy and his anxiety not to be misunderstood and misrepresented. It was with the utmost reluctance that he

---

[10] Cf. Jan den Tex, *op. cit.*, pp. 10 and 21; and H. G. Hubbeling, *Spinoza*, p. 92. See also Leo Strauss, *Spinoza's Critique of Religion* (New York, 1965) and his account of the criticism of Spinoza by Hermann Cohen, *op. cit.*, pp. 15-28. Cf.: "The situation in which Spinoza finds himself . . . cannot be grasped except in the light of that fundamental character of his philosophy, which one may describe, in agreement with Dilthey, as 'two-sided,' or with Cohen, as 'ambiguous." *Ibid.*, p. 227.

replied to de Velthuysen's criticisms or Burgh's self-righteous exhortations to recantation. He refused to allow even Leibniz, on too brief acquaintance, to see the draft of the *Ethics* (Cf. *Ep*. LXXII), and he adjured the friends for whom he wrote the *Short Treatise* to take the greatest care to whom they imparted his views, and to do so only with the welfare (*heyl*) of others as their object, and the assurance that the reward of their labour would not be lost.[11]

That nothing in the *Theologico-Political Treatise* is seriously at variance with the doctrine of the *Ethics,* or is irreconcilable with it, is apparent from Spinoza's defence of the former in his letters to Oldenburg (*Epp*. LXXIV, LXXV, LXXVII and LXXVIII), to some of which reference has already been made in our discussion of Spinoza's theory of human responsibility. I shall return to them in the sequel and shall try to show as I proceed that the coherence of Spinoza's teaching remains unbroken by the doctrines of the *Theologico-Political Treatise*.

4. Revealed Religion and Superstition

Professor Leo Strauss seems to attribute to Spinoza a vaccilation between, on the one hand, the identification of revealed religion with superstition and, on the other, the toleration of religion, as piety and obedience, in part as a political expedient and in part as an inferior substitute for rational understanding.[12] But neither does Spinoza halt between two opinions, nor does he hold either of the views precisely as they seem here to be attributed to him. Certainly he bitterly opposed and sharply criticized superstition of every kind, but he was far from reducing religion to this product of fear and imagination. Again what he sees as true and universal religion is not simply a device on the part of a skilful and unscrupulous ruler (as Strauss describes it) to keep the multitude within bounds.[13] Indeed, he maintains that religion achieves the same end as rational understanding, and that there is no conflict between revelation and reason. The pious who obey the laws of God experience contentment and peace of mind, as well as those who, through clear and distinct understanding of the nature of God and his law, attain to the intellectual love which is eternal blessedness.[14]

Strauss' interpretation is difficult to follow for it is not clear whether he is simply being inconsistent in his account of Spinoza's doctrine, or is attributing the inconsistency to Spinoza. At times he seems to maintain

---

[11] *K.V.*, II, xxvi, *ad fin.*
[12] Cf. *op. cit.*, Chs. viii & ix.
[13] Cf. *op. cit.*, p. 223.
[14] Cf. *T.Th.P.*, XV and Spinoza's note XXXI.

that for Spinoza religion (especially revealed religion) is simply superstition, at others that Spinoza held a purified and simplified form of religion, standing "midway between philosophy and superstition" (op. cit., p. 246), to be salutary. That it is so, however, is said to be "the fundamental dogma of theology," one "not accessible to reason." And so, on the next page, Strauss argues that even this form of religion is founded upon superstition. As this exposition frequently quotes Spinoza's own phrases, it might be assumed that it is intended as a statement of Spinoza's view. But it is a view which, in its main tenets, Spinoza explicitly repudiates. It could, therefore, be taken simply as an inference from Strauss' interpretation of Spinoza's doctrine to which he thinks Spinoza should be committed.

That Spinoza explicitly repudiated the imputed doctrine is apparent from his reply to de Velthuysen who attributed to him virtually the same position. Velthuysen says ". . . in order to avoid the fault of superstition, he seems to me to have cast off all religion." (*Ep*. XLII). Spinoza replies:

> "What he understands by religion and what by superstition I do not know. Does he, I ask, cast off all religion who maintains that God must be acknowledged as the highest good and that he must be loved as such with a free mind? and that in this alone our highest felicity and highest liberty consist? further that the reward of virtue is virtue itself, and the punishment of folly and weakness is folly itself? and lastly that everyone ought to love his neighbour and obey the law (*mandatis summae potestatis obedire*)?" *Ep*. XLIII.[15]

From the way in which Spinoza speaks of superstition it is clear that he intends to distinguish it from, rather than to identify it with, true religion, and that he regards superstitious practices and rites as pseudo-religion – *religio vana*, as opposed to *religio vera* (Cf. Preface to the Theological Treatise). The cause of superstition is insecurity and the inability of men to carry out their projects in the pursuit of their own interests by any sure plan, so that they are constantly thrown from one extreme to the other of hope and fear. In prosperity they have little or no recourse to religion of any kind, but in adversity they seek desperately for some assurance and help, and are prepared to believe any stupidity from which they can derive comfort, or to be terrified by anything which is unusual and is taken as a sign of impending misfortune. Hence the widespread belief in signs and portents as indications of the displeasure of the gods with human misdemeanours, demanding their expiation by

---

[15] Cf. *Ep*. LXXIII; "I regard the chief difference between religion and superstition to be this, that the latter has ignorance, but the former wisdom as its foundation."

sacrifices and prayer. Such, says Spinoza, are the beliefs which men embrace who are prone to superstition *and averse to religion*.

As we saw earlier, the main, or sole, causes of the inanities of superstition are men's ignorance, their liability to imagination and their subjection to passion. The pursuit of uncertain ends (prompted by passive desires), and ignorance of the causes of events, lead to disappointment and frustration and consequent conflict of emotions; this is both the result and the cause of imaginative vagaries of which superstition is the fruit.[16] But this is not what Spinoza understands by revealed religion, whether revealed by reason, or, as he also thought possible, by imaginative presentation. How the latter is compatible with Spinoza's theory of knowledge, will presently be considered; but, whatever the source, a revelation of God's law can hardly be the same thing as the "delirium and insanity" which Spinoza derides as superstition.

Strauss presumably thinks that revealed religion cannot be anything other than superstition, because Spinoza has said that imagination is the source and the only source of error. What reason demonstrates Strauss does not view as religion at all. Wisdom, he contends is the one alternative to religion which Spinoza leaves open to man (Cf. *op. cit.*, p. 216). Revealed religion, on the other hand, uses the imagination as its medium, and as imagination is the source of superstition, the two must be the same. So, says Strauss, "revealed religion, the concern of the many slavish and impotent, lives for the temporal and in the temporal," whereas theory, or wisdom, lives in and for the eternal (*op. cit.*, p. 218). Again "revealed religion is a product of the imaginative-affective life..." (*ibid.*).

All this has some plausibility until we notice Spinoza's assertion that what the Scripture reveals is not *the truth*. Prophecy, he holds is not philosophy. It merely inculcates beliefs which will lead men to piety and justice. And it is in this that true religion consists; nor, despite all the imaginative media involved, is it wholly alien to wisdom.

> "It is therefore not to wonder at that the Prophets, who were concerned with the common welfare, not that of the few, commended so strongly humility, penitence, and reverence. For in truth those who are subject to these emotions can be led much more easily than others, so that at length they may live according to the direction of Reason, that is, so that they may be free and enjoy the life of the blessed." (*Ethics*, IV, liv, S.)

The multitude of men are inevitably subject to passion and live mainly under the sway of imagination, accordingly they are by nature prone to

[16] Cf. *Ethics* I, App. and pp. 126-8 above.

superstition. Very few have ability unassisted and by their own strength of mind to reach *scientia intuitiva* and philosophical wisdom. How then can the mass of humanity be saved? Spinoza's answer to this question is that there is a way, even at the level of imagination by which even the majority of people could be led to live the kind of life conducive to reflection and contemplation. This is the way of faith and piety, love of one's neighbour, social harmony and justice. And men are led to it by prophecy, the record of which is to be found in the Bible. Our first step, therefore, in seeking to understand the nature of revelation is to consider the status and validity of the Scriptures and the proper method by which they should be interpreted.

5. Biblical Criticism

There can be no question as to the primacy of reason. When Blyenbergh writes of the two rules in accordance with which he endeavours to philosophize, one being clear and distinct understanding and the other the revealed word of God, and gives precedence to the latter, doubting what seems clear if it conflicts with what he finds prescribed in the scripture, (*Ep.* XX), Spinoza expresses a fundamental difference of opinion as to these very principles. If he has found a firm proof of anything, he says, he can never entertain any thoughts which cause him to doubt it, and he does not fear that anything in the scriptures will conflict with it – even though he confesses that he does not understand them – because truth cannot conflict with truth (*Ep.* XXI).[17] In fact, he claims that he has never found anything in what the scriptures expressly taught which did conflict with reason or that reason did not support, still less anything from which it followed that human reason is corrupt (*T.Th.P.*, Praef.).

Moreover, the primacy of reason is inescapable, for if the scripture teaches the word of God, we can accept it as doing so only in the light of reason. There must be some criterion for distinguishing the true from the false canon and there are none which can be validated except on rational grounds. Miraculous origins or signs are of no avail, for what is and what is not a genuine miracle only reason could decide. We shall see, however, that miracles can reveal no truth about God nor about the authenticity of prophecy. For (among other reasons) the Bible itself teaches that there are false prophets and that false prophets can perform miracles with the purpose to deceive; [18] thus, by the Bible's own teaching,

[17] Cf. *Cog. Met.*, II, viii to which reference is made in the letter.
[18] Cf. *T.Th.P.*, VI; Deut. XIII.

miraculous accoutrements are no valid criterion of divine inspiration, and if it were there would still be need of a reason why we should take it to be such.

If sanctity is claimed on the ground of intrinsic merit, that must be demonstrated rationally. If a document is said to be divine because its teaching is true, that must be shown on rational grounds, for then truth cannot be based on inspiration without question-begging; if because its teaching is morally sound and admirable, a rational criterion of moral rightness is needed, and if none is forthcoming the claim can be made indiscriminately.

Thus, in Spinoza's terms, it must be by the natural light that we assess and examine the scriptures and if we should find in them anything that is contrary to reason we can refute it with the same liberty that we refute illogicalities in the Koran or the Talmud (*Cog. Met.*, II, viii). Accordingly, Spinoza lays down principles of criticism and interpretation which, he says, do not differ from those that govern the investigation and interpretation of nature (*T.Th.P.*, VII).

The first rule to be observed is that what the scripture teaches can be sought only in the scriptures themselves. Secondly, as the scriptures do not themselves define the subjects about which they discourse, we must elicit the definitions from them by comparing what is written of the same subjects in different places. That in which the majority of the relevant texts agree must then be taken as the correct meaning and this must then be used to interpret obscure or ambiguous passages or those which mutually conflict. Next, we must beware of confusing the sense of a statement with its truth and of reading into it our own reasoning, but must investigate every passage solely in terms of the language used and reasoning based upon the scripture itself. Fourthly, the words actually used must be taken in their literal meaning, even if they conflict with reason, and may be regarded as metaphorical (however seemingly rational) only if they conflict with what we have found them to mean most generally throughout the text. For instance, when Moses is reported as saying that God is fire, we can decide whether or not this is meant literally, not by considering whether it is rational, but only by comparing it with what Moses says elsewhere and more generally about God. And as he is also reported in many places as saying that God has no likeness to anything visible, we may judge which statements are most probably meant literally and which metaphorically.

Finally, we must bear in mind the special characteristics of the language in which the text was originally written and from which it may have been translated. If, for instance, the original language was Hebrew, we must not be misled by differences of sense or connotation between words or phrases in our own language and their Hebrew equivalents. There may also be peculiarities of syntax which make exact translation difficult and actual translations misleading. Considerations of language, however, are really historical. For in what language a text was originally written, what its peculiarities were, and whether or not what we have is a translation are historical questions. This brings us to what is perhaps most important and most remarkable in Spinoza's critical procedure: his insistence upon regarding the Bible as an historical document and the method of historical criticism and investigation that he propounds. This again is an essentially rational approach.

The Bible, we are told, is divinely inspired; it contains the word of God; those who wrote down its contents were under divine influence. How do we know all this? Is it on authority, and, if so, on whose? That of the Bible itself – but how is that established, except by investigating its origins and sources, how and by whom it was written, whether the authors themselves claimed divine inspiration and what were the bases of their claim if they made one? Or perhaps the authority is the Church. If so whence derived? – the Pope, who traces his claim back to St. Peter. But this itself is an historical claim demanding examination, as is that made on behalf of St. Peter himself. All the questions raised by any claim to an authority derived from tradition or the special status of an ancient document are historical questions and the claims cannot be validated without historical evidence, whatever other criteria may also be invoked. The demand for historical evidence is thus a rational demand.

"In spite of the brilliant work which made Spinoza the founder of Biblical criticism, the general tendency of the Cartesian school was anti-historical," writes R. G. Collingwood.[19] It might equally truly be said that in spite of the anti-historical tendency of Descartes (well demonstrated by Collingwood) and his strong influence upon Spinoza, the method of Biblical criticism which Spinoza developed makes him one of the founders of critical scientific history. For he was among the first to maintain, in effect, that the available documents (in this case, the books of the Bible) may not be accepted at their face value. If they are to be understood properly their history must be known, and this is not stated in them, not even when the purport of the text seems to reveal it. We must seek from internal and external evidence by whom the book was written and in what language, whether or not it was later corrected or

---

[19] *The Idea of History* (Oxford, 1946), p. 63.

modified by others, how competent such persons may have been to correct alleged errors, whether it had been translated from some other more original text, and how it came to be accepted as one of the sacred writings. We must ask, and seek to discover, how the books were collected into a single corpus, if each of them is a unitary work or possibly a compilation of writings by different authors. Then also we must know the characters of the authors and what their intentions were in writing before we can clearly understand the meaning of what they have written. Further we must know what were the circumstances in which the books were written, what were the manners of the society in which the authors were educated and what degree of erudition they display, as well as to what manner of people the writings were addressed. Only in the light of such historical knowledge can we decide what they meant; and only when we have done all this can we tell what in the scriptures is prophecy, or even what is meant by the term as used by the authors of the texts. The claims to authenticity based on a tradition (such as the pharisaic) or on the infallibility of a pontiff (like the Roman Catholic) cannot be allowed, for we find contradictions in the first and disagreements among those who profess to adhere to the tradition, and denial of the second by some who defer to more ancient authorities.

The criteria for deciding many of these issues Spinoza does not specify. For instance how are we to decide what were the manners of the time, the kind and degree of education received by an author or whether an extant text is a translation and, if so, from what language? But he does make one specially interesting suggestion: that one can properly understand what a writer means only when one knows the circumstances in which and the influences under which he was thinking and what his intentions were. In other words, we may not simply accept what is written but must ask why the author says what he does. We must try to reconstruct his thought. According to Collingwood, this is precisely the aim of scientific history and his view is, by implication, anticipated in the *Tractatus Theologico-Politicus*.

Spinoza himself proceeds always (or mainly) from internal evidence, and he seeks agreements and consistencies within the texts. If he finds them he credits the sense of the passages concerned. On the other hand, where he finds conflicts and disagreements he tends to suspend judgement. In general, the implication of both his statements and his procedure is that convergence and coherence of evidence is a sign of reliability whatever the source of the evidence may be. But the ultimate criterion always held in reserve is what is acceptable to reason. Statements that are incredible in the light of scientific knowledge he refused to accept, though he admits the possibility of their becoming acceptable if a reasonable explanation could be discovered; and whatever involves internal contradiction is naturally to be ruled out.

I shall not exemplify Spinoza's critical procedure in any detail. My aim is rather to state the results he obtains by its use. But I shall allow myself one illustration. The Pentateuch, he argues, could not all have been written by Moses. Deuteronomy, for instance, clearly says that Moses was not permitted to cross the Jordan (Chs. XXXI, XXXII). If this was so, the preface to Deuteronomy, could not have been written by Moses, for it states: "These be the words which Moses spake unto all Israel beyond Jordan in the wilderness . . ." Again, in Deut. XXVII (and Josua VIII, 37), it is stated that the entire book of Moses was inscribed upon an altar which was built of only twelve stones, from which it follows that the book must have been much shorter than the Pentateuch. Further, the final chapter of the Book describes the death of Moses, his burial and the mourning of the children of Israel for thirty days thereafter, none of which could have been written by Moses himself. Where reference is made to Moses in the third person, Spinoza avers that the text must have been written by another writer. In Genesis, XII, 6, telling of Abraham's journey through the land of the Canaanites, the narrator adds "the Canaanite was then in the land," which is evidence that the verse was written at a time when the Canaanites had been driven out, and that was after Moses' death. Likewise, in Deut. III a parenthesis is inserted stating that the bed of Og the King of Bashan still remains in Rabbah, indicating that the author was speaking of an antiquity, and was not writing at the time of the events recorded or soon after them. Moreover, such statements and phrases as, "Moses was very meek, above all men which were upon the face of the earth" (Numbers, XII, 3), "Moses, the godly" (Deut., XXXIII, 1) [20] and "there hath not arisen a prophet since in Israel like unto Moses" (Deut. XXXIV, 11), could hardly have been written by Moses himself, but are obviously praises and tributes written by somebody else – and written, moreover, very much later, for the writer of the last statement says also: "but no man knoweth of his sepulchre unto this day." By such critical examination of texts Spinoza attempts to decide on the date and authorship, considering always what is consistent and compatible both in the scripture itself and with what is alleged of it, and accepting nothing that involves a contradiction.

[20] In the Authorised Version: "Moses, the man of God."

6. Prophecy

Anything by which we participate in the divine nature might be called prophecy, and as everybody has "objectively" in his mind an idea of God, and as the true nature of the intellect is to frame true ideas, one could call natural knowledge prophecy, for the more we know of nature the more we know of God.[21] But this sort of knowledge is available to all and can be accepted by any who can follow the demonstrations, and the masses therefore regard it as commonplace, preferring what is rare and strange. They reserve the word prophecy, therefore, for what is revealed by other means and exclude ordinary scientific and philosophical knowledge.

Thus, applying his methods of research and interpretation to the Bible, which, he says, is the only source of prophetic revelation available, Spinoza finds first that by "prophet" what is meant is "interpreter" and that the prophets interpreted to the people what was revealed to them by words or signs, either actual or imagined, though the latter is often taken to be real by the prophet himself.

The prophets were not endowed with superhuman minds but were gifted with an ability to discern, through the media just described, certain truths which neither they themselves nor the generality of persons were able to reach by pure reasoning, but which they embraced by pure faith. It is not altogether clear whether Spinoza meant that what was revealed in this way exceeded the capacity of the intellect as such, or merely that it was beyond the individual capabilities of the persons who accepted it by pure faith. If he meant the former he might be accused of inconsistency; but I think, and shall try to show, that there can be little doubt he meant the latter.

He speaks of "other causes and media by which God revealed those things to men which exceed the limits of natural knowledge, and even those which do not exceed it (for nothing prevents God from communicating to men by other means the same things that we know by the natural light)." (*T.Th.P.* I). This makes it quite clear that what is revealed by prophecy can also be revealed by the natural light, and from what we have already seen of Spinoza's doctrine, that the intellect of man once purified of imaginal elements is identical with at least part of the intellect of God, it would seem unlikely that he should maintain that truths beyond those available to the intellect might be revealed by other means. This is the more improbable since he goes on to say that

---

[21] Cf. *Ethics*, V, xxiv, I, xxv, C; *T.Th.P.*, IV.

the medium of prophecy is the imagination, and elsewhere he identifies that as the source of error.

The prophets, he says, perceived revelations of God by the help of the imagination, that is, mediated by words or images, real or imaginary. For instance, his future military leadership was revealed to Joshua by the vision of an angel bearing a sword; Isaiah saw an image of the Lord sitting on a very high throne with the people of Israel immersed in the mire far below and stained with the filth of their sins. Such visions were merely in the imagination of the prophets, but in other cases they heard actual voices and saw signs. This is the only description of prophecy we get from scripture and we have no right to invent any other. The scripture says nothing of the cause of these signs and visions except that the prophets were filled with the spirit of God, which, Spinoza maintains, is only the Hebrew way of saying that they had unusual and remarkable virtue and genius. To say that the cause was the power of God (as many do) would be idle, because that is the cause of everything and provides no specific explanation but is only a confession of ignorance. To know the cause, however, is unnecessary for the interpretation of the scripture, which does not concern itself with causes. What we can safely conclude is that prophecy is revelation through imagination, and as words and images can be combined to produce "many more ideas than can be derived purely from those notions and principles upon which all our natural knowledge is erected," the prophets were able to perceive many things outside the limits of the intellect.[22]

Now we know from other investigations how prolific of ideas the imagination can be, but we have been told that these ideas are none of them adequate, clear or distinct. So what the prophets perceived could not have been the truth as it is cognized by God – or even as it may be known by man "through the adequate idea of the formal essence of one of God's attributes." But the multifarious ideas producible by the imagination can easily comprise quantitatively many more things than the individual imagining (the prophet) could deduce *geometrico ordine*, and there is no reason why imagination should not (in ways which we may not be able to explain) make a specially gifted person aware of truths which could in principle also be rationally known. For Spinoza says that the prophets did not know clearly and distinctly the truths which were revealed to them and of which they felt subjectively certain. This certainty, he says, was not mathematical (or philosophical) but was only moral certainty and was experienced only after the prophet had been given a

[22] *T.Th.P.*, I.

sign. Thus Abraham demanded a sign to assure him of God's covenant, Moses was given a sign, and Gideon asked for a sign "that I may know that it is Thou that speakest with me." Such signs could never produce mathematical certainty, for there can be false prophets, some despite their own conviction.[23] The test of authenticity, we shall see presently, is neither the sign nor the prophet's vision but the nature and effect of his message.

When Spinoza says that prophecy may reveal truths beyond the limits of the intellect, what he means is that by images and words the prophet is led to accept and to teach truths which the prophet himself was incapable of deducing logically from first principles or reaching by *scientia intuitiva*. The scriptures make it quite apparent that prophets were not people of superior intellect. Some of them were uneducated country folk, even Hagar the handmaid of Abraham was among those who had the gift. And, he points out, men of great imaginative power seldom excel in intellectual ability, while those with greatest intellectual acumen are often deficient in imagination, tending, in any case, to keep it under restraint (*ibid.*). All this comports with what Spinoza says elsewhere about imagination; for instance, in *Ethics* II, xvii, Schol., he allows that if we do not take the imaginative idea for more than it really is, we could view the power of imagination as a virtue of our nature. What the imagination presents in itself, what is positive in it is not false, only its omission of the wider context of relationships without which it is apt to be misinterpreted. But there is nothing to prevent imaginative visions leading us to believe in ultimate truths like the existence of God and the necessity for righteousness as a condition of salvation. It may be beyond our ability and knowledge to explain how this occurs and it may be beyond the capacity of those so persuaded to deduce the truths rationally which they are thus led to believe, but the truths themselves do not conflict with what is discoverable by the natural light.

When we realize further what the content of prophecy is shown to be (by a proper interpretation of what scripture teaches), it becomes clear that there is no inconsistency in Spinoza's teaching. Diligent search through the biblical texts makes it apparent that the prophets were not philosophers and were not propounding philosophical science. This may be the character of the wisdom literature such as Proverbs and Ecclesiastes and the Wisdom of Solomon, but Solomon was not and did not profess to be a prophet. The sole aim of prophecy, Spinoza maintains, is practical and its content is purely moral precept: to Love God and one's

[23] *Ibid.*, II.

neighbour; in the words of Jeremiah (IX, 23): "let him that glorieth glory in this, that he understandeth, and knoweth me, that I am the Lord [Jehovah] which exerciseth loving kindness, judgement and right-eousness in the earth: for in these things I delight, saith the Lord [Jehovah]"; and again (XXII, 15-16), "He judged the cause of the poor and the needy; then it was well. Was not this to know me? saith the Lord [Jehovah]." Examples of this in the prophetic writings are numerous, and Spinoza quotes many to show that the common doctrine of the prophets, in which they all agreed, was that "the knowledge of God" meant primarily just and charitable living, the teachings of Jesus being no exception. Prophecy, Spinoza holds, exhorts to the good life, it does not propound philosophical truths.

On other matters the opinions of the prophets diverge widely, on whether or not God is corporeal, whether or not he has human attributes, and similar matters. Further, they speak in very various styles, depending on their own social background and the intelligence and experience of the people they are addressing. Moreover, as imagination is the source of their vision, and as imagination is inconstant, the gift of prophecy tends to fluctuate even in a single individual and the type of image and meta-phor used varies greatly. Spinoza concludes, therefore, that prophecy is not the exposition of theoretical truth and should never be taken as such, but is moral teaching, adapted in its mode of expression to the culture and capacity of its audience, and variously expressed according to the personal views, the education and the social background of the prophet.

The presumption of a second inconsistency in Spinoza's position may thus be removed. He has asserted that God does not act *sub specie boni* with specific purposes in view, but that the divine will and the divine intellect are one. How then, it may be asked, can God be said deliberately to reveal himself, his laws and his wishes to specially selected persons? Moreover, if we say that there are moral laws which God prescribes we think of him as a ruler and judge, which Spinoza has said is an error. This error, however, is to be attributed to the imagination of the prophets and to their habit of adapting their teaching to the capacity and beliefs of their audience; and it is an error which does not affect the moral efficacy of their exhortations, for their sole object is to inculcate obedi-ence, justice and charity. There is a valid sense in which the moral precepts may be called "the law of God," justification for which has al-ready been made plain (in the *Ethics*) and to which I shall shortly revert.

God's will and power, as has been said, are the ultimate cause of all things and of all ideas. There is, therefore, nothing inconsistent in attributing to the will of God the occurrence in finite minds of imaginative ideas, or the ability of individuals to apprehend in and through such ideas certain truths which might also be reached by reason but which the individuals concerned do not or cannot demonstrate for lack of the appropriate intellectual bent. The psychological explanation of the gift of prophecy we do not know, of the proximate causes of finite ideas we are often, in fact usually, ignorant, and to say simply that they issue from God's nature, or are caused by his power, is true but not particularly enlightening, because it applies equally to all finite things. In short, the gift of prophecy is like the gift of poetry or music; not everybody possesses it and we cannot explain why some people have the special talent and others do not, but to describe it as a mode of revelation to the prophet of the nature and will of God does not conflict with Spinoza's main doctrine.

7. The Election of the Jews

Two questions arise from this account of prophecy Spinoza's treatment of which are worthy of note. First, does the exceptional prophetic genius of the Hebrew people, as evidenced in the scriptures, justify their claim to have been specially chosen by God? Secondly, as the prophet requires a sign to assure him of the revelation, and as the sign may nevertheless turn out to be spurious, we may call in question the status of miracles. I shall confine myself here to the first question and shall turn to the second in the following section.

The idea that God has singled out one nation for special favour or precedence is for Spinoza altogether unthinkable. Not only is God no anthropomorphic ruler exercising arbitrary choice and bestowing special favours on men or nations with capricious predilection, but even if he were, such selection of one nation for exclusive beneficence would make no sense and confer no advantage. True happiness and blessedness, he says, consists solely in the enjoyment of good not in elation at the fact that others are excluded from it. Nobody is better or wiser or more virtuous for others being less so, in fact, we have already seen that the contrary is true; and whoever rejoices in his superiority over others is to that extent malicious and vicious (*T.Th.P.*, III). God, therefore could not promise any people exclusive wisdom for their special benefit.

Further, wisdom and morality depend on human nature which is the same in all men, irrespective of nationality, and, whatever anybody does, is appointed by God. Nations are distinguished from one another solely by their laws and customs and the structure of their societies, but neither by their native intelligence nor their natural virtue. This opinion is specially notable for it is, once and for all the rejection and condemnation of racialism. Spinoza had good cause to realize that discrimination on the pretext of racial superiority is as prevalent among the persecuted, and as pernicious, as among the persecutors. The Jews, persecuted as an inferior and pariah race by non-Jews, could be equally exclusive and intolerant as a self-styled élite. They expelled him from their community for his denial of their divine election and his refusal to conform to religious observances in which they thought themselves privileged and in which he no longer believed, and they hounded him out of Amsterdam (by denouncing him to the city authorities) simply because he held to his own convictions. In the same way his own forebears had been hounded out of Spain and Portugal by the Inquisition, but their own suffering had not taught them forbearance.

The scripture, he shows, gives ample evidence that the ancient Hebrews were exceptional neither in wisdom nor in righteousness, that the gift of prophecy was not vouchsafed exclusively to them, for it was displayed also by gentiles (such as Baalem), and even Abraham deferred to the laws of Abimelech. Moreover the prophets themselves taught that God's providence and dispensation was equally bestowed on all men, as was later the teaching of the Gospel and of Paul.

The only acceptable interpretation, therefore, that can be given to the doctrine of election is that the ancient Hebrews were especially fortunate in the laws given them by Moses and the social order in which they resulted. This, despite their waywardness and frequent lack of wisdom enabled them to overcome their enemies and maintain a stable kingdom for a long period. In this sense only might they be considered as chosen by God, a belief they themselves embraced because they realized their own persistent good fortune in war and politics. The persistence of the Jewish race in modern times, despite their expulsion from their homeland and the loss of their political order, Spinoza attributes to their exclusiveness and the consequent hatred and persecution of them by other nations, which has segregated them, as has their persistence in their religious rites and especially in the custom of circumcision which marks them off from other peoples. In fact, unless the foundations of their religion should emasculate their minds, he declares, so changeable are the affairs of men that they might yet again rebuild their state (*imperium*) and once more be "chosen by God" (*ibid.*).

Let us now turn our attention to miracles.

8. Miracles

A miracle is sometimes defined as an event which produces faith in those who experience or accept its occurrence as actual. So far as a sign may serve to induce a prophet and his audience to believe that his message is a divine revelation, this definition would apply and would probably have been acceptable to Spinoza. But it in no way establishes the reality of miraculous events as those which are not subject, or are contrary, to the laws of nature and are produced directly by arbitrary acts of the divine will. Spinoza rejects this conception of miracle emphatically. For him, the law of nature is the law of God's nature, and for God to act contrary to that would be for him to contradict himself, or for his nature to be other than it is, which is unthinkable. A miracle, therefore, is not an event contrary to the laws of nature, for there are no such events, but is only one which men cannot explain because its natural causes are unknown to them.

Whether or not a miracle induces people to believe in prophetic utterances as divine, it can in truth teach us nothing about God's existence or his essence. People who believe on account of miracles are simply following their imaginations and their passions (wonderment and fear), so that strictly belief in miracles or in doctrine on the strength of miracles is mere superstition. Certain knowledge of God's existence and his essence is either self-evident or deducible from first principles the truth of which nothing can conceivably shake. If anything should occur contrary to the laws of nature, it would contradict these first principles and so shatter the very basis of our knowledge of God and his essence.

The more we understand of nature and of particular things, the more we know of God, and from what is unintelligible to us, as must be an event contrary to natural law, we can learn nothing. What we understand is what we can comprehend in the system of nature, in the light of God's essence, for without that nothing can be or be conceived. Clearly then, a miracle which, by its very definition if defined as contrary to nature, is unintelligible, can teach us nothing of nature – or of God.

How, then, must the reports of miracles in the Bible be understood? First, we must realize that the scripture does not teach science and does not attempt to explain events by natural causes. Secondly, its language and style are adapted to the beliefs and understanding of the people to whom it is addressed, being often poetic to move them more strongly. Thirdly, little reflection is needed to show that in many instances the events described were natural and could be naturally explained – for example, the rainbow as a sign to Noah, Saul's search for his father's asses and their recovery, or the change of heart of the Egyptians towards the Israelites. In other cases though the natural explanation is not apparent to us we may nevertheless assume that there was one (so far as the report of the event is true).

The report, however, may not be true, though it could genuinely have been believed by the narrator. Moreover, the scriptures themselves bear witness that there are false prophets and that "signs" may be given to deceive people. Apart from that, writers commonly interweave their own beliefs with what they offer as a plain report of fact, and imaginings are sometimes confused with perceptual experiences. In a letter to Oldenburg, Spinoza explains that he accepts the descriptions in the Gospels of Christ's passion and death, and the fact that the disciples believed what they wrote about his resurrection. But, he adds, it in no way detracts from the teaching of the Gospel to maintain that in this last they could have been deceived, as were so many other prophets concerning allegedly miraculous events which they report (*Ep.* LXXVIII). The true test of revelation is not the report of signs and wonders that accompany prophecy, but the actual content of the teaching. What induces men to believe it is another matter, but the psychological causes of belief are no less produced by God.

9. *The True and Universal Religion*

In the fourth chapter of the *Theologico-Political Treatise* Spinoza briefly summarizes the teaching of the *Ethics* that our supreme good requires the perfection of what he here calls "our better part" – the intellect.[24] If we wish to seek our surest advantage, we must try above all things to perfect the understanding as much as possible. Certainty and the removal of doubt, he continues, depend solely upon our knowledge of God; thus our supreme good both depends on and consists in such knowledge. Love of God, being the love of a perfect object makes man correspondingly more perfect. Accordingly, whatever is the means to this supreme object may be called God's law.

What the true prophets all agree in teaching is that the love of God leads to salvation and that love of one's neighbour, justice and mercy are God's commandments. This, they teach, is truly the law of God, written not on tablets of stone, nor in a certain set of books, but in men's hearts. It is a doctrine that can be understood by the simplest people and is the

---

[24] Cf. *loc. cit.*: "*Cum melior pars nostri sit intellectus, certum est si nostrum utile revera quaerere velimus, nos supra omnia debere conari, ut eum quantum fieri potest perficiamus; in ejus enim perfectione summum nostrum bonum consistere debet.*"

authentic and universal teaching of the scriptures. This, then, is the criterion of genuine prophecy. If any other oracle is pronounced, inconsistent with this message, it is spurious. "Wherefore, the divinity of the Scripture ought to be founded upon this alone, that it teaches true virtue. And that can be established only from Scripture. For if that could not be done, we could not, without great prejudice, accept it and testify to its divinity" (*T.Th.P.*, VII). Once again, the ultimate court of appeal is reason, for that the love of God and man and righteous living are the means to salvation is what reason demonstrates. But not everybody can discover or even follow the demonstration and to some this truth is revealed imaginatively without rational support. Such are the prophets; and those who accept their message as the divine will and command do so by faith. If they also carry out their precepts in practice they shall win salvation, for "faith if it have not works, is dead in itself."

This is the essence of the true and universal (or Catholic) religion the precepts of which Spinoza states (in *T.Th.P.*, XIV) as follows:

1. God Exists: that is, a supreme being in the highest degree just and merciful, the true exemplar of life. Whosoever does not know or believe that such a being exists cannot obey him or acknowledge him as judge.
2. God is one, and devotion, admiration and love towards him is absolutely to be required.
3. He is omnipresent and nothing is hidden from him. If any believes otherwise he will doubt of the equal justice with which God directs all things.
4. God has supreme dominion over everything.
5. The worship of God consists solely in obedience to his law, solely in justice, charity and love of one's neighbour.
6. All who live in accordance with these principles are saved and those who follow the dictates of selfish pleasure are lost.
7. Finally, God forgives the sins of the penitent.

These precepts are indispensable to the good life, but a knowledge of their rational basis is not; and the scriptures, which teach them, are addressed not to the learned but to the multitude, who would, if they did not believe and honour them, be led astray by the temptations of sensual pleasure.

The person who observes the moral law through faith in God on the plane of imagination would, it seems, enjoy a beatitude dependent solely on his virtue but not founded in any rational contemplation of God's essence. But Spinoza has demonstrated that because of man's inevitable finitude he must always be subject to the passions, which can be overcome only by countervailing emotions, either such as are excited by fear of penalties or hope of rewards, as in political life, or else the active emotions of adequate knowledge. And he has said that obedience through fear (and equally, we may presume, through avarice) is rather slavery than true virtue. How, then, does the man of faith achieve salvation unless he too can attain to the intellectual love of God?

The answer to this question is, I think, to be found in the final paragraph of Ch. XV of the *Treatise* and Spinoza's note thereon, taken in conjunction with the Scholium to Prop. liv of *Ethics* IV (quoted above) [25] and the Scholium to Prop. x of *Ethics* V. These passages tell us (i) that passions such as humility, penitence and reverence, commended by the prophets, incline people towards more rational living, (ii) that so long as we have no perfect knowledge of the passions our best course is to live according to certain set rules committed to memory and applied so as to keep evil passions in check and to encourage virtuous action, (iii) that revelation teaches what reason does not perceive, namely, that simple obedience is the path to salvation and that this can be effected by the special grace of God which is inscrutable to reason. Here again, Spinoza seems to be referring to the reason of the person accepting revelation by faith only, for he has himself shown by reason in the *Ethics* that simple obedience is the way to salvation. But one who cannot follow this reasoning may still believe what revelation teaches – that by the special grace of God salvation is granted to those who obey his law. In the note Spinoza adds "Revelation, not reason, can teach us that it is sufficient for salvation or beatitude to embrace divine decrees as laws or commands (*mandata*) and that it is not necessary to conceive them as eternal truths."

To obey in simple faith, however, is not slavery because, as the scriptures teach, the law must be in our hearts and observance of it must itself be seen as salvation. It is its own reward. And to be so disposed to honour it is itself to enjoy the grace of God. The truly devout love God and follow his behest (to love their neighbours, living in peace and charity) through that love and loyalty and not through fear. They give willing service without expectation of reward.

Nothing beyond this is essential, not ritual observances, nor the acceptance of special historical narratives, nor the adherence to theological dogmata (although the former may be of some help in exciting the imagination and retaining the fidelity of the vulgar); and whosoever abides by these principles has in him the spirit of Christ and is saved, be he Jew, Christian or Turk. So radical a doctrine was more than Spinoza's contemporaries could stomach, whether they belonged to the Synagogue, to

[25] P. 209.

the Roman Catholic or to the Protestant persuasion, and even his tolerant and broadminded friend Oldenburg had serious doubts.

10. Spinoza's attitude to Christianity

Though he became estranged from Judaism, Spinoza never formally embraced Christianity, for reasons which are perhaps already sufficiently apparent. Nevertheless, he studied the New Testament closely and includes it in what he refers to as the scriptures. He clearly held that it was inspired in precisely the same sense as any other part of the Bible to which his criteria of authenticity apply. Moreover, he says in the *Tractatus* that Christ was unique among prophets in that the nature and the law of God (as defined above) were revealed to him directly without the need of visions or of signs. He grasped them *pura mente* without intermediary symbolism, and in his very person he revealed to men the way of salvation.[26]

Further what he sets out as the true catholic religion and the law of God is what Christ taught, and is what Spinoza also at times describes as "the spirit of Christ" as well as "the holy spirit." For instance, he writes (in *T.Th.P.*, V): "He who is completely ignorant of [the Scriptures], and none the less has the right opinions and a true principle of living, is absolutely happy (*beatus*), and truly has in himself the Spirit of Christ." In the *Short Treatise* he gave the name "Son of God" to each of the infinite modes, so that the divine intellect is termed a "son of God," and in a letter to Oldenburg (*Ep.* LXXIII) we find: "I say that it is not entirely necessary to salvation to know Christ according to the flesh; but we must think far otherwise concerning that eternal son of God, that is, the eternal wisdom of God, which has manifested itself in all things, especially in the human mind, and most of all in Jesus Christ."

There is a sense, therefore, in which he considered Jesus to be divine, to have been in his own person a revelation of God's nature and the expression of divine wisdom, but in a manner not impossible also for others, at least in some degree. For the eternal wisdom is one with that intellectual love by which God loves himself and in which the virtuous and the philosophical can share.

But Spinoza declares that he cannot understand the doctrine "which certain Churches add" to this, that God took upon himself human nature. "Indeed, to confess the truth, they seem to me to speak no less absurdly than if someone were to tell me that a circle assumed the nature of a square." (*Ibid.*) No tales of miracles can serve to convince him of any

---

[26] Cf. *T.Th.P.*, I and IV.

such absurdity, not even the allegation of the resurrection itself. Nor does he consider other current dogmas of the various Churches, or the beliefs and practices of professing Christians, to be anything better than superstition. They have, he says, by relying solely on miracles, that is appeals to ignorance, the fountain of all wickedness, "turned their faith, even though it is true, into superstition." (*Ep*. LXXIII).

The Gospel accounts of Christ's passion and death he was prepared to take literally, but in the stories of the resurrection he finds only symbolic truth. The resurrection, he says, was really spiritual, and was revealed to the disciples in ways adapted to their comprehension and beliefs. Their experiences of the risen Christ were visions and apparitions in which they sincerely believed, but in truth Christ rose from the dead (in the sense in which he himself says, "Let the dead bury their dead") [27] only in that his mind and spirit are eternal and transcend all temporal things, as the holiness of his life and death and teaching may enable others to do who follow his example (*Ep*. LXXV). For man, though but a finite mode of substance, is not wholly limited to the finite and the temporal, but has in him immortal longings which can unite him with divinity and admit him to eternal life.

[27] i.e., let the earthly rites of burial be performed by those who are immersed in finite and transitory affairs.

CHAPTER XI

HUMAN IMMORTALITY

1. The final Problem

We have found it possible to resolve the many contradictions which *prima facie* seem so blatant in Spinoza's philosophy. The rigidity of his method and its discursive rationalism we have found not incompatible with his representation of the highest form of knowledge as intuitive. The reconciliation is found in a conception of truth as a coherent *discursus* embracing an all-inclusive whole. His apparent atheism and naturalism is not really in conflict with his constant insistence on the fundamental necessity of the nature and existence of a transcendent God. His unrelenting determinism is, despite all appearances, consistent with free action and moral responsibility and with what is the only valid and defensible conception of teleology. His explicit denial of the reality of good and evil is, nevertheless, consistent with his moral outlook and his delineation of a true and a supreme good for mankind. And his polemics against superstition are yet in conformity with his respect for and advocacy of a true and universal religion. But there remains one problem still to face, and perhaps the most difficult of all: How is the finite mind of man – the idea of a body, which is a finite mode of extension, limited and determined both spatially and temporally – reconciled, through an adequate knowledge of nature or substance, with the infinite and eternal being of God?

My object in this chapter is to consider this final question. In effect, Spinoza's answer to it is his doctrine of human immortality, which is, in many ways, the most puzzling and controversial of his entire system. The mind or soul of man, he tells us is a mode (or idea) in the Attribute of Thought (God's attribute), of which the object is a mode of Extension (another of God's attributes) and nothing else.[1] The soul is the idea of the body, and as the body is altered so is the mind affected. If the body is

---

[1] Cf. *Ethics,* II, xiii.

destroyed the mind is likewise.[2] Nevertheless, the mind can be united not only with its body, but also, through its adequate ideas, with the infinite essence of God; and, through the third kind of knowledge, *scientia intuitiva*, with its corollary, the intellectual love of God, the mind of man may be united with God himself and his infinite intellect, thus it may become immortal (*onsterfelijk*) and eternal (*aeterna*). We must ask whether Spinoza's account of the relation of body and mind is, or can be understood to be, compatible with any such notion of immortality for the soul; whether in view of his theory of body-mind relation any notion of immortality can be seen as acceptable.

This is really the focal and fundamental problem of Spinoza's, and indeed of all, philosophy, for it involves the relation of time and the temporal to eternity, of the finite to the infinite, the nature of the immanence of the latter in the former, and the possibility of self-transcendence by the former to comprehend the latter in knowledge. To some extent we have touched already on all of these aspects of the problem, but they are all summed up in the problem of immortality. Some effort will therefore be needed to throw still more light on these issues in order to discover whether the notion of immortality is to be made intelligible, or if it must be rejected as altogether untenable. We must both consider Spinoza's theory, what it actually means, whether he has made it coherent or, if not, whether without doing violence to its main principles it can be coherently understood; and we must make some attempt, however halting and inadequate, to cope with the problems in themselves.

2. *Traditional ideas of Immortality*

There have been, in the past, two predominant ways of conceiving human immortality. The first is to regard human personality as consisting of two separable parts, each in some sense complete in itself, a material body and an immaterial soul. On the death of the body, the soul is then thought of as being released, and, in a disembodied state, as continuing to live for an indefinitely long time, as it had done in the past. The second way of regarding immortality is that adopted in the Christian creeds, which envisage a soul separable from the body, but consider the resurrection of the body essential for the preservation in an after-life of the individuality of each particular person. The soul here does not die, as the body does, but presumably remains after bodily death in some state of suspended existence until such time as it can be reunited with the

---

[2] Cf. *K.V.*, II, *Voorreeden*, footnote: *Ethics*, II, xiv et seq.

resurrected body, now somehow rendered indestructible so that the person can live on for ever.

Spinoza's theory, at least *prima facie*, seems incompatible with both of these conceptions. He maintains first that the soul is the idea (which constitutes the human mind) of which the object "is a body, or a certain mode of extension actually existing, and nothing else" (*Ethics*, II, xiii). If and when the body ceases to exist, therefore, it should follow that its idea ceases to exist likewise – except in the rather special sense that every mode of Extension and of Thought exists eternally in God. This latter existence, however, cannot be equated with human immortality in particular, because it applies to all finite entities without exception, whether they are modes of Extension or of Thought. The eternal existence of the modes in God's eternal and infinite attributes pertains to God. It is not the *continued* existence in time of any one of them beyond its allotted span, and thus by no means is it the continued existence of a human person enjoying successive experiences after the death of his body. It seems to follow, further, from the Scholium to Prop. xiii of *Ethics* II, that body and mind are inseparable and co-terminous. There Spinoza asserts that the relation between them is no different from that between any other *idea* and its *ideatum*: "For of everything there must necessarily be given an idea in God, of which God is the cause, in the same manner as there is an idea of the human body." The only difference between man's mind and the ideas in God of other things is what follows from the difference between the human body and other bodies, the former being, for the most part, more complex. As the human body is more apt than others for doing and suffering many things at the same time, so the human mind is more apt to perceive many things at the same time.

Similarly, we are told in the *Short Treatise* that as the body suffers changes caused by other bodies, so these changes are felt by the soul as sensations (Pt. II, Introd., footnote) and also that the soul, being an idea of the existence of some thing (*Zaak*) in Nature, endures and changes according as that thing endures and changes (Pt. II, App.). But in both of these contexts Spinoza qualifies his statement in a way which he then uses to prove human immortality. To this qualification I shall return presently. What is to be noted here is that the doctrine of body-mind relationship is so conceived that the mind (the idea of the body) cannot be separated from the body and can exist only if and when the body exists. It should follow that the immortality of the soul, if it is to be affirmed at all, cannot be conceived, as it was by Plato in the *Phaedo*, as the continued existence of a disembodied soul after the death and dissolution of the body.

Nor is the notion of a resurrection of the body anywhere suggested by Spinoza and it would seem impossible in his system. For the existence of each finite thing (according to him) is necessarily caused in the succession of finite causes which flow endlessly from God's infinite being; and no cause is mentioned, or seems to be contemplated, which could reconstitute exactly so complex a body as the human organism, once its dissolution has been brought about by other necessary causes. That such reconstitutive causes might be included in God's infinite reality is conceivable, but Spinoza never considers the possibility, nor is there anything in the nature of things as we experience them that requires us to assume the actuality of such causes. However that may be, Spinoza's account of human immortality does not include or require the resurrection of the body as a particular mode of extended substance, though it does, as we shall see, require a special interpretation of the nature and status of individual bodies and a transformed idea of them.

So far, however, we can say that Spinoza's theory of body-mind relationship is in conflict with both the most usual traditional forms of the notion of immortality, and would seem to exclude the possibility of any kind of "life after death." Yet Spinoza, in the Scholium to Prop. xx of *Ethics,* V, says: "And with these (demonstrations) I have dealt with everything that concerns this present life. . . . It is, therefore, time now that I should pass to those matters which pertain to the duration of the mind without relation to the body." And in the 23rd Proposition of the same Part he declares: "It is not possible for the human mind to be absolutely destroyed with the body, but something of it remains which is eternal." The first statement is significant, not simply because no existence of the mind without relation to the body should be possible consistently with what we have been told earlier, but also because reference is made to it specifically as "duration." It would, however, be quite consistent with this statement subsequently to deny that the mind endures at all without relation to the body; and this is precisely what Spinoza does say in the Scholium to the 23rd Proposition: "Our mind . . . can be said to endure, and its existence can be defined by a certain time, only so far as it involves the actual existence of the body." Nevertheless, he maintains in the same place that "we feel and know (*experimur*) ourselves to be eternal." How is all this to be understood so that it is self-consistent?

3. A Common Interpretation of Spinoza

Most commentators resolve the difficulties first by contending that the reference to "this present life" in the Scholium to Proposition xx, in Part V of the *Ethics,* is a concession to ordinary parlance or a "momentary slip," [3] and to the mind's duration without relation to the body as a use of "duration" different from that in which he distinguished it from "eternity." Joachim explains [4] that Spinoza is not quite consistent in his use of this word. While, as a rule, he refuses to predicate duration of what is eternal and identifies the former with persistence in time, he also regards duration as that of which time is the measure. Time results from the subdivision of duration into periods. But this sub-division is the work of *imaginatio,* for strictly duration is indivisible (like Extension generally); [5] and when adequately conceived all its "parts" are seen as coaeval. It then becomes identical with eternity, or, as Joachim puts it, is "the general term of which eternal existence and temporal existence are forms" (*Loc. cit.*).

Spinoza's otherwise clear distinction between duration and eternity can then be taken seriously, and his attribution to the human mind of "immortality" (a term he uses himself only once in the *Ethics*) is explained as the identity of its adequate ideas with the eternal and infinite intellect of God. There are two ways, Spinoza remarks, in which we conceive of things as existing, either so far as they exist in relation to a certain time and place, or so far as they are contained in God, and follow necessarily from his the divine nature (*Ethics* V, xxix, S.). When we conceive things as existing in this second way we do so *sub specie aeternitatis* and our knowledge of them is not limited by temporal bounds. The adequate ideas in human knowledge are thus eternal. In *scientia intuitiva* man achieves an adequate knowledge of the essence of things through an adequate idea of the formal essence of certain of God's attributes,[6] and such adequate ideas as constitute this third kind of knowledge (as well as such adequate ideas as constitute the second, scientific kind – *ratio*) are eternal and timeless. And as the ideas in which these forms of knowledge consist are part of the complex idea which is the human mind, there must be some part of it "that remains eternal" when the human body dies and passes away. The use of the word "remains" here is again

---

[3] Cf. Joachim, *Study,* p. 296. Joachim, nevertheless, points out that for Spinoza "this present life" would naturally mean "our life so far as we are imaginative," i.e. the life of *Imaginatio,* associative thinking, passion and illusion.

[4] *Op. cit.,* pp. 294 ff.

[5] Cf. *K.V.,* I. ii, and p. 52f above.

[6] *Ethics,* II, xl, S 2.

regarded as a slip or a concession to ordinary language. It is repeated by Spinoza in subsequent propositions, but there is no need to understand it otherwise than as meaning that there is something eternal in the human mind besides what ceases to "endure" when its body dies (as we say in arithmetic: $15 \div 6 = 2$, remainder 3). The eternity of the "immortal" part of the human mind or soul is thus not a continued duration after the death of the body, but a quality of being.

What corresponds in extension to the eternal part of the human mind is then not the human body as a finite mode merely, or as imagined in the first kind of knowledge (*imaginatio*), but the human body as adequately understood in the second and third kinds of knowledge. As so understood it is an eternal consequence of God's infinite, immanent causality, and must be conceived in its proper place in the total scheme of things, through an adequate idea of the formal essence of (presumably) the attribute of Extension. In as much as adequate ideas are identical with God's, their counterpart in extension will not be any merely finite mode but the whole extended world – *facies totius universi* – for all modes of Extension are mutually connected in the infinite series of causes which flow of necessity from God's nature; and Spinoza explains at some length how simple bodies become included in more complex bodies in a hierarchy that eventually includes the whole of nature.

This interpretation of Spinoza's doctrine, or something very similar to it, is accepted by all the best known commentators. Joachim expounds it with admirable clarity; L. Roth and Ruth Saw do not depart from it; Stuart Hampshire adheres to it; and much the same view, with minor variations, is taken by John Caird and A. E. Taylor.[7] Indeed, there is a great deal in the Spinoza text to support it and it must be treated with respect. I shall not discuss the views of these commentators individually, nor shall I consider at this point the implications for morality and religion of the conception of human immortality involved. It would be better first to discuss the conception itself, for it leaves difficulties unresolved and significant implications in Spinoza's theory undeveloped.

4. Difficulties and Criticisms

In the first place, with all due respect to Joachim, as one of the most accurate and careful scholars who has commented on the *Ethics*, we

---

[7] Cf. H. H. Joachim, *op. cit.*, Book III, Ch. IV; Leon Roth, *Spinoza* (London, 1945), pp. 140-163; Ruth Saw, *The Vindication of Metaphysics* (London, 1951), pp. 128-136; Stuart Hampshire, *Spinoza* (London, 1946), pp. 126-132; J. Caird, *Spinoza* (London, 1910), Ch. XVI; A. E. Taylor "Spinoza's Conception of Immortality," *Mind*, V, 18, (N. S.), 1896.

have already found that it is not wholly correct to attribute the idea of the human body as a finite mode of Extension in interaction with other finite modes, merely to the confusion of *imaginatio*. "The modes are not 'parts' of Substance," writes Joachim, "The oneness of the modes in God is more intimate than the oneness of parts in a whole ... It is the separation of the modes from God (as if they were 'parts' of a whole) which causes the inadequate understanding of the imaginative consciousness, for which Reality becomes a world of finite things." [8] Joachim is certainly right to insist that for Spinoza the finite modes are not separable from God, as material "parts" may be imagined as separable from a material whole – that conception of whole and parts is certainly inadequate to Spinoza's substance. And Joachim, too, is fully aware that the unity of the modes in substance does not preclude or cancel out their multiplicity.[9] But if it is an imaginative error to think of the modes as separable parts, it is not simply an error to think of them as finite and as distinguishable within the unity of substance. (Joachim, of course, is not suggesting that it is, but he does not offer a clear alternative to the imaginative error which will preserve the "reality" of the finites and of the distinctions between them). And though it may well be only for imaginative consciousness that Reality is *merely* a world of finite things, there really is in a legitimate sense a world of finite things contained in the infinite reality of substance.

The finite modes really are finite in so far as they are determined by other finite modes and in whatever other ways they may be determined, (e.g. by their specific attribute). And these determinations follow necessarily from God's essence and are produced, as are all changes and events in time, by his immanent causation. It follows that the finiteness of man's body is not a figment of the imagination or simply a misconception, nor are the facts of its coming into existence at his birth and passing away at his death. The same applies to his mind as the idea of his (finite) body. It is really finite and its limitations follow necessarily from the nature of things. His finiteness is no misconception, though we can (if only for that reason) entertain misconceptions about it. We cannot, therefore, simply dismiss the notion of the body as a finite mode, nor of the mind as dependent on, or correlative to, it, as inadequate ideas typical of *imaginatio*. The finite body and the idea of it, which according to Spinoza, constitutes the human mind are actual factors in the nature of substance. They are parts of nature, and, even though their essence cannot be adequately

[8] *Op. cit.*, p. 229.
[9] *Op. cit.*, p. 300.

understood in isolation from the rest of nature, and can be adequately understood only in their essential and inseparable relation to the other parts and to nature as a whole, yet they cannot be dissolved away into substance as a single, seamless, undifferentiated unity excluding finiteness and temporal change. The character of the finite, as finite, remains in contrast and in opposition to the eternal and infinite, and the problem of reconciling them in the divine nature cannot be side-stepped.

Secondly, to understand what Spinoza means by human immortality, no obvious help is to be gleamed from the assertion, which he does indeed reiterate, that the idea of the finite human body exists eternally in God and, like the existence of the body itself as a finite mode of Extension, follows necessarily from God's infinite essence. For this is true of all finite bodies and all the ideas of them. Their essences are all eternally contained in God and the ideas of them are all eternally in God's infinite understanding. If this sort of eternal being is all that is involved in man's immortality he is no more immortal than a fish and rather less so than a piece of granite.

Similarly, it does not help to insist that an adequate idea of the body involves its relations to all other bodies and so involves an adequate idea of the whole of nature; and that such an adequate idea of nature would be itself an infinite and eternal idea. Because such an infinite and eternal idea would be the intellect of God and not of man, which, for all his accomplishments, remains finite. True, Spinoza does assert, and with reason on his principles, that in so far as man achieves adequate knowledge his mind becomes united with that of God; but this would seem to be, surely, only to a limited extent, and it is not easy to understand how one can enjoy immortality only to a limited extent, or be eternal only in a limited sense. Would any such limitation not involve us in a flat self-contradiction? Yet, as Spinoza's very philosophy exemplifies, according to its own principles, man does frame more or less adequate ideas of nature and of the essence of God. Again we are faced with the problem: How are we to reconcile the finite with the infinite? Spinoza's doctrine of human immortality is an important aspect of his answer to the question.

Some may wish to object that the difficulty I have raised is spurious, for Spinoza repeatedly asserts that things vary in degree according to the amount of reality their essence includes, and the essence of the human mind is intelligence, and it embraces more of reality the more it conceives things *sub specie aeternitatis*. It could therefore be eternal in a degree, or to the extent to which its ideas were adequate, and to that extent it would be immortal. In short, as Plato and Aristotle alleged, not the whole human soul, but only its thinking part is immortal – in Spinoza's terminology the part that consists of adequate ideas. Undoubtedly this objection has some weight, but now we are involved in another difficulty (or perhaps the same one over again, seen from a new angle). The personality of man is a single whole and does not consist of separable parts, even though it includes many distinguishable functions and traits. The category of whole and part is as inappropriate to the mind as Joachim explained it to be inappropriate to the nature of Spinoza's substance. We cannot, therefore, intelligibly maintain that the human soul is immortal only in bits and pieces, and that some parts die with the body while others do not. If it lives at all it must live as a whole. Thus though it is legitimate to hold that we can attain to the truth or to goodness in varying degrees, it hardly seems proper to maintain that we can, *qua* individuals, enjoy eternal life only in some degree of eternity inferior to the eternity of substance, or only in certain parts of our conscious being.

Further, a frequent objection to Spinoza's theory, which the interpretation outlined above would encourage, is that it rules out any semblance of individual, or personal, immortality. For what is said to be immortal is only adequate knowledge of things viewed *sub specie aeternitatis,* a set of eternal truths identical for all minds as for God's and with as little personal idiosyncrasy as he possesses. If this is all that is immortal, the objectors complain, it is not what we think of as the human individual. Moreover, Spinoza says quite plainly that it does not include memory,[10] which seems an indispensable condition of personal identity. The whole doctrine, therefore, seems to be more a denial of human immortality than an affirmation and explanation of it, and though it may be true that in the final analysis all men are but mortal, it is at best misleading to call the demonstration of this fact a theory of human immortality.

5. Idea as Transcendent

How far is it possible to extract from Spinoza's writings answers to these objections and a solution to this problem? The first clue to follow is one suggested in the previous section, that the mind is a single, indivisible whole. Spinoza has told us that the human mind is the idea of the body; and in the 32nd Epistle he says that "the human body is a part of Nature" and "the human mind ... also is a part of Nature: since I maintain that there exists in Nature an infinite power of thinking, which, so far as it is infinite contains in itself objectively the whole of Nature and

---

[10] Cf. *Ethics* V, xxi, xxiii, S, and xxxix.

whose thoughts proceed in the same way as Nature which, to be sure, is its *ideatum.*" This power of thinking is undoubtedly the intellect of God – a system of ideal modes, or ideas, corresponding to the extended modes, or bodies, which constitute the physical world. None of these is a mere collection or congeries of separate or separable items (though the modes in each attribute are distinguishable and ordered as a system of inter-related terms). The world of extended things, we learn from this letter, as from the *Korte Verhandeling* (and elsewhere), is an indivisible whole, and the order and connection of things is the same as the order and connection of ideas.

In the same letter that I have quoted above Spinoza goes on to say "the human mind is the same power [of thinking] not in so far as it is infinite and perceives the whole of Nature, but in so far as it is finite and perceives only the human body, and in this way I declare that the human mind is part of a certain infinite intellect." But the contents of the divine intellect, as follows both from what Spinoza says in this epistle and from his general position stated repeatedly in various works, constitute an indivisible and systematic whole; and from what he says further about ideas it becomes apparent that any adequate idea belonging to this system will, in a significant sense, comprehend the whole of it.

For ideas are not static pictures or replicas, in some different medium, of the extended things; they are their "minds" or consciousness, just as the idea of the human body is its mind and consciousness. But the idea of a relatively simple body, like a stone or a coprolite, taken simply in and by itself, is so rudimentary and inadequate that it hardly merits the name "mind" at all, though Spinoza is prepared to concede it in some degree.[11] The human body, however, is far more complex and is "apt to do and suffer many things," hence its mind (or idea) is equally complex and is highly developed.

We must not, however, think of ideas or minds as mere reproductions, in the attribute of Thought, of the essences of their corresponding bodies. They are awarenesses, self-conscious and self-illuminating. Every idea implies an *idea ideae*; every knowing a knowledge that one knows, and though each such *idea* is, according to Spinoza, formally distinct from every other (as an act of consciousness), the *idea* and the *idea ideae* are "objectively" identical and are both substantially one and the same with their (physical) *ideatum.*[12] Each is a mode under a different attribute of the same identical substance. The nature of this dual unity we have al-

[11] Cf. p. 77f above.
[12] Cf. *Ethics* II, vii, xxi, and xliii; *TdIE*, VI, 35, and above, p. 88.

ready examined and shall consider more closely below, but first I wish to draw attention to the fact that consciousness, the basic sense of Spinoza's *idea,* even at its most primitive level, is never, *qua* consciousness, confined or limitable to a bare particular of any sort. Its most elementary object is and must be at least a particular distinguished from a background, or set in a context. An entity's idea or consciousness of itself must and can only be its awareness of itself in distinction from something else, and so must any awareness of anything whatsoever. Consciousness, therefore, is always not merely self-consciousness (*idea ideae*) but is also self-transcendent, and tends to comprehension of some whole to which its object belongs. If this point is taken along with what I have just cited about the wholeness and indivisibility of the infinite power of thinking and of its object, very significant consequences ensue for the human mind which will illuminate Spinoza's doctrine of its capacity for eternity.

6. *Time and Eternity*

In section 8 of Chapter V we saw that temporal sequence could be conceived on two levels: either the phenomenal, at which things and events appear to us in haphazard order and are strung together seriatim by the imagination, or else as a real series of finite causes and effects issuing from the eternal and infinite essence of God and ordered by the unchanging *Gestalt* of the whole of the extended universe. On the first level time is a mere aid to the imagination whereby we divide and measure the duration of things conceived as a sort of quantity of existence (*Ethics* II, xlv, S). On the second level time is the coming to be and passing away of finite modes of substance in infinite causal succession, in which both their persistence in being for as long as they last and their successive transition from one to another follow from the eternal necessity of the nature of God (*ibid.*). The eternal nature of substance transcends the temporal series (in ways which we noted), but the temporal sequence is nevertheless governed by and summed up in the *facies totius universi* so that it actually constitutes it, as the metabolic and physiological processes in a living organism constitute its stable form. The finite modes are to the *Gestalt* of the whole universe much as matter is to form in the philosophy of Aristotle. They are distinguishable but not separable and each makes the other *what* it is (as, for Aristotle, both matter and form determine the nature of substance). The "face" of the whole universe, however, is an infinite mode issuing immediately from motion-and-rest, and identical with it in reality, and that is also an infinite mode following immediately from the essence of substance, as expressed under the attribute of Extension. The temporal series and the eternal mode are thus two aspects of the same substantial reality.

All this is equally true under the attribute of Thought, the modes of which are identical in substance with those of Extension. Thus the eternal essence of God contains or expresses itself in and through both infinite and finite modes in all its attributes, and the temporal succession among the finites is the direct manifestation of its immanent causality. Time and eternity are, therefore, not separable, but are alternative aspects of the unitary being of substance.

Furthermore, within the flux of finite modes that is governed by the principle of order immanent in it so as to constitute the face of the entire universe as one unchanging infinite whole, there are modes on different levels of complexity and having different degrees of perfection or completeness. Under Extension these are bodies having less or more aptitude for doing and suffering many things at once. The ideas of such bodies, under Thought, are their minds, and are correlatively less or more capable of thinking. The finite modes which constitute bodies come and go in constant temporal flux, but the more complex and "perfect" are to a higher degree self-perpetuating, and the gradation of such perfection is continuous right up to the infinite mode, if Spinoza is to be believed (Cf. *Ethics* II, Lem. vii, S.). In the same way, we may understand how ideas range on different levels of perfection from inadequate to adequate, and while the former are transitory and finite, constituting the psychic life of the soul (the "stream of consciousness"), they contribute nevertheless to the generation of the latter, which are ideas of the eternal – or of things under the aspect of eternity (*sub specie aeternitatis*). We have seen how this is effected, through self-reflection and the inherent self-transcendence of consciousness (*cogitatio*). In the finite and transitory modes God's causality is transient but it is always and in all modes also immanent, and this immanence becomes manifest in adequate ideas which comprehend the structure of infinite modes.

It is clear that an adequate idea of an infinite mode and of the relation to it of its constituent finite modes cannot be merely one of those finite modes. Strictly, the idea of the infinite mode is itself an infinite mode of Thought, as the idea of the *facies totius universi* is the infinite intellect of God. Nevertheless, men whose minds are the ideas of finite bodies can know more than those finite bodies alone. All they know is mediated through their bodies, and the vehicle of all their knowledge is the stream of psychical states which constitute their minds, but their bodies register effects from the whole of the physical world and the causality of God is immanent in them; so their minds become capable, to the extent that their bodies are more versatile, of framing ideas, more or less adequate, of the entire world of nature, of God and of his attributes. These ideas are as much God's as our own, and, so far as they are adequate, are identical with God's. Hence they are eternal. Such ideas are those which span the entire temporal order and view it *sub specie aeternitatis,* for, as Hegel says, "time itself in its concept is eternal"; [13] and time, we have seen, is itself eternity in complementary aspect. Thus when Joachim says that Spinoza uses the term "duration" in two senses, one as that "quantity of existence" which the imagination divides up into fictitious temporal spans or measures, and the other as the whole, which, when adequately conceived, is eternity, he is right. Duration may well be regarded as the general term of which temporal existence and eternal being are specific forms, but such a view must not mislead us into thinking that what is eternal endures through time, for endurance through time is precisely what the eternal transcends. Nor is eternity a sort of parallel time series accompanying duration, nor yet a second duration beyond it. All these imaginative representations are strictly inconceivable; for temporal predicates apply only to the finite; the eternal is the infinite as such.

7. *Mind as Idea of Body*

Let us now return to Spinoza's doctrine of the relation of the human body to its mind. First, our ideas are the awareness of our bodies and nothing else. We feel and are conscious of the activities, passivities, and functionings of our bodies, and of other bodies only as and through our own. Our awareness of the world is thus at the same time our awareness of the body, and it is only by making distinctions, in an appropriate and systematic way, within this total self-awareness, that we distinguish what belongs to our own bodies from what pertains to others. According to Spinoza, we make these distinctions well or ill according as we think adequately or inadequately; and we do the former in so far as we are active (and *vice versa*), and the latter so far as we are passive – so far as our body suffers effects from interaction with other bodies. Though Spinoza frequently writes as if action depended only on adequate ideas, and as if inadequate ideas resulted only from bodily passivity, to understand him aright we must realize that activity and passivity are each one and the same in both body and mind. It is, then, only so far as we think adequately that we make the right distinctions between our own body and others and conceive their mutual relations correctly.

[13] *Encyclopaedia of Philosophical Sciences,* § 258, *Zusatz.*

Next, we have noticed that the body is strictly and in fact related in some way to everything else in the extended world, and all these relations must, therefore, be registered in idea either as passions or otherwise. In *imaginatio* ideas are confused and false but they are nevertheless consequences of the impingement of external things upon the body. Thus even so far as its confused ideas are concerned, the mind embraces and reflects the whole of nature.

But each thing endeavours, so far as it is in itself, to persevere in its own being, and this *conatus* is the actual essence of the thing itself involving indefinite time. The mind, both in its confused and in its adequate ideas, is aware of this *conatus* (*Ethics* III, ix.), which is nothing less, in the last resort, than the power of God himself; and it is by virtue of the *conatus* that the mind advances from *imaginatio* and confused ideas to adequate knowledge in the forms of *ratio* and *scientia intuitiva*. The human mind, therefore, as the idea of the body, embraces within its consciousness all the affects of the body and all its relations with the rest of the world, and so is all-inclusive even in its passions and its confused ideas. Its *conatus* is towards action and so impels it to develop (in ways the detail of which we have already examined) [14] towards the perfection of its own being in the intellectual love of God. The result of this development is not just the supplementation of confused ideas by a new set of adequate ideas; it is the transformation of the entire personality on its emotional and practical side, as well as in its theoretical content. Adequate knowledge is not simply part of the mind beside and separable from inadequate ideas still harboured within it. Adequate knowledge is an order of activity, different from the passivity of *imaginatio,* which annuls all cognate confused ideas, transforms the passions into healthy, positive and beneficent emotions, and divisive and turbulent motives of action into love and compassion. All this, moreover, is the product of the *conatus in suo esse perseverare* of the individual, which is the very power of God (the Holy Spirit) working within him.

This transformation is of mind and body in one. Spinoza quite explicitly says that "he who has a body capable of many things, has a mind of which the greater part is eternal" (*Ethics* V, xxxix), having already stated that the attainment of the third kind of knowledge implies the mind's knowledge of itself and of its body *sub specie aeternitatis*. (*Ibid.,* xxx). This knowledge of the body is surely no mere way of viewing it, as might be some inadequate imagination of it. It must be a conception of the body as it really is in nature, the more so as the initial feeling of the

[14] Cf. pp. 103ff and 166ff above.

body in *imaginatio* was already a confused awareness of the *facies totius universi* (construed however as the common order of nature), which has become progressively clarified into a true and adequate knowledge of God. It is in this way that our minds are part of that infinite power of thinking in nature of which Spinoza writes in Epistle XXXII.

The body is thus revealed as the vehicle of God's own self-revelation in and through the mind of man. The power of God, causing the infinite system of modes which is nature, and working immanently throughout that system produces man's body, as it produces all others, and *pari passu* produces man's mind, the idea of his body, which it then urges through a process of internal development from *imaginatio* to *scientia intuitiva* and to a revelation of God's own infinite and eternal nature, the supreme object of perfect and unadulterable love. It is the love of God himself, by which in one and the same act he loves himself and his creation, including man. In short, it is a union or self-identification of man with God.

This knowledge and love of God, the eternal and infinite substance, transforms all man's emotions and actions, and constitutes the life of blessedness, which is the highest virtue, the final object of rational desire, as well as the completest and most adequate knowledge of nature. This *is* man's immortality, and its special character follows from the nature of self-consciousness, which, as was said above, is no inert replica of the extended world, but is an active self-awareness of the body, that embraces in its purview and comprehension all its relations to other bodies and the infinite, eternal character of the essence of substance to which it belongs – "proceeds from an adequate idea of the formal essence of certain attributes of God to the adequate knowledge of the essence of things" (*Ethics*, II, xl, S 2).

Consciousness is self-transcendent. It cannot exist simply in space and time and at the same time be aware, as it is, of the inter-relations of all parts of space and time. It cannot be limited within a restricted space or period, and also know the relations of that restricted space and period to the rest of the extended world. In order to enjoy that knowledge it must somehow be identical with its object(s), as it is impossible for the body as a finite mode of Extension to be identical with its causes and effects. Although the body is related to all other bodies and registers within itself their effects, it can do so only if it is distinguished from them as the mind cannot be distinguished from them if it is to be conscious of them. Spinoza insists that *idea* and *ideatum* are identical; but a finite mode of Extension cannot be similarly identical with other finite extended modes with which it is in spatio-temporal and causal relations, though it can be, and is, inseparably continuous with them. The mind, on the other hand, in knowing these relations and their systematic integration into one individual has as its *ideatum* the whole extended world (*totius facies universi*), transcends all spatial and temporal limits and is one with the whole eternal structure.

The coming to be and passing away in time of finite things in the material world, are then seen as a partial feature or aspect of a single, indivisible, infinite and absolute totality – the eternal being of God-or-Substance. They are not unreal, for they do proceed necessarily from the divine essence. They are actual elements within the reality of nature and do constitute the modes of substance under a real and necessary attribute of God. Only for the imagination are they merely fleeting episodes of ephemeral significance. Their finiteness is not illusory, for their mutual determinations are essential to the multiplex unity of substance. But their temporal existence in itself is not of ultimate significance, for they can neither be nor be conceived except through the infinite being of God, in which they all live and move. To understand the world in this way is to conceive things adequately and is the part of *scientia intuitiva*; and any mind that has perfected its knowledge to this degree has transcended the finite nature of its body, and the transient existence of things in space and time in a synoptic awareness of "all time and all existence."

It follows, as Spinoza says, that "the human mind cannot be absolutely destroyed with the body, but there is something besides (*aliquid remanet*) which is eternal." It transcends, in its consciousness, the temporal as well as the spatial limits of the body, while yet being identical in substance with the body, as its idea, its "psyche" or conscious life. The body is the condition of the mind's existence, but its ideal, its conscious, character is transcendent, for this transcendence is typical of all consciousness, even of *imaginatio*. There is a valid sense, therefore, in which every mind is both finite and in some degree eternal. All ideas are on the one hand part of the psychical stream which is the counterpart of the body, yet, on the other hand, all consciousness is in some degree transcendent of its immediate object in time and space; and to the extent that it is not limited, as its body (*qua* finite mode of Extension) is limited, it participates (if we may, like Plato, use a term which is not wholly appropriate) in eternity. For to be aware of spatio-temporal relations is, of necessity, not to be merely one term in any such relation. To be conscious of space and time is to transcend space and time – to be eternal. To be adequately conscious of the whole structure of nature as it really is, to know it *sub specie aeternitatis* as God knows it, is to be united with God and to share (if, again, so inappropriate a word may be permitted) in his eternal being.

8. Misinterpretations and Misconceptions

Obviously this eternal reality cannot be an extended duration. If this is the nature of man's immortality it cannot possibly be an "after-life" or temporal existence prolonged beyond the temporal existence of the body. Such a misconception of immortality is not only common among the unphilosophical but is even attributed confusedly to Spinoza by some commentators. Among these perhaps H. A. Wolfson is the worst offender, for his rendering of Spinoza's theory of immortality is riddled with mistakes, some involving technicalities which it would not be profitable to detail here. "The mind, according to Spinoza," Wolfson writes, "is not merely a physiological function of the body which is born with the body and which must completely disappear with it. This is only true of some of its functions. But in its thinking essence it comes from above, . . . it is a mode of the eternal and infinite attribute of thought. That part of mind existed from eternity prior to the existence of its particular body, and it remains to eternity even after the death of the body." (*The Philosophy of Spinoza*, II, p. 291f.).

That the mind in any part or activity is "merely a physiological function of the body" is at best a *suggestio falsi* far from Spinoza's contention; and this is the sort of error to which we found Wolfson prone in an earlier context (see p. 168f above). Nor does its thinking essence "come from above" (whatever that may be taken to mean). The mind as a whole is the idea of the body, for Spinoza, the mode of substance, in Thought, of which the body is the mode in Extension. They are both the same thing (*res*). And the mind as a whole (not just part of it) is related to the infinite intellect of God in the same way as the body is related to the face of the whole universe. There is no question of some parts of the mind disappearing with the body (the imaginative and the passionate) while other parts continue to exist thereafter. Certainly, the body and the psychical functioning of the mind, involving memory and imagination, are co-terminous. But what "remains," what is not accounted for, simply by psychical functioning, is the eternal truth of adequate ideas, *imaginatio, ratio* and *scientia intuitiva* are not parts of the mind but are grades of knowledge. The last two are eternal, but for that very reason we cannot say that they are "prior to" or "remain after" the birth and death of the body, for "in eternity there is no *when, before* or *after*." (*Ethics* I, xxxiii, S 2; *Cog. Met.* I, iii).

The eternity of the mind's adequate thinking is not an extended duration beyond the temporal limits of mortal existence. For the mind transcends the body just because its consciousness is *not* in time and so far as it does *not* endure. It transcends time and space in the sense that time and space are *for* it and it is not in them. Consciousness embraces time and space as orders or wholes, and so is aware of the place, within these orders, of the body, of which the human mind in its psychic or imaginative phase is the conscious life. The human mind is thus both finite and potentially infinite, both the idea of a finite mode of Extension (and thus itself a finite mode of Thought) and, nevertheless, in being idea, capable of adequate knowledge of the total scheme of things, in which it is self-transcendent and eternal.

The objection may be repeated that this conception of immortality dissolves away human individuality, which, in accordance with this view, cannot survive the body. What "remains," if we follow Spinoza, is the impersonal eternal essence of Substance with which the mind in *scientia intuitiva* has become identified. This must inevitably be the same for all minds, for there is only one infinite being, as Spinoza spares no effort to demonstrate; and to become identified with it must be to become wholly absorbed into it and as a distinct individual to be obliterated by it.

Wolfson, noticing that this kind of eternity might be attributed equally to the body as to the mind (in the manner we noticed on p. 234 above), alleges that Spinoza conceives of a personal immortality in which something peculiar to the individual persists after, as it had existed prior to, the existence of the body.[15] In all this he misinterprets Spinoza's actual statements by reading them in the light of doctrines taught by his mediaeval predecessors (Gersonides, Crescas, etc.), in a way which, all the evidence seems to show, Spinoza never in the least intended. Throughout his discussion Wolfson confuses eternity with duration in the sense of temporal succession. He speaks of "the thinking essence" of the human mind coming from and returning to God – "both mind and body," he says, "Spinoza will admit, come from God, and unto God shall they return" (p. 294). But Spinozistically this is nonsensical. Everything is in God and cannot "come from" him, as there is nowhere away from God for it to go or come. Similarly, it cannot "return to" that substantial whole which it could never have left. The eternity, whether of the essence of the body or of the mind, is not a coming and going to and from God. It is a non-transitional being. Consequently it could make no sense for Spinoza to speak of the eternal part of the mind as existing prior to

[15] Cf. *op. cit.* II, pp. 295 and 318 ff.

the body, as Plato thought, or as persisting after it (Cf. Wolfson, *op. cit.*, p. 296); nor is it compatible with Spinoza's theory of body-mind relation.

If then anything peculiar to the finite individual is in any sense eternal, it cannot be in a sense in which it *temporally* survives that individual's death and continues thereafter to exist as it did "during his lifetime" (*op. cit.*, p. 295). Similarly it reveals complete misunderstanding to write (as Wolfson does) of "the short tract of time during which it [the mind] is encased in a body" as "only an episode in its history." The mind viewed *sub specie aeternitatis* is not a history containing episodes, or at most its history so far as it has one is exhausted, in that view, by what is here described as "the short tract of time." The eternity of adequate thought is not a tract of time, long or short; though all history and all its episodes can be comprehended in thought as an eternal consequence of God's eternal essence. It is odd that Wolfson can write so ineptly of Spinoza's meaning and persist in this confusion up to the very point where he quotes (apparently with approval) Spinoza's own criticism of it:

"If we attend to the common opinion of men we shall see that they are indeed conscious of the eternity of their mind, but they confuse eternity with duration, and attribute it to imagination or memory, which they believe remains after death." (*Ethics* V, xxxiv, S).

The objection, however, that Spinoza's view of immortality annihilates human individuality is misconceived. Immortality, we have seen, is not a matter of the "survival" by any personality of his body. Nothing "remains" in the sense of continuing *in time*. What remains when we have accounted for the mortal form of experience is an eternal awareness of God's essence and the complex system of the world. It is an awareness enjoyed in his own person by each and every individual who attains to adequate knowledge, and it transforms and perfects his personality by developing it to its fullest moral capacity. So far from being lost or swallowed up in the boundless ocean of substance, the individual personality becomes whole, internally harmonious and perfectly self-determined. The limitations of bodily life are clearly understood in their relation to the rest of nature – nothing is blurred or obliterated – but these limitations are no restriction to the mind's self-awareness as a necessary and intimate pulse in the total life and consciousness of the universe. Temporal transience is not felt as an irremediable handicap or an inescapable confine.

9. Blessedness

All that Spinoza writes in the final propositions of the *Ethics* about human blessedness and the eternal nature of man's mind follows from what has here been set out. "The greatest endeavour of the mind and its greatest virtue is to understand things by the third kind of knowledge." (*Ethics* V, xxv). This kind of knowledge gives the greatest satisfaction (*ib.* xxvii). From it necessarily arises the intellectual love of God (*ib.* xxxii, C.), which, though eternal, has all the perfections of love, for as pleasure is the transition to a greater perfection so the actual enjoyment of perfection is the condition of blessedness (*ib.* xxxiii, S.). This is the highest good possible and the enjoyment of it cannot be surpassed. It is not a reward for virtue but is virtue itself (*ib.* xlii). For even if we did not know that our mind is eternal, so far as it thinks *sub specie aeternitatis,* we should still value most highly charity, justice, piety and religion (*ib.* xli); and what is thus good in itself requires no subsequent guerdon to make it attractive. It would be ridiculous to imagine that any gratification of the appetites or indulgence of lesser desires, for however long a period, could be more satisfactory and could thus serve as a recompense for virtue. Equally absurd is the assumption that men can become truly virtuous through fear of eternal punishment. Nothing is more ludicrous than to speak as if virtue were a hardship to be endured for the sake of carnal pleasures promised later, or to escape greater pains threatened in an everlasting after-life.

Further, a mind that understands the eternal nature of things and its own place in the total scheme, which thus enjoys God's knowledge of himself and is eternal in the knowledge of his eternal essence will be unconcerned about the temporal limits of the body. Its concern for the life of the body will be to understand its place in nature adequately and truly, and to act accordingly. Its longevity or otherwise will therefore become of minor importance. The actual time and eventuality of its death will have little significance, once the third kind of knowledge and the intellectual love of God have been attained. "So far as human bodies are capable of many (acts), there is no doubt but that their natures can be referred to minds which have a great awareness (*cognitio*) of themselves and of God, and of which the greater part and the most important (*praecipua*) is eternal, and that therefore they should scarcely fear death." (*Ethics,* V. xxxix, S.). For death will have been transcended in the sublime contemplation of the totality of being – the infinite and eternal reality of God.

EPILOGUE

CHAPTER XII

SPINOZA IN RETROSPECT

Anxiety about the slings and arrows of outrageous fortune is scarcely sensible for one who believes that all events are determined by eternal laws. He will find it futile to worry about anything beyond that for which he is personally responsible, and if he is responsible only for actions based on, and expressive of, clear and distinct knowledge, he will not be given to futile remorse or unproductive regrets about passionate and unwise conduct committed in the past. Responsible action, moreover, will be simply the natural and unimpeded activity of the intellect following its own laws and principles – free, in the sense that it is self-determined and unimpeded by passion, not in any sense of indeterminate arbitrament. The free man, cognizant of the wholeness of nature and the over-riding importance of synoptic awareness, will be unmoved by the trivial inconveniences of daily occurrence, which seem frustrating only by reference to shortsighted affective judgement. He will be tolerant of his neighbour's petty misdemeanours and recalcitrance. He will be generous and charitable and will in consequence enjoy peace of mind. Such joyous tranquillity, neither ascetic nor libidinous, is what Spinoza's philosophy offers. It has much in common with, though it also differs in significant ways from, the doctrine of the Stoics, whom Spinoza admired; but how far is it acceptable to the modern mind? How far is it a dated outlook restricted to the conditions and limitations of a bygone age? How far an impossible ideal founded upon a misconception of the nature of man and the world?

There can be little doubt that contemporary man, bewildered by practical problems almost inconceivable for Spinoza and without any stable assurance about ultimate ends, has yet not abandoned the search for the kind of ultimate satisfaction which Spinoza envisions. Modern youth seeks it in odd places, but it is still the desired goal. Nor is what Spinoza recommends in conflict with the scientific spirit of our age, or of his own – for that spirit was born and nurtured just prior to and during his life-time, and, in large measure, it is the new scientific outlook that his philosophy expresses. Bacon and Descartes are his mentors at least as much as Maimonides and Crescas. Nevertheless, contemporary science is very different, both in its fundamental presuppositions and in its achievements, from seventeenth century science. How much could any philosophy in harmony with it have in common with Spinoza's? Or if, as some contemporary philosophers maintain, the scientific adventure leads only to a dead end and is self-frustrating, or as others do, that it has no ultimate objective validity, can Spinoza's unshakable conviction of final truth find favour in a modern ear?

Every philosopher is an expression and a reflection of the age in which he writes; but the greatest philosophers are not limited to such reflection. Their insight carries them beyond historical confines to truths that are universal to all ages. Undoubtedly Spinoza is one of these. He is, indeed, in many ways, a typical product of his day. He had absorbed and digested the various streams of learning then current, the Mediaeval, both Jewish and Christian, the Cartesian, that of the Italian Renaissance and the efflorescence of the new science. He reacted as vigorously against Aristotle and the ancients as did Descartes or Hobbes, and he was equally convinced of the certainty of mathematical knowledge and the efficacy of strict mathematical deduction. But the grasp and penetration of his thought went beyond the limitations which these very convictions imposed upon his contemporaries. The very method which he believed to be and called geometrical transforms itself in his hands into something far less rigid and abstract; and the mechanism and determinism which was typically inherent in seventeenth century scientific thinking reveals new and pregnant implications in his application of it. These he never had time to develop fully, but we have seen how the germs of an evolutionary theory reveal themselves in such indications as he has given of the trend of his thinking.

Similarly, in spite of frequent and understandable misinterpretation, his conception of determinism is by no means purely mechanistic, as is that which persisted long after his time and is even current in many quarters today. Bodies, in his view, increase progressively in complexity and versatility – become more capable of doing and suffering as they become more complex – until a stage is reached at which their activity, though still determined, is determined by their own comprehensive systematic structure (their "perfection"), so that it becomes free action. That this is true in the physical world is never explicitly stated or explained by Spinoza, but his theory of free intellectual action is quite definite and that, in view of the conception of body-mind relation he entertains, involves a physical counterpart, though it is never fully elaborated.

The doctrines adumbrated are, moreover, compatible with recent developments in physics and biology, as I have tried in places to suggest, and the fact that Spinoza can so coherently combine them with ethical, metaphysical and theological concepts in a single system gives pointers to modern philosophers that they do ill to neglect. For they have as yet failed to integrate their own philosophical ideas, whether epistemological or ethical, with the world-view of twentieth century science, and hints taken from Spinoza, who himself had far less to go upon, might even today not prove unfruitful.

The materialist-mechanistic conception of the physical world as matter and motion is typical of the 17th century. One finds it explicitly set out by Hobbes:

"The universe, that is, the whole mass of all things that are, is corporeal, that is to say, body...; also every part of body is likewise body,... and consequently every part of the universe is body, and that which is not body is no part of the universe." [1]

And Spinoza adopts this conception for one attribute of Substance, at least as a point of departure. Extension specifies itself immediately as matter and motion, which is its proximate infinite mode. But he immediately goes beyond the limits of 17th century thought in his denial of Descartes's view of extension as inert (Cf. *Epp.* LXXXI and LXXXIII) and his dynamic conception of it as a power of God. Further, though he defines primary bodies purely in terms of matter and motion, which is again in keeping with seventeenth century science, he contemplates a progressive scale of complication which is no mere aggregation, but at each step becomes more holistic with the structure of the totality governing the nature and behaviour of the parts.

This latter characteristic, which we have found pervasive in Spinoza's thinking, is premonitory of modern ideas. In the view of contemporary physics the impressive feature of physical nature is what Sir Arthur Eddington called "the wide inter-relatedness of things." [2] Space and time, velocity and distance, mass and charge, field and matter, wave and particle, atomic structure and chemical affinity, are mutually so bound together that none of them could be other than it is without changing

---

[1] *Leviathan*, XLVI.
[2] *The Expanding Universe* (Cambridge, 1933) p. 120.

all the rest. Consequently the unity of the universe has been generally emphasized by many outstanding scientists, apart from Eddington, E. A. Milne, Albert Einstein and W. D. Sciama in particular. Similarly the biological conception of eco-systems leads to the notion of what Pierre Teilhard de Chardin calls the biosphere as a single organic whole. Spinoza's teaching with respect to the "face" of the entire universe is wholly consonant with these twentieth century ideas and his illustration of it in the thirty-second letter is extraordinarily modern in tone.[3]

A corollary of Spinoza's determinism by which his contemporaries were repelled is no more likely to attract modern readers. He repeatedly insists that all events occur in accordance with the eternal and immutable laws of Nature, so that nothing could have happened otherwise than it has done and everything that will happen in future will be completely determined by adequate causes. This seems to imply an inevitability of historical process uninfluenceable by human deliberation. Theories of historical inevitability have been harboured and advocated by other, more recent, thinkers, like Tolstoy or Marx, not always consistently, and they have aroused strong and determined opposition by others, like Sir Isaiah Berlin, who maintain that history is made by human action and that man has power and freedom to influence its outcome. But the implication of fatalism in Spinoza's position is to be repudiated, as it was by its author.

We have seen that Spinoza denied freedom of the will in the sense of indeterminate choice, but also that this did not involve denial of human responsibility nor the impossibility of affecting the actual course of events by deliberate action. The complete determinateness of things does not prevent men from acting purposively. As Spinoza writes to Oldenburg (*Ep.* LXXV), "whether we do what we do necessarily or contingently, we are led nevertheless by hope and fear." Human actions are among the causes which determine events, and although they are not themselves uncaused, the more rational they are the more are they free, in the sense which Spinoza adopts. Moreover, it does not follow from the statement that everything happens in accordance with universal and unchangeable laws, that the future is fixed and predetermined apart from human intervention, for that too follows the laws of nature, as Spinoza conceives them.

We have argued that not all determination is of the mechanical kind and, whatever Spinoza may have thought of mechanism, he certainly did not think, or maintain, that human action was *mechanically* determined.

---

[3] See p. 65ff above.

It is no fair or accurate interpretation of his description of psychological causation to say that it is mechanistic, and rational determination certainly is not. The eternal and immutable laws of God themselves, though they may include the laws of mechanism, are not necessarily, and not plausibly, restricted to the laws of physics. We have seen good reason to suppose otherwise. From all this, then, it would follow that the course of history may be completely determined, but the future need not be in the least inevitably fixed in a way that makes it impossible for human action to affect it. Nor need human action, in order to do so, itself be uncaused or indeterminate – quite the contrary.

Nobody would wish to argue that any event, once it had occurred, let us say the election of an American President, had been or could have been uncaused, or that it was not affected by human action. We might say that it could have been otherwise and that another candidate might have won, but only if the causes had been otherwise (e.g. if people had not voted as they did). So even had the outcome been different it must equally have been determined. And the same will be true of any future event. If the causes and actions of the relevant people are appropriate at the time, it will be such-and-such; but if they are otherwise, it will be otherwise. What the causes will be we do not know. We may, on the basis of such evidence as is available to us, try to predict; and if we know a great deal about the probable causes, the intentions and characters of the people involved and the attendant circumstances, our prediction may be tolerably good; but only if we were omniscient would it be certain. Being omniscient would involve knowing precisely the workings of every mind of every person concerned in the occurrence, which would in no way imply that none of them could act rationally and responsibly. Still less would it imply that none of them could influence the event. So Spinoza's contentions that God knows everything and that his knowledge and his creative power are identical, and, further, that being perfect and infinite he could not have done anything other than he has done, could all still hold good without modifying our usual and normal beliefs concerning the way historical events occur and are brought about by human action.

We all conceive the past as settled and unalterable. "What's done cannot be undone." And it is the past that constitutes history. Accordingly, while history is a record of changes, it does not itself change. When Spinoza speaks of nature as a whole, as determined and eternally what it is, he includes (of necessity) the whole of history, past and future. But this puts all events in the category to which those we now call past belong. The whole of history, as contained in Spinoza's God, is seen *sub specie aeternitatis* and contingency cannot enter into it. But that in no way alters or invalidates the idea of history as an ongoing, temporal process, with a future still unrealized at any particular point in time. That idea is limited to time and is subject to our metaphysical conception; but if we adopt a Spinozistic position, that does not commit us to any belief in the futility of human action, in the inevitability independent of such action of as yet unknown future events, or in our impotence as mere men to affect, indeed to create, the course of history.

This conclusion is reinforced by the interpretation I have given to Spinoza's doctrine of the *conatus* as a dynamic urge on the part of the individual to increase its power of spontaneous action. But this doctrine also has been variously understood; some might hail the *conatus* as a forerunner of the modern psychological doctrine of drives in animal behaviour, and so to some extent it is. But many contemporary psychologists (though by no means all – and doubtfully even a majority) interpret living behaviour more mechanistically than Spinoza does, adhering more persistently to the seventeenth century outlook, than he himself. In this they are behind their own times because the physical basis of mechanism, which was established in Spinoza's time and had its hey-day in the period immediately succeeding, has today been completely superseded and in modern physics is altogether obsolete. Spinoza's development of the *conatus* doctrine, however, as we have seen, is essentially teleological, and in this his view is nearer to those of *Gestalt* psychologists and the ethology of men like N. Tinbergen, W. H. Thorpe and Conrad Lorenz than to the behaviourism of B. F. Skinner.

My interpretation of Spinoza's use of the *conatus* has been questioned (in private discussion) by my colleague Professor W. A. Sturm, who points to the sixth and seventh propositions of Pt. III in the *Ethics* as indicating that Spinoza meant by perseverance in its own being, a static unchanging persistence within the set limits of the thing's essence. This, indeed, is how Spinoza is commonly understood. But it seems to me clearly impossible to interpret him in that way without involving him in intolerable inconsistency. For he says that the awareness of the *conatus* on the side of Thought is the same thing as appetite and desire, in which case it cannot be a mere inert persistence in the *status quo*. And he insists that all men have a desire to acquire what is useful, explaining further that what is useful is what increases one's power of action. The *conatus,* therefore, must be an endeavour to increase one's power, and this is the sense Spinoza gives it in every context, whether he is dealing with the strength of the passions, the power of the intellect, or motives determining men's political acts. Moreover, the *conatus* is in all things, not only in man, and the inference ought then to be warranted that all things, each according to its degree of complexity or "perfection," will display a dynamic or appetitive tendency. This may very well be the source of Leibniz' belief that appetite was inherent in every substance, as his doctrine of *vis viva* may also owe much to Spinoza.

It may, nevertheless, still be questioned how Spinoza's philosophy can afford any help in the face of the grave problems which I outlined in my opening pages. It should, however, be obvious to any reader who has persisted to this point that these problems are not the result merely of science and technology, but of the way in which they are used by men. They are the outcome of what Spinoza called imaginative thinking and the blind desire that is its consequences. The remedy for these is no different today from what Spinoza advocates. It is the propagation of what he showed to be the true and universal religion – the practice of justice and generosity – and the resolute pursuit of reason in politics and practical affairs as well as in the search for knowledge, both as indispensable to practice and for its own sake. The detailed application of this doctrine to contemporary difficulties must be worked out by each and every individual who becomes convinced of its truth. No attempt can be made to do it here. Even so, the persistent modern critic will continue to raise objections.

Spinoza's view of men as led by blind desire will appeal to many modern readers as borne out by our most common experience, and his contention that this is not to be ridiculed, condemned nor deplored, because it is natural and inevitable, will find ready acceptance as sensible and realistic. But Spinoza's faith in the competence and the efficacy of reason, even as accompanied by active emotion, is less likely to find modern adherents. Spinoza would say that it was not faith but knowledge, clearly and distinctly intelligible and capable of indubitable proof. All this, the great majority of modern philosophers (as well as non-philosophers) will reject. Some will say simply that reason never will and never can have sufficient appeal to men, or sufficient driving force even when it does appeal, to overcome the passions; and that Spinoza is much nearer the mark when he says that to believe men involved in the affairs of state will be governed by reason is to dream of a golden age or of a fairy tale. Others will say (following Bertrand Russell) that he places too much trust in the efficacy of pure logic, which is limited in its applicability, cannot discover truth (or for that matter any matter of fact) and may be misleading in its very subtlety unless carefully checked and supported by observation. Yet a third group of philosophers will maintain that reason is a merely mechanical technique applicable only to a projected objective world which excludes what is most intrinsically real and important, the existential, felt, lived subjectivity of the self. To live according to reason is an option open to man, they will say, but only one of many. It offers a cold and limited prospect and is not necessarily attractive. But whether one opts for it or for some other way of life is a matter of free choice, which cannot be pre-empted or annulled because freedom is the very being and essence of man's consciousness by virtue of which he is and feels himself to be, human.

With much of this Spinoza would himself have been in sympathy. Certainly men are, he would agree, for the most part led by blind passion. They are and can never cease to be parts of nature, finite modes, almost completely and inevitably overwhelmed by the influence of external causes and only under the most special conditions their own masters. Nevertheless, it can be demonstrated that those special conditions may, with great difficulty and only very seldom, be realized, for the most excellent things are as hard to come by as they are rare. He would agree also that the sort of logic Russell decries is worth very little. He would have called it a mere aid to the imagination, but he would think little better of what can be learned by mere observation – though he was not above appealing to experience. Reason for him is no mere calculus, it is a comprehensive intellectual grasp of the significance of things in the light of the whole of reality – wisdom, not mere ratiocination. Again, there are indeed other options open to men than a life of reason, and what makes man human is indeed his self-awareness, his capacity to frame true ideas and his knowledge of the infinite. But this is no mere freedom of arbitrary choice. That is sheer illusion, resulting from ignorance, not conscious self-awareness (*cognitio*). The freedom of the mind is self-determination and that proceeds only from systematic thought.

It is, however, just this last assertion that modern philosophers, be they analytic or existentialist, will vigorously deny. Systematic thinking, if that means the construction of a speculative system like Spinoza's, is for all of them no better than a procrustean bed. It is not simply that the real is too rich and various to be contained in it, but that our minds have not the means *a priori* to construct any such system which could be true of the world. What we know of things we can discover only by patient observation, and the fruits of that are little enough compared with what still remains to be learnt. Spinoza's claims smack too much of overweening arrogance – though in his actual life he was the meekest and most unassuming of men. He claims to be able to comprehend, at least in principle, the infinite nature of God, identified as the nature of the whole universe (not alone physical, but in its infinity). If this is not omniscience it comes near to it, and who dare make such a claim, even if only to a potentiality of realization?

But this is not Spinoza's claim. He avers only that adequate knowledge involves the admission in principle of the existence of an infinite whole, not the detailed knowledge of it.[4] And he requires all knowledge to be related to this indispensable presupposition. The alternative is to reject all system and any final criterion by which to judge. For if we do not judge the acceptability of theories (be they scientific or philosophical) by reference to some system sufficiently coherent to maintain itself intelligibly in our minds, we have no ground on which to criticize and no right to pronounce upon, to accept or reject, any. The extreme relativist is debarred by his own doctrine from claiming a privileged knowledge or a superior standard by which to pronounce Spinoza's theory unacceptable. For the relativist, man must be the measure of all things, each for himself, and none may reject what any accepts. For him there can be no universal principle of decision and so neither truth nor untruth. He is thus committed to scepticism, and the consistent sceptic can but be dumb. Moreover this conclusion follows, not only from Spinoza's theory, but from that of the relativist himself.

Of those who say that reason is but one of many options and not necessarily the best, we must ask by what criterion they would have us decide, first whether what they tell us is true, next, if it is, which alternative is preferable. If they have a reason for their contention and refer us to that, then the contention itself must be false, for we can accept no reason simply as one of a number of equally appealing options. We must accept it, if we do, as over-riding all other possible opinions – as cogent. If other options are equally open to us it is equally open to reject their reason; in which case it could not be compelling, and so no reason at all. If we accept it and allow that other options are open because they can show us good grounds for that opinion, we must still seek grounds for choosing to live otherwise than rationally; and if the grounds for doing so are rational we shall not have chosen to live otherwise. But if they are not rational they will not be grounds and we shall have none for our choice. It will be mere caprice. If we are asked to reject rationalism and to accept the view of the antirationalist for no reason at all, we

---

[4] Cf. *K.V.*, II, xxii, and p. 109 above.

can do so only from prejudice, and what claim then should our (or their) theory have to be philosophical or scientific that could not equally be made for any whim or fancy, however wild or wayward.

Reason, however, as advocated by Spinoza, is not the cold, dry dance of bloodless categories usually assumed by those who raise objections. It is comprehensive thinking ardently pursued by one who seeks, and loves the search, for ultimate satisfaction of spirit, both intellectual and moral. This ardour and this devotion, consuming the whole mind, is apparent from the first in the proemium to the *Treatise on the Improvement of the Intellect* and emerges in full diapason in the fifth Part of the *Ethics,* not as riotous enthusiasm or fulsome sentimentality, but as the measured cadence of the confident yet sober march of triumphant reason.

BIBLIOGRAPHICAL APPENDIX

The original editions of Spinoza's works, published by Rieuwaertz in the year of his death (1677) and the immediately succeeding year (1678), were in Latin, as he wrote them, and in Dutch translation by H. Glazemaker:
B. D. S. [Benedict de Spinoza], *Opera Posthuma, quorum series post praefationem exhibitur.*
De Nagelaten Schriften van B. D. S. als Zedekunst, Staatkunde, Verbetering van 't Verstant, Brieven en Antwoorden.

The best modern editions are:
J. Van Vloten et J. P. N. Land (Eds.), *Opera Quotquot reperta sunt* (Hague, 1914), and Carl Gebhardt (Ed.) *Opera* (Heidelberg, 1924).

A list of Spinoza's extant writings has been given in the preface to this volume with the exception of:
Stelkonstige Reeckening van den Regenboog (Algebraic calculation of the Rainbow),
Reeckening van Kanssen (Calculation of Chances), and
Compendium Grammatices Linguae Hebraeae (Hebrew Grammar).

Among the most important Spinoza bibliographies are:
Oko, Adolph S., *The Spinoza Bibliography* (Boston, 1964).
Catalogue van de Bibliotheek der Vereniging Het Spinozahuis (Leyden, 1965).
The earliest and most famous biographies are those of J. M. Lucas and Johannes Colerus. Both have been translated by Professor A. Wolf, the former under the title of *The Oldest Biography of Spinoza* (London, 1927) and the latter as an appendix to the translation of the *Short Treatise of God, Man and His Wellbeing* (London, 1910). In Wolf's edition of *The Correspondence of Spinoza* (London, 1928) there is a useful and interesting introduction giving brief accounts of all of Spinoza's correspondents as well as a description of the seventeenth century scene.

Other important works on Spinoza and Spinozism (a selection from an enormous bibliography) are the following:

(1) Mainly historical (but including some commentary):

Chronicum Spinozanum (5 vols.) Hagae Comitis 1921-1927.

Feuer, L. S., *Spinoza and the Rise of Liberalism* (Boston, 1964).

Fischer, Kuno, *Spinozas Leben, Werke und Lehre* (Heidelberg, 1946).

Freudenthal, J., *Die Lebensgeschichte Spinozas in Quellenschriften* (Leipzig, 1899).

Meinsma, K. O., *Spinoza en zijn kring* (Hague, 1896).

Vries, Theun de, *Baruch de Spinoza* (Hamburg, 1970).

(2) Commentaries:

Bidney, D., *The Psychology and Ethics of Spinoza* (New Haven, 1940).

Caird, J. *Spinoza* (London, 1910).

Hallet, H. F., *Aeternitas, a Spinozistic Study* (Oxford, 1930).

—, *Benedict de Spinoza* (London, 1957).

—, *Creation, Emanation and Salvation, a Spinozistic Study* (Hague, 1962).

Hampshire, S., *Spinoza* (London, 1946).

Hubbeling, G. H., *Spinoza* (Baarn, 1966).

—, *Spinoza's Methodology* (Groningen, 1964).

Huan G., *Le Dieu de Spinoza* (Paris, 1913).

Joachim, H. H., *A Study of the Ethics of Spinoza* (Oxford, 1901; New York, 1964).

—, *Spinoza's Tractatus de Intellectus Emendatione* (Oxford, 1940).

Kline, G. L., (Ed.) *Spinoza in Soviet Philosophy. A Series of Essays* (London, 1952).

Mac Shea, R. J., *The Political Philosophy of Spinoza* (New York, 1968).

McKeon, R., *The Philosophy of Spinoza. The Unity of His Thought* (New York, 1928).

Parkinson, G. H. R., *Spinoza's Theory of Knowledge* (Oxford, 1954).

Pollock, F., *Spinoza, his Life and His Philosophy* (London, 1899).

Powell, E. E., *Spinoza and Religion* (Boston, 1941).

Roth, L., *Spinoza, Descartes and Maimonides* (Oxford, 1924; New York, 1963).

—, *Spinoza* (London, 1945).

Saw, Ruth L., *The Vindication of Metaphysics* (London, 1951).

Strauss, L., *Spinoza's Critique of Religion* (New York, 1965) being a translation of *Die Religionskritik Spinozas* (Berlin, 1930).

Wolfson, H. A., *The Philosophy of Spinoza*, 2 Vols. (Harvard Univ. Press, Cambridge, Mass. 1934; New York, 1960).

(3) The annual papers issued by the Society of the Spinozahuis under the title *Mededelingen vanwege het Spinozahuis*, are of considerable interest and value. Those I have consulted are:

C. A. Crommelin, *Spinoza's Natuurwetenschappelijk Denken* (1939).

Ch. H. van Os, *Tijd, Maat en Getal* (1946).

B. H. Kazemier, *De Staat bij Spinoza en Hobbes* (1951).

C. W. Monnich, *De Verhouding van Theologie en Wijsbegeerte in het Tractatus Theologico-Politicus* (1958).

Theun de Vries, *Spinoza als Staatkundig Denker* (1963).

Jan den Tex, *Spinoza over de Tolerantie* (1967).

(4) Translations into English of Spinoza's works:
The Chief Works of Benedict de Spinoza, translated into English from the Latin, with an introduction by R. H. M. Elwes, 2 Volumes; London, George Bell & Sons, 1889; New York, Dover Publications, 1955.
Spinoza's Short Treatise on God, Man and His Well-Being, translated and edited with introduction and commentary and a life of Spinoza, by A. Wolf; London, A. & C. Black, 1910.
The Correspondence of Spinoza, translated and edited with introduction and annotations, by A. Wolf; London and New York, Lincoln MacVeagh, 1927.
Ethic of Benedict de Spinoza, translated by W. Hale White and Amelia H. Stirling; London, T. Fisher Unwin, 1894.
The Ethics of Spinoza and de Intellectus Emendatione, translated by A. Boyle, with an introduction by G. Santayana; London and New York, Everyman Library, 1910.
Early Philosophical Writings, The Cartesian Principles and Thoughts on Metaphysics, translated by F. A. Hayes and David Bidney; Indianapolis & New York, Liberal Arts Press, 1963.
Benedict de Spinoza, The Political Works, The Tractatus Theologico-Politicus in part and the *Tractatus Politicus* in full; edited and translated with an introduction and notes by A. G. Wernham; Oxford, at the Clarendon Press, 1958.
Spinoza Selections, edited by John Wild; New York, Charles Scribner, 1930.
The Philosophy of Spinoza, selected from his chief works, with a life of Spinoza and an introduction by Joseph Ratner; New York, The Modern Library, Random House, 1954.

INDEX

Abstraction (*abstracta*), 23, 27, 50, 52, 63, 143.
Acquiescentia in se ipso, 116, 164.
Action, 110, 118f, 145, 160, 178;
  free, 250;
  of the body, 85;
  of the mind, 85, 91, 105, 169;
  power of, 114, 118, 144ff, 148f, 161, 165, 172, 194, 254.
Activity, 89ff;
  same in body as mind, 239.
Advantage (see also Expedience, Profit), 174, 201;
  relation to good, 147ff.
Aeternitas (see Eternity).
Aeternatatis sub specie, 107n, 156f, 171, 231, 234f, 239, 253f.
Affect, *110–119*, 166.
Affectio, 110, 158, 166.
Affirmation, 89f, 93, 134.
Aiken, H., 181n.
Althusius, 182.
Ambition, 163f, 170.
Amsterdam, xii, xiv, 206, 220.
Analytic philosophy, 6, 256.
Anger, 117.
Animositas, 119.
Anselm, 40.
Appetite, 112, 254f.
Aristocracy, 197.
Aristotle, 83, 114, 235, 237;
  Nicomachean Ethics, 114n, 149n;
  on moral weakness, 149f;
  on pleasure, 114.
Aron, R., 181n.
Association of ideas, 93.
Atheism, xv, 46f, 205;
  absurdity of, 33–47.
Attributes, 38f, 42, 49, 50–54, 55, 59f, 131, 169;
  infinity of, 64ff, *69–74*;
  ideas of, 202;
  not *ens rationis*, 50;
  not property, 41, 72f;
  real differentiations, 82.
Augustine, 104.
Austin, J., 192.
Auxilia imaginationis (see also Imagination), 100.
Axiom, 21f.
Ayer, A. J., *The Problem of Knowledge*, 22n.

Bacon, F., 250.
Bad, see Evil.
Balling, P., 10n.
Batuscheck, E., 71n, 89.
Beatitude, see Blessedness
Bell, D., 181n.
Benevolence, 116, 170.
Bentham, J., 192.
Berlin, Sir Isaiah, 252.
Bible, 210
  historical document, 212.
Biblical criticism, 210–214.
Biocoenosis, 68.
Biology, 67f. 251.
Blackstone, Sir W., 192.
Blessedness, 158, 162, 180, 204f, 207, 223, 241, 246.
Blok, P. J., *History of the People of the Netherlands*, xviin.
Blood, 65f.
Blyenbergh, W. van, 60, 154, 156, 210.
Body, 56, 65, 67, 77ff, 80, 238;
  human, 69, 72, 121, 236,
    adequate knowledge of, 240,
    finite mode of Extension, 101, 160, 227, 233f, 241,
    part of nature, 235,
    relation to mind, 74, *77–79*, 166, 227ff, 230, 236, 251,
    substantial identity with mind, 79, 82ff, 87f.
Bouwmeester, J., 10n.
Boxel, H., 124.
Bradley, F. H., 131.

Buridan, J., 135.
Burgh, A., 109, 207.

Caird, J., 4, 19f, 28, 49f, 54, 59, 159, 232;
  Spinoza, 20n, 49n, 232n.
Calvinists, xvii.
Camphuyzen, D. R., 7n.
Carnap, R., 4.
Casearius, xiv.
Causa sui, 35, 41f, 44, 57, 64, 73, 119, 122, 130.
Cause, 23, 42f, 102, 129f;
  adequate, 110, 180;
  efficient, 51, 128;
  final, 126;
  free, 48, 51, 122, 130, 136;
  immanent, 17, 57, 67, 233;
  inadequate 110;
  proximate, 57;
  supernatural, 62;
  transient, 57f.
Chance, 124.
Charles II, xvii.
Cheerfulness (*hilaritas*), 163f, 177.
Christ, 222, 225;
  spirit of (see also Holy Spirit), 202, 224ff
Christianity, 33, 35;
  Spinoza's attitude to, 225f.
Cohen, H., 206n.
Colerus, J., xi, xvi.
Collegiants, xiiif.
Collingwood, R. G., 5, 212f;
  Essays in the Philosophy of History, 5n;
  The Idea of History, 212n;
  The Idea of Nature, 5n;
  The New Leviathan, 81n;
Commiseration, 116, 177.
Common properties, 24, 106f.
Communis ordo naturae, 57n, 62, *98–103*, 156, 160.
Compulsion, 122, 124.
Conatus, 103, 105, *110ff*, 118, 121, 128, 132, 144, 149, 150, 155, 160f, 166f, 176, 182, 186, 202, 205, 240, 254;
  foundation of virtue, 172;
  same as essence, 103, 110, 155, 202, 240, 254.
Conception, 16n.
Condé, Prince of, xviif, 182.
Consciousness, 80, 85, 101, 236f;
  not in time, 244;
self-reflective, 87, 103, 121, 125;
  self-transcendent, 238, 241f;
  stream of, see Psychical.
Contract, social, 183.
Copernican revolution, 5.
Cosmological argument, 46.
Court, J. de la, xv.
Crescas, Chasdai ben, xii, 244, 250.
Cruelty, 117.

Death, 173, 176, 246.
de Broglie, Louis, 27;
  The Revolution in Physics, 27n.
Deduction, 21–27, 250.
Definition, 21;
  rules for, 18.
Democracy, 194, 197.
Denial, 89f, 134.
de Ruyter, Admiral, xvii.
Descartes, R., xiv, 18, 23, 26, 30, 36, 39ff, 44, 52, 55ff, 61, 64, 72f, 84, 90f, 104, 166, 250f;
  anti-historical tendency, 212;
  Meditations, 44, 73n, 91n, 104n;
  on body and soul, 74;
  on error, 91;
  on free-will, 91, 97, 133ff;
  on imagination, 91;
  on pineal gland, 166;
  Philosophical Works (Haldane & Ross), xiv, 40n;
  Principia Philosophiae, 52n;
  Replies to Objections, 40;
  Rules for the Direction of the Mind, 91n.
Desire, 112, 114, 118, 120, 122, 148f, 161, 182, 254.
Despair, 3ff.
Determination (see also Negation), 36, 124f, 130, 250, 252;
  not compulsion, 122.
Determinism, see Determination
Devil, 136, 148.
de Vries, Isaac, xvi, 10n.
de Vries, Simon, xvi, 10n, 58, 82.
de Vries, Theun, 197n.
de Witt, C., xvii, xviii.
de Witt, J., xiv, xvii, xviii, 182, 206.
Dialectic, 109, 125.
Dilthey, 206n.
Doubt, 93, 98, 134.
Duration, 99f, 230f, 239.

Eddington, Sir A., 27, 56, 68, 251f;
  The Expanding Universe, 27n, 251n.
Einstein, A., 26, 59, 252;
  The World as I See It, 27n.
Emotion, 110;
  active, 118f, 150, 168.
Empiricism, 12, 22, 95.
Enden, Clara Maria van den, xii.
Enden, Francis van den, xii.
Entia rationis, 25, 49f, 52, 80, 82, 142.
Environment, internal, 79.
Envy, 120, 185, 203.
Epiphenomenalism, 85.
Erdmann, J. E., *A History of Philosophy*, 49n
Error, 92ff, 98, 168;
  as privation, 98, 136.
Essence, 39, 61, *63*, 67, 111, 154, 254;
  formal, 16, 63;

objective, 16, 63.
Eternal things, 23f, 27, 50, 58, 60, 107.
Eternity, 107, 231, 242ff;
 not to be confused with duration, 239,
  244f;
 relation to time, 237ff.
Euclid, 17, 21, 28f, 108.
Evil, 80, 114, 126, *141–159*;
 absolute, 156;
 ens rationis, 80;
 mere negation or privation, 136, 151, 153;
 reality of, 152–159;
 relative, 142, 146, 151.
Existence, 61;
 contingent, 43, 45;
 necessary, 43.
Existentialism, 6, 7, 256.
Expedience, 147ff.
Experience, 8, 15, 22f.
Extension, 20, 33, 39, 52f, 55ff, 58, 61, 64ff,
 69–74, 80, 99, 101, 130, 168, 204, 232;
 attribute of, 227, 231, 238;
 mode of, 80, 101, 168, 204, 229, 232.
Ezra, Ibn, xii.

Fabritius, J. Ludovicus, xvi.
Facies totius universi, 56f, 59, 67f, 101ff, 128,
 130, 157, 232, 237f, 241, 242f, 252.
Faith, 205, 215, 221, 223, 255.
Falsity, 16.
Fate, 123f, 252.
Fear, 117, 178.
Feeling, 81, 166.
Feuer, L. S., xv;
 Spinoza and the Rise of Liberalism, xivn, 192n.
Fiction, 93
Findlay, J. N., 43n.
Fluctuatio animi (fluctuation of the mind), 115,
 122.
Fortitudo, 119, 190.
Freedom, *122–126*, 130, 173, 176, 178f, 180,
 201;
 of choice (see also Will), 256;
 of mind, self-determination, 256;
 of speech and expression, 194f;
 of religion, 205;
 of thought, 194;
 of will, see Will;
 political, 196f;
 the end of the state, 195.

Gabriol, Ibn, xii.
Galileo, 26.
Gaudium, see Joy
Generositas, 119.
Geometrical order, 17f, 20, 160.
Geometry, 19, 28f, 250.
Gersonides, xii, 244.
Geulinx, A., 84
Geyl, P., *History of the Low Countries*, xviin.

Gloria, 116.
Glory, (see *Gloria*), 204.
God-or-Substance, 18f, 28, *31–74*, 45, 80,
 130, 145, 155, 162, 242, 253;
 action of, 125, not *sub specie boni*, 127, 218;
 attributes of, 23, 36f, 48, 49, 109, 202;
 causality (creativity) of, *48–74*, 80, 122f;
 definition of, 18, *38*;
 essence of, 23, 51, 109, 152, 234, 245,
  same as power, 48;
 existence of, 28, 33, *39–46*, 221, proofs of,
  40–46;
 grace of, 224;
 idea of, 17, 24, 35f, 86, 104, 202, 215;
 infinite idea of, see Infinite;
 intellect of (see also Infinite intellect), 89,
  119, 234, 236, 243;
 intellectual love of, 202ff, 224, 225, 240,
  246;
 law of, 183f, 218, 222;
 love of, see Love;
 of purer eyes than to behold evil, 159;
 personality of, 38;
 power of, 26, 51, 74, 123, 155, 218, 240,
  251, same as essence, 48, 111;
 son of, 202, 225;
 spirit of (see also Holy Spirit), 216;
 unity of, 49, 54;
 will of, 51n, 136, 218, the refuge of ignorance, 127.
Good, 80, 114, 126, *141–152*, 153, 161;
 common, 192, 203;
 ens rationis, 80;
 relative, 142, 146;
 supreme, *143ff*, 173, 187, same for all men,
  173, 180;
 true, 143ff, 168, 201.
Green, T. H., 186f, 198;
 *Lectures on the Principles of Political Obliga-
  tion*, 186n.

Habbakuk, 159n.
Hague, xivf, 182.
Hallet, H. F., 81n, 118;
 Benedict de Spinoza, 59n, 44n.
Hampshire, S., 4, 61n, 62n, 232;
 Spinoza, 61n, 62n, 232n.
Hanson, N. R., 12n;
 Patterns of Discovery, 12n.
Harris, E. E., 82n, 129n;
 Annihilation and Utopia, 200n;
 Foundations of Metaphysics in Science, 82n,
  129n;
 Fundamentals of Philosophy, 95n;
 Hypothesis and Perception, 12n, 43n;
 Revelation through Reason, 153n;
 The Survival of Political Man, 200n.
Hatred, 114ff, 118, 120, 166, 169, 177;
 of God impossible, 203.
Hebrew, 212, 216.

Hegel, G. W. F., 13, 24, 36, 50, 121, 239;
  Encyclopaedia of Philosophical Sciences, 239n.
Heidegger, M., 4, 5n, 12;
  Holzwege, 5n.
Heidelberg, xvi.
Heisenberg, W., 27;
  Philosophical Problems of Nuclear Science, 27n;
  Physics and Philosophy, 27n.
History, 181, 212, 245, 252ff, 254.
Hobbes, T., 114, 179, 181ff, 185, 187, 190ff,
  196, 250f;
  Leviathan, 114n, 179n, 183n, 184n, 185,
  251n.
Holy Spirit, see Spirit.
Honour, 8, 177, 179.
Hope, 177.
Horkheimer, H., *The Eclipse of Reason*, 13n.
Huan, G., *Le Dieu de Spinoza*, 49n, 51n, 71n.
Hubbeling, H. G., 4, 25, 28f, 167, 182, 206;
  Spinoza, 21n, 49n, 206n;
  Spinoza's Methodology, 20n, 25n, 40n, 49n,
  167, 183n, 197n.
Hudde, J., xvii, 69.
Human nature, *119–122*, 144, 182;
  ideal or exemplar of 144f;
  law of, 184.
Human bondage, 122, 160–166.
Humanity, 163.
Hume, D., xi, 13, 42, 95, 147;
  Treatise of Human Nature, xi and n.
Humility, 177.
Husserl, E., 4, 5n;
  Die Krisis der Europäischen Wissenschaften, 5n.

Idea (*idea*), 16ff, 72, 84ff, 89, 118, 125, 167,
  169;
  abstract, 85;
  adequate, 90, 96, 105, 109, 113, 118, 157,
  168, 236, 238, free 125;
  ambiguity of, 85;
  cause of, 95;
  inadequate, 91f, 96f, 106, 113, 157, 168,
  236, 239;
  not passive or inert, 65, 236;
  of body, 77;
  transcendent, 235ff.
Idea ideae, 16n, 69, 71, *87–89*, 104, 112, 121,
  236f.
Idealism, 12, 159.
Ideatum, 16f, 25, 72, 77, 80, 86, 82, 88, 121;
  identical with idea, 236, 241;
  of the infinite power of thinking, 236.
Image, mental, 89.
Imaginatio (see also Imagination), *93–103*,
  104, 109, 112, 142, 145, 146, 152, 156, 158,
  164, 166f, 233;
  transcendence of, 241f.
Imagination (see also *Imaginatio*), 19, 54, 59,
  62, 91f, 93, 102, 107, 126, 128, 143, 153,
  155, 163, 168, 171, 204, 237, 240;

aids to, 141, 143, 146;
attributed to God, 127;
cause of superstition, 209;
medium of prophecy, 216, 218;
not *per se* false, 92, 217;
order of, 93;
source of error, 92, 209, 216.
Immortality, xiii, 175, 180, *227–246*, 241;
  mentioned only once in the *Ethics*, 231;
  personal, 235, 244f;
  traditional ideas of, 228ff.
Induction, 25.
Infinite Idea of God, 37, 57, 65, 67.
Infinity, 28;
  relation to finite, 227, 234.
Inquisition, xii, 195, 220.
Intellect, 15, 18, 92f, 105, 134f, 204.
  essence of, 205;
  essence of the human mind, 105f, 172;
  infinite, 49, 51, 57, 65, 70f, 80, 89, 105,
  228; order of, 172.
Israel, Rabbi Manassah ben, xii.
Israelites, see Jews.

Jealousy, 115, 117, 203.
Jelles, J., 10n, 206.
Jesus (see also Christ), 218.
Jews, xiii;
  election of, 219f.
Joachim, H. H., ix, 19f, 49f, 52n, 54, 59,
  94ff, 97f, 110n, 112, 159, 231ff, 239;
  Logical Studies, 96n;
  Study of the Ethics of Spinoza, 19n, 20n, 49n,
  50n, 56n, 58n, 59n, 71n, 96n, 110n,
  114n, 231;
  Spinoza's Tractatus de Intellectus Emendatione,
  20n, 94n, 95n;
  The Nature of Truth, 96n, 97.
Jonas, H., 5n, 12;
  The Phenomenon of Life, 5n.
Joshua, 214, 216.
Joy, 113, 177.
Judaism, xiif, 33, 35, 225.
Justice, 148, 255.

Kant, I., 24, 121, 147, 179, 189.
Kerckrink, D., xiii.
Knowledge, 15ff, 255;
  adequate, *103–109*, 149, 155, 164f;
  best kind (see adequate, and *Scientia intuitiva*), 16;
  first kind, see *Imaginatio*;
  fourth kind, see *Scientia intuitiva*;
  goal of reason, 201.
  of God, 149, 165, 173, 180;
  of good and evil, 162, 165, 171;
  primacy of, 15;
  second kind, see *Ratio*;
  third kind, see *Scientia intuitiva*.
Koran, 211.

Kuhn, T., *The Structure of Scientific Revolutions*, 12n.

Laetitia (see also Pleasure), 165n.
Lakatos, I., *Criticism and the Growth of Knowledge*, 12n.
Language, 6.
Law, 173, *188–196*;
  civil, 183;
  criticism of, 195;
  idea of, 189;
  of Nature, see Nature.
Leibniz, G., xi, xviii, 43, 65, 255.
Leonidas, 175.
Leyden, xiv.
Life, 12;
  after death, 230, 243, 246;
  eternal, 226;
  good, 180, 223.
Light, divine, 205;
  natural, 205, 210, 215, 217.
Locke, J., 95.
Logic, 21, 255f.
Lorenz, C., 254.
Louis XIV, xviif.
Love, 9, 114ff, 118, 159n, 166, 169, 203;
  more powerful than hatred, 117, 182;
  of an infinite object, 9;
  of finite objects, 177;
  of God, 149, 165, 180, 217, 222, 241,
    goal of reason, 201.
  intellectual, see God, 202ff.
Lucas, J. M., xiif, xix, 15.

McKeon, R., *The Philosophy of Spinoza*, 21n.
Macchiavelli, N., 181.
Maimonides, xii, 250.
Marx, K., 3, 252.
Mathematics, 19, 30, 107, 250.
Measure, 80, 100.
Memory, 89, 243.
Mechanism, 128.
Metaphysics, 6, 28f, 60;
  combined with ethics and theology, 251.
Method, 11f, *15–30*, 160, 250.
Meyer, Ludovicus, 10n, 30, 100.
Milne, E. A., 252.
Mind, 78;
  all things beminded, 80;
  fluctuation of, see *Fluctuatio*;
  human, 69, 90, 103, 236f, 244;
    as idea of body, 80ff, 239–243;
    as finite mode, 101, 226, 233f,
    idea of, 87f,
    identity theory of relation to body, 82f
      (see also Body);
    part of nature, 235.
Miracles, 47, 210, 219, *221f*, 226.
Modes, *50–57*, 60, 110f;
  finite, 55–57, 58, merely appearance, 54

infinite, 23, 48, 55–57, 58, 130, 131, 225,
  of Extension, 65f, 67,
  of thought, 65;
  not 'parts' of substance, 233.
Monarchy, 190f, 197;
  absolute, 190;
  constitutional, 191.
Morality, 160ff.
Moral weakness, 149–152.
Mortiera, Rabbi Saul Levi, xii.
Moses, 211, 214, 217, 220.
Motion, 56, 77.
Motion and rest, 56, 59, 65, 77f, 101, 237.
Musgrave, A., *Criticism and the Growth of Knowledge*, 12n.
Multitudo libera, 190.

Natura Naturans, *48–51*, 62, 125.
Natura Naturata, *48–51*, 62, 103, 125, 131.
Naturalism, 33f.
Nature, 22, 34ff, 141, 145, 221;
  common order of (see *Communis ordo*), *98–103*, 241;
  identified with God, 33f;
  laws of, 61f, 252.
  Law of, 179, *183–188*, 192.
  Right of, 183–188;
  State of, 183, 185, states in, 192.
Necessity, 21ff, 43;
  not opposed to freedom, 124;
  opposed to chance, 124.
Negation, 20, 36f, 38f, 122.
Netherlands, xii, 182, 197.
Newton, Sir Isaac, 26.
Nominalism, 25, 27, 51.
Novalis, 33.
Number, 100.

Oates, Capt L. E. G., 175.
Occasionalism, 84.
Oldenburg, H., 131, 205, 207, 222, 225, 252.
Ontological argument, 40–45.
Oosten, J., 123, 205n.
Orange, William III of, xiv.
Order, 127f, 131;
  of idea same as of things, 18f, 26, 52, 70f, 84f, 166.
Organism, 67, 78, 129.
Ovid, *Metamorphoses*, 165n.
Pain (*tristitia*), 113ff, 122, 154f, 156f, 161f, 166, 176;
  caused by God, 203.
Pantheism, 33ff, 103.
Parallelism, 84f.
Parkinson, G. H. R., *Spinoza's Theory of Knowledge*, 49n.
Part, 35;
  and whole, 19, 52.
Passion, *110–122*, 148, 154, 160, 170, 178;
  cause of superstition, 209;

mastery over, 166–172, 203.
men always subject to, 160, 165, 173, 182f, 223.
Passivity, *89–98*, 110;
   same in body as in mind, 239.
Pauli, W., 68.
Paul, St., 189, 220; *Epistle to the Romans*, 165, 189.
Paulus, Prof., xix.
Pentateuch, 214.
Perception, 16n.
Perfection, 17, *39*, 44, 118, 126, 130, 142, *144ff*, 158f, 150;
   degrees of, 125, 132, 154, 159, 238, 255;
   identified with power, 51;
   transition to greater or lesser, 114, 156, 162.
Peter, St., 212.
Phantasia, 91.
Philosophy, 19;
   and religion, 210f;
   and theology, 205;
   fundamental questions of, 6f;
   spring of, 6, 8ff.
Physical world, 77, 79f.
Physics, 56, 59, 60, 68, 251, 254;
   contemporary, 56;
   laws of, 253.
Plato, 8, 13, 14, 109, 152, 153n, 181, 235, 242, 245;
   on good and expedient, 147ff;
   on moral weakness, 149–152;
   on the Good, 173;
   on Virtue as knowledge, 173;
   Crito, 176; *Gorgias*, 147n, 149n; *Meno*, 149n; *Phaedo*, 147n, 229; *Republic*, 109n, 147n, 178n; *Sophist*, 44.
Pleasure (*laetitia*), 8, 113ff, 122, 154, 157, 161f, 166, 176f, 202f.
Political theory, 181f.
Politics, *181–200*, 255.
Pollock, Sir F., 83, 85;
   Spinoza, His Life and Philosophy, 83n.
Pope, 212.
Popper, Sir K., 12;
   The Logic of Scientific Discovery, 12n.
Pride, 116, 163, 170, 177f.
Privation, 98, 136, 142.
Profit, 143.
Prophecy, 205, 210, *215–219*;
   criterion of, 223;
   exceeds capacity of intellect, 215ff;
   exhorts to good life, 217f;
   not philosophy or science, 209, 217.
Prophet, 209;
   has not superhuman mind, 215, 217;
   means 'interpreter', 215.
Psyche, 242.
Psychical stream, 242ff.
Purpose, 126, 129.

Racialism, 220.
Ratio, 13, 19, 21, 98, 105, *106f*, 112, 145, 167, 170;
   eternity of, 231.
Rationalism, 13, 22, 51, 257f.
Reality (see also Perfection), 17, 78f, 114;
   degrees of, 74, 78f, 132, 164.
Reason (see also *Ratio*), 13, 168, 178, 209, 256;
   conflict with revelation, 207;
   demonstrates means to salvation, 223;
   dictates of, 172ff, 186;
   efficacy of, 255;
   law of, 183f, 185;
   life of, 178–180;
   not dance of bloodless categories, 258;
   only possible in society, 189;
   one of many options, 257;
   power of, 168;
   primacy of, 210, 213;
   those who despise, 205.
Reflection, 16ff.
Regulus, 175.
Relations, 25, 141f.
Relativism, 4, 257.
Relativity, 59.
Religion, 3f, *201–226*;
   true and universal, 202, 207, 209, 222ff, 225, 255.
Repentance, 116, 177.
Responsibility, 132f, 155, 207, 252.
Revelation, 205, 207, 222;
   teaches path to salvation, 224.
Rieuwertz, J., xiv.
Rijnsburg, xiv, 7n.
Roth, L., 4, 232;
   Descartes, Spinoza and Maimonides, 30n, 133n;
   Spinoza, 30n, 232.
Rousseau, J. J., 196;
   Contrat Social, 196n.
Russell, Bertrand, 255f.

Salvation, 11, 175, 202, 217, 222f;
   for the majority, 205, 224;
   knowledge of Christ according to the flesh unnecessary for, 225.
Sartre, J. P., 4, 149.
Saw, Ruth, 232;
   Vindication of Metaphysics, 232n.
Scepticism, 18, 46, 104.
Schuller, Dr. G., xiiif, 10n, 70.
Sciama, D. W., 27, 252;
   The Unity of the Universe, 27n.
Science (see also Method), 12, 19, 107, 255;
   contemporary (see also Biology and Physics), 250.
Scientia intuitiva, 13, 19, 21, 98, 102, 105, *107ff*, 130, 142, 145, 158, 165, 202ff, 205, 228, 242, 246;

eternity of, 231.
Scripture, 205, 209f, 213;
  including New Testament, 225;
  not addressed to the learned, 223;
  universal teaching of, 223.
Secondary qualities, 90, 110.
Self-love, 116, 120, 163.
Self-regard, 152, 175.
Self-sacrifice, 174ff.
Selfishness, 151f, 174f, 204.
Seneca, 193.
Sensation, 81, 86, 89.
Shame, 116, 178.
Shelley, P. B., *Prometheus Unbound*, 159n.
Signs, 208, 215ff, 219, 222, 225.
Sin, see Vice.
Skinner, B. F., 254.
Smart, J. J. C., 43n.
Society, 137, 183, 189.
Socrates, 8, 175.
Sorrow (*dolor*), 113.
Sovereignty, 188–193, 199;
  absolute, 190f;
  juristic theory of, 190, 192;
  of the people, 190;
  rights and powers of, 191ff;
Spijck, van der, xii, xvi, xviii.
Spinoza, B. de, 7, 8;
  alleged atheism, 33
  life of, xi–xix;
  method of, 11; see Method
  no ascetic, 10, 178;
  philosophy not 'out of date', 4f;
  rationalism of, 13;
  relevance of, 9f;
  terminology of, 5;
  writings of, ix–x,
    Opera (van Vloten and Land), x,
    Cogitata Metaphysica, x, 38, 64n,
    Epistolae, x, *Ep*. X, 58, *Ep*. XII, 52n,
      100, *Ep*. XIII, xiv, *Ep*. XXIII, 154f,
      Ep. XXXII, 56n, 65, 83, 119n, 241,
      Ep. XXXV, 41, 52n, 69n, *Ep*. XLII,
      34n, 123, *Ep*. XLIII, 124, 208, *Ep*.
      XLVII, xvi, *Ep*. XLVIII, xvi, *Ep*.
      LIV, 38, *Ep*. LVI, 124, *Ep*. LX, 55,
      Ep. LXIII, 59n, 70, *Ep*. LXIV, 56f,
      69n, *Ep*. LXV, 69n, 70, *Ep*. LXVI,
      69n, 70, *Ep*. LXXXI, 56n, *Ep*.
      LXXXIII, 56n, 79;
    Ethics, x, xv, 5, 10, 18, 20f, 28f, 40, 43f,
      49, 51, 53, 55, 60ff, 64, 67, 78f, 87f,
      92, 94f, 104ff, 112f, 120, 122, 128,
      130, 134, 136, 143f, 158f, 160, 167,
      173, 182, 186, 200f, 202f, 205ff, 209,
      258;
    *Korte Verhandeling van God, de Mensch, en
      dezelfs Welstand*, ix, xiii, 9, 20, 40, 53,
      56, 86, 108, 118, 136, 158, 177, 201,
      225, 229, 236;

Nagelaten Schriften, xix, 79n;
Opera Posthuma, xix, 79n;
Principia Philosophiae Cartesianae, ix, xiiif,
  5, 40, 44n, 56n;
Short Treatise, see *Korte Verhandeling*;
Tractatus de Intellectus Emendatione, x,
  xivf, 8, 16ff, 20, 25, 28, 50, 63, 87f,
  107, 144, 177, 201f, 258;
Tractatus Politicus, x, xviii, 186, 196, 197;
Tractatus Theologico-Politicus, x, xv, xvi,
  xviii, 10, 123, 176, 187, 194, 197, 202,
  205ff, 213, 224.
Spinoza, Gabriel de, xvi.
Spinoza, Michael de, xii.
Spirit, holy, 202, 204f, 225.
State, 181–200;
  in state of nature, 192;
  limitation of powers of, 193f.
Stoics, 166.
Stouppe, J. B., xviii.
Strauss, L., 207, 209;
  Spinoza's Critique of Religion, 206n.
Strawson, P. F., *Introduction to Logical Theory*,
  21.
Sturm, W. A., 254.
Substance (see also God), 35, 100, 125, 131,
  152;
  created, 64, 73;
  definition of, 41;
  distinctions in, 49ff;
  division of, 52f.
Superstition, 10, 12, 127f, 137, 178, *207ff*,
  221, 226.
Supposal, see Fiction.
Synagogue, xiii, 15, 205f, 224.

Talmud, 211.
Taylor, A. E., 232.
Teilhard de Chardin, P., 252.
Teleological argument, 46.
Teleology, 20, 46, 125, *126–132*, 147, 254.
Tex, J. den, 194n, 206n.
Theology, 205;
  with metaphysics and ethics, 251.
Thorpe, W. H., 254.
Thought, 39, 49, 52f, 54, 56, 60, 64f, *60–74*,
  80f, 84, 168, 254;
  attribute of, 227, 238
  mode of, 101, 229.
Thucydides, 181.
Time, 80, *98–103*, 231;
  ens rationis, 80, 100;
  eternal in concept, 239;
  product of *imaginatio*, 99f, 231;
  relation to eternity, 228, 237ff.
Tinbergen, N., 254.
Titillation (*titillatio*), 163, 176.
Tolstoy, L., 252.
Treaties, 193, 199.
Tristitia, see Pain.

Tschirnhaus, W., 55, 57, 61, 69f, 72, 79.
Tyranny, 193f.

Universals (*universalia*), 23, 27, 50f, 67, 106.
Unselfishness, 151f.

Value, 6;
    psychological, 6;
    relation to fact, 147.
Van Beuningen, xviin.
Van Beverningh, xviin.
van Os, Ch. H., 101.
Velthuysen, L. de, 123, 205n, 207f.
Vice (see also Evil), 148;
    its own punishment, 148.
Virtue, 148, 161f, 164, 173, 224;
    as highest good, 180;
    definition of, 162
    its own reward, 136, 148, 174, 178, 180,
        246;
    no hardship, 246.
Vis viva, 65, 255.
Voorburg, xiv.

Watt, A. J., 61n.
Wernham, A. G., 197f;
    Benedict de Spinoza, the Political Works, 197n.
Whole and part, 19, 52, 54, 64ff, 233, 235.
Wickedness, see Vice.
Will, 112, 126, *132–137*;
    General, 196;
    free, 7, 20, 47, 73, 91, 97, 123, 129, 149f,
        168, 252, critique of Descartes's theory
        of, 133ff;
    of God, 51n, 136;
    same as intellect, 135.
Windelband, W., 71n, 89.
Wittgenstein, L., 4.
Wolf, A., 56n.
Wolfson, Abraham, xi;
    Spinoza, A Life of Reason, xin.
Wolfson, A. H., ix, 162, 168f, 243ff;
    The Philosophy of Spinoza, 49n, 162n, 168n,
        243.

Zeno, 100.